Beginning moderni

MANCHESTER
1824

Manchester University Press

Beginnings
Series editors: Peter Barry and Helen Carr

'**Beginnings**' is a series of books designed to give practical help to students beginning to tackle recent developments in English, Literary Studies and Cultural Studies. The books in the series

- demonstrate and encourage a questioning engagement with the new;
- give essential information about the context and history of each topic covered;
- show how to develop a practice which is up to date and informed by theory.

Each book focuses uncompromisingly upon the needs of its readers, who have the right to expect lucidity and clarity to be the distinctive feature of a book which includes the word 'beginning' in its title.

Each aims to lay a firm foundation of well-understood initial principles as a basis for further study and is committed to explaining new aspects of the discipline without over-simplification, but in a manner appropriate to the needs of beginners.

Each book, finally, aims to be both an introduction and a contribution to the topic area it discusses.

Also in the series

Beginning modernism

Jeff Wallace

Manchester University Press
Manchester and New York
distributed in the United States exclusively by Palgrave Macmillan

Published by Manchester University Press
Oxford Road, Manchester M13 9NR, UK
and Room 400, 175 Fifth Avenue, New York, NY 10010, USA
www.manchesteruniversitypress.co.uk

Distributed in the United States exclusively by
Palgrave Macmillan, 175 Fifth Avenue, New York,
NY 10010, USA

Distributed in Canada exclusively by
UBC Press, University of British Columbia, 2029 West Mall,
Vancouver, BC, Canada V6T 1Z2

British Library Cataloguing-in-Publication Data
A catalogue record for this book is available from the British Library

Library of Congress Cataloging-in-Publication Data applied for

ISBN   978 0 7190 6788 4   hardback

ISBN   978 0 7190 6789 1   paperback

First published 2011

Typeset
by Servis Filmsetting Ltd, Stockport, Cheshire
Printed in Great Britain
by Bell & Bain Ltd, Glasgow

For Fran, with love and thanks

Contents

Figures

Every attempt has been made to contact the copyright holders.

Acknowledgements

For their invaluable help, I would like to thank Carmel Barber, Steve Blandford, Alex Goody, Sue Holdway, Rod Jones and Fiona Reid. It is difficult to imagine a more patient and helpful editor than Matthew Frost, and thanks are also due to Kim Walker for her assistance in the final stages. I think I borrowed the idea of the Glen Baxter drawing from Roger Webster, with whom I first taught modernism a long time ago. Nina Wallace and Robin Wallace persuaded me at crucial stages that the first chapter at least was readable and comprehensible. Finally, I want to thank all the undergraduate students at the University of Glamorgan with whom I shared and discussed ideas about modernism over a period of some twenty years. They have been a great inspiration to write *Beginning Modernism*. Were they to read this book they would probably find some familiar material, and they would, I hope, still want to argue with it.

1

Introduction

Modernist studies past and present

What was, or is, modernism? Let us begin with some proposals. Modernism is the concept used to describe an extremely diverse range of innovative and experimental practices in literature, the visual and plastic arts, music, film, design and architecture, covering very broadly the period 1880–1939. The term itself began to emerge in various contexts in the 1920s; Brooker, for example, locates it first in 1927, in the title of Robert Graves and Laura Riding's *A Survey of Modernist Poetry* (Peter Brooker, ed., *Modernism/Postmodernism*, Harlow, Longman, 1992, p. 6). From around the 1950s onwards, it began to be used more consistently in Anglo–American academia as a description of early twentieth-century experimentalism in art and culture. Modernism is, however, less a single consistent 'movement' than a retrospective category for relating together a variety of movements, artefacts, artists, thinkers and cultural practices, some of whom might have been surprised to find themselves thrown together under the banner of 'modernism'.

The purpose of *Beginning Modernism* is to provide a point of entry into the study of this exciting and highly important, yet bewildering and often contradictory cultural and historical phenomenon. Like other books in the *Beginnings* series, *Beginning Modernism* is primarily aimed at the student of literature. Modernism is, however, by its very nature multifaceted, and characterized by the invention, dissolution and recombination of genres and their boundaries. *Beginning Modernism* will, then, help you to an understanding of

key developments in modernist literature, while encouraging you to
relate these to other, diverse yet now familiar instances of modernism, such as the Eiffel Tower or Charlie Chaplin's movies, Antoni
Gaudi's *Sagrada Familia* cathedral in Barcelona, Igor Stravinsky's
Rite of Spring or Pablo Picasso's *Les Demoiselles d'Avignon*, not to
mention reinforced concrete and the Model T Ford.

Because of the complexity of the subject, there are many other
guides to modernism available, and some of these are listed in the
'Selected reading' section at the end of this chapter as valuable com-
panions to the present book. The distinctive features of *Beginning
Modernism* are as follows:

- Each chapter aims to carefully 'talk' you into, and through,
  certain issues in modernism.
- An emphasis on the close reading of texts, written or visual,
  in order to give you confidence with the detailed handling of
  modernist materials.
- The provision of further selected reading for each aspect of
  modernism, pointing the way to further valuable sources rather
  than trying to comprehensively cover and summarize a particular
  field.
- A sense of current developments in modernist studies.
- Regular 'Stop and think' sections, designed to encourage your
  active involvement in debates around modernism.

I began with a few basic proposals. However, like any major
'ism', modernism tends to blur at the edges, both chronologically
and semantically, as soon as you begin to look at it closely. Let
us take periodization. My suggested dates, 1880–1939, are quite
broad, and in your own reading around modernism, you will soon
discover a range of alternative suggestions within those dates. There
are more radical alternatives, even to the idea that modernism is
fundamentally an early twentieth-century phenomenon. Marshall
Berman's influential *All That Is Solid Melts Into Air: The Experience
of Modernity* (London, Verso, 1982), argues that the great modernist writers were actually located in the mid-nineteenth century: Karl
Marx, Charles Baudelaire and Nikolai Gogol, for example. One can
encounter the view that modernism originates in 1857 with the publication of Baudelaire's *Les Fleurs du mal* and Gustave Flaubert's

novel *Madame Bovary*. At the other end of the spectrum, the influential German thinker Jürgen Habermas famously maintained that the 'project of modernity' is far from over, his argument being often used to support claims that it is too early to proclaim the death of modernism at the hands of a condition of contemporaneity we now call 'postmodernism' (Habermas, 'Modernity – An Incomplete Project', in ed. Hal Foster, *Postmodern Culture*, London, Pluto, 1985, pp. 3–15).

Perhaps, in order to say *when* modernism was, it might help to define more closely *what* modernism was. But again there are a number of possibilities. Having taught undergraduate courses in modernism for over twenty years now, I'm aware of the tendency for some students to feel – at any point in the course! – that modernism as a concept is just too slippery for comfort. An essay such as Susan Stanford Friedman's 'Definitional Excursions: The Meanings of *Modern/Modernity/Modernism*' (*Modernism/modernity* 8:3, September 2001, pp. 493–513) provides a good analysis of this inherent slipperiness. By way of response to those students, I began a while back to offer in my teaching a very provisional definition of the *meaning* of modernism, which we would then go on to explore, and which I present here as another opening gambit: *modernism is the moment at which art stops making sense*. It seems, in other words, to become the conscious goal of the writings, ideas and art forms we now call modernist to make the familiar unfamiliar, to disrupt or shatter our accepted forms of representation and understanding, to introduce *difficulty*.

> Let us go, then, you and I,
> When the evening is spread out against the sky
> Like a patient etherised upon a table;

T.S. Eliot's famous early poem, 'The Love Song of J. Alfred Prufrock' (1915), begins, as a song should, in a regular, lilting metre. The second line rhymes, maintaining the trace of a song-like pattern even if the rhythm begins to falter, and we sense something slightly awry in the wording (how exactly can evening, which is a general condition or concept, be 'spread out' against the sky?). But it is the simile in the third line that shocks us – perhaps even now – into a recognition of something radically new.

STOP and THINK

You may have come to this book because you are studying a course on modernism, or simply because you want to find out about an area that is unfamiliar or daunting. Assess your own assumptions about what modernism is:

- What kind of movement is modernism? Wide? Narrow? Open and democratic? Closed and elitist?
- What kinds of artistic and cultural forms do you associate with modernism?
- Who uses the word, and with what kinds of connotation (positive? negative? uncertain? ambiguous?)
- Is modernism the same as 'modern art'? What connotations does this phrase bring with it?

Now read the following statement by the Russian modernist thinker Victor Shklovsky (1893–1984) from his essay 'Art as Technique' (1917):

> Habitualization devours works, clothes, furniture, one's wife, and the fear of war . . . And art exists that one may recover the sensation of life; it exists to make one feel things, to make the stone *stony*. The purpose of art is to impart the sensation of things as they are perceived and not as they are known. The technique of art is to make objects 'unfamiliar', to make forms difficult, to increase the difficulty and length of perception because the process of perception is an aesthetic end in itself and must be prolonged. (quoted in V. Kolocotrini *et al.*, *Modernism: An Anthology of Sources and Documents*, Edinburgh, Edinburgh University Press, 1998, p. 219)

- Is Shklovsky right about the power of habit in human life?
- Can or should art take on the role that Shklovsky assigns to it? What other roles might there be for art?
- Can you think of any specific examples of forms or works of art that have, for you, worked in the way Shklovsky suggests?
- Do the conditions of 'modern life', however we define that, make the role Shklovsky assigns to art more or less important?

Figure 1 Pablo Picasso (1881-1973): *Les Demoiselles d'Avignon* (Paris, 1907)

According to Peter Ackroyd, when T.S. Eliot's poem was first shown in 1917 to Harold Monro, a prominent publisher of new Georgian verse, Monro returned it with the declaration that it was 'absolutely insane' (Peter Ackroyd, *T.S. Eliot*, London, Abacus, 1985, p. 55). A similar effect may be attributed to Pablo Picasso's famous *Les Demoiselles d'Avignon* (Figure 1), first exhibited in 1907. Menace and inscrutability are still communicated by an image in which African tribal art combines with Cubist technique, and in which the range of distortion across the faces of the five naked prostitutes is matched by the warped and fragmented space they inhabit. Igor Stravinsky (1882–1971) introduced into classical music unprecedented forms of dissonance, strange and unsettling to trained and untrained ears alike; there was uproar in the Théâtre des Champs-Elysées, Paris, when his *Rite of Spring* was first performed there by Sergei Diaghilev's Ballets Russes company in Paris on 29 May 1913. Similar consternation was prompted when Marcel Duchamp named a public urinal basin *Fountain* and offered it to an exhibition of contemporary art in New York in 1917.

This version of a modernism defined by difficulty or by a rupturing of common sense is often referred to as 'high modernism', and was the dominant tendency when literary modernism began to be studied in universities, from around the mid-twentieth century. In recent years, however, this definition has come to be challenged as emerging out of a kind of self-fulfilling logic: modernism had been constituted, in other words, *through* the careful selection of works of difficulty. In his book on the English novel between 1895 and 1920, David Trotter proposes to abandon, as a 'blatant mystification', the 'explanatory and evaluative' concept of modernism as a dramatic rupture, on the grounds that 'nobody has been able to say exactly what the force or event *was* which caused writers to write in a certain way' (*The English Novel in History 1895–1920*, London and New York, Routledge, 1993, p. 4).

A 'new modernist studies' has arisen, richly diversifying the kinds of cultural production that could be described as modernist, and thereby unsettling the notion, of which we will read much in due course, of modernism as distantly superior to the burgeoning of early twentieth-century mass society and popular cultural forms. Much of the transformative energy of the new modernist studies has come from the United States, perhaps best exemplified by the journal *Modernism/modernity*, published by Johns Hopkins University Press for the Modernist Studies Association since 1994, and in which recent special issues have examined topics such as mass communications, film, Jewish modernism, transnationalisms, and fascism (I refer periodically to material from *Modernism/modernity* throughout this book, and I strongly encourage you to browse the journal if possible). Douglas Mao and Rebecca L. Walkowitz have proposed the concept of 'bad modernisms', based on a 2002 conference emphasizing the determinedly disobedient and recalcitrant aspects of the modernist endeavour and as an antidote to the sometimes decorous institutionalizing of 'high modernism'. Their edited volume (*Bad Modernisms*, Durham and London, Duke University Press, 2006) consistently undermines the high–low cultural divide and demonstrates the elasticity of the concept of modernism, for example in Lisa Fluet's essay entitled 'Hit-man modernism', which weaves modernist texts into an account of the hired killer figure in the violent 'pulp modernism' of B-movies, or Monica Miller's essay on the figure of the black dandy. In a collection of essays on the subject of 'Gothic Modernisms', Kelly Hurley sees the Gothic as a category that deconstructs the distinction between high and popular modernisms; as part of her study of William Hope Hodgson's novel *The Night Land* (1912), Hurley observes that some of the most innovative, anti-realist fiction in Britain is to be found 'amongst popular genres – Gothic Horror, sensation fiction, science fiction – at the *fin de siècle*' ('The Modernist Abominations of William Hope Hodgson', in *Gothic Modernisms*, eds Andrew Smith and Jeff Wallace, Basingstoke, Palgrave, 2001, pp. 129–49).

Behind these new developments lie pioneering accounts of gender and modernism, such as those by Sandra Gilbert, Susan Gubar and Bonnie Kime Scott, focusing primarily on the retrieval of previously marginalized women modernists; studies, particularly those of Lawrence Rainey and Ann Ardis, using concepts of class and social distinction to critically question the idea of high modernism; and explorations of the complex ethnic diversity of modernism. Rainey in particular has done much to demystify or demythologize 'high' modernism by emphasizing, along the lines of Pierre Bourdieu's sociological concept of 'cultural capital', that the economic value of modernism might be linked to conditions of rarity and obscurity or inaccessibility. On this logic, for example, T.S. Eliot could wish his landmark poem *The Waste Land* (1922) to be 'successful, but not too successful'! (Lawrence Rainey, 'The Cultural Economy of Modernism', in ed. Michael Levenson, *The Cambridge Companion to Modernism*, Cambridge, Cambridge University Press, 1999, p. 51). A different kind of unsettling or complication of Eliot's reputation forms part of Michael North's groundbreaking study *The Dialect of Modernism: Race, Language and Twentieth-Century Literature* (Oxford, Oxford University Press, 1998). North continues a process of reclaiming the Harlem Renaissance, a black cultural movement in

1920s New York, from white historical condescension, by arguing that the widespread use of 'negro' dialect was a necessary factor in the modernisms of writers such as Eliot, Gertrude Stein and Ezra Pound, as well as a complex artistic strategy in Harlem writers such as Langston Hughes, Claude McKay, Jean Toomer and Zora Neale Hurston (see my section on Primitivism in chapter 4 for a more detailed account of North's crucial argument).

What then are some of the key issues now shaping the field of 'new modernist studies'?:

- *Gender and sexuality*. Modernist studies have benefited as much as other areas of literary studies from the rapid expansion of scholarly interest in questions of gender and sexuality. In a collection of essays entitled *Modernist Sexualities* (eds Hugh Stevens and Caroline Howlett, Manchester, Manchester University Press, 2000), Hugh Stevens argues that high modernism is a product of the primarily white and male viewpoints of literary criticism from the 1950s to the 1970s, for which the difficulty of the modernist artefact proved a suitable subject for the masculine exercise of professional critical rigour. The associations of modernism with a particularly masculine ethos of aggressive rupture and renewed classicism, typified by approaches to the 'men of 1914' (T.S. Eliot, Ezra Pound, F.S. Flint, T.E. Hulme, for example), have been strenuously challenged, and the concept of modernism opened up to the rich and diverse work of women, gay and lesbian writers in the period. An index of such changes can be found in the output of the American critic Bonnie Kime Scott, from her counter-emphasis on the 'women of 1928' (Virginia Woolf, Rebecca West and Djuna Barnes) and anthology *The Gender of Modernism* (1990) to the much more recent sequel anthology *Gender in Modernism* (2007), more diverse than its predecessor (and including, as its blurb puts it, 'authors dismissed as sentimental'!), and reflecting an interest in the ambiguity of sexual identity increasingly deriving from the perspectives of gender studies and queer studies. *Beginning Modernism* takes it as read that no barriers of gender or sexuality now exist in the critical treatment of modernist artists, however significant such barriers might have been in the moment of modernism itself. Nevertheless, important ground-clearing scholarly work continues in the latter area, focusing, for example, on the relationship of women to modernity, and on the ways in which women's intellectual work required them to renegotiate the boundary between public and private spheres. See, for example, Alice Gambrell's study of women as 'insider-outsider intellectuals' in *Women Intellectuals, Modernism and Difference: Transatlantic Culture, 1919–1945* (Cambridge, Cambridge University Press, 1997), or eds Ann L. Ardis and Leslie W. Lewis, *Women's Experience of Modernity 1875–1945* (Baltimore, Johns Hopkins University Press, 2003).

• *Geography*. To my opening questions, when and what was modernism?, contemporary modernist studies adds a third: where was modernism? The long-established answer to this question would be: in the great European cities, and in New York. The importance of metropolitan milieus for the cultures of modernism is unquestioned, as chapter 5 of this book will indicate. But modernist geography now largely consists in the attempt to rectify the strongly Euro-American bias of previous studies in two main ways: first, by making visible the modernisms of, for example, India, East Asia, the Caribbean and Mexico; and second, by emphasizing the *transnational* character of modernism. In the case of India, for example, Dipesh Chakrabarty's *Provincialising Europe: Postcolonial Thought and Historical Difference* (Princeton, NJ, Princeton University Press, 2000) shows the emergence of a 'high modernist' response to modernity in the Bengali intelligentsias of the nineteenth and twentieth centuries. Amit Chaudhuri has also consistently sought to reinscribe an Indian tradition of modernism as a humanism of 'high seriousness', for example in the poetry of Rabindranath Tagore (who was highly influential on W.B. Yeats), as a necessary counterweight to the excessively Rushdiesque 'post'-modernizing of twentieth-century Indian writing; see for example his essay 'Cosmopolitanism's Alien Face', *New Left Review* 55, Jan./Feb. 2009. Laura Doyle and Laura Winkiel's edited volume *Geomodernisms: Race, Modernism, Modernity* (Bloomington, Indiana University Press, 2005) is another pioneering study of the diversifying geographies of modernism. It is likely that future developments in modernist studies will also include the increasing availability of works in

translation, counter-colonizing the canonical space still largely
monopolized by the great works of Euro-American modernism.

- *The everyday*. Modernist studies has been increasingly preoccupied with what the French cultural theorist Michel de Certeau
calls the 'practice' of everyday life. The rapid transformations
of early twentieth-century modernity are primarily felt in actual
daily events and routines: walking and travelling, inhabiting
houses and apartments, working, eating and drinking, shopping,
communicating, being entertained. While modernism in design
and architecture was oriented towards the rationalization and
reorganizing of the everyday, modernist literature develops new
methods of foregrounding the everyday. The time span of a single
day in James Joyce's *Ulysses* (1922) allows an extraordinary attention to the minutiae of daily life, from making breakfast, visiting
the toilet and shopping to fantasizing, masturbating and being
unfaithful. The same structure in *Mrs Dalloway* (1925) allowed
Virginia Woolf the opportunity to emphasize the importance for
an individual woman of being able to move freely between the
public and private spaces of city and home. Products of technology, from tinned food to typewriters and motor cars, carry a new
significance. These kinds of emphasis have led modernist studies away from a narrowly literary or aesthetic methodology and
towards an interdisciplinary practice more akin to cultural studies. See, for example, Bryony Randall, *Modernism, Daily Time
and Everyday Life* (Cambridge, Cambridge University Press,
2007), Morag Shiach, *Modernism, Labour and Selfhood in British
Literature and Culture, 1890–1930* (Cambridge, Cambridge
University Press, 2004) or Tim Armstrong, *Modernism: A
Cultural History* (Cambridge, Polity, 2005).
- *Technology*. While the considerable impact of new technologies in modernity, and on modernist thinkers, has long been
acknowledged, recent work has begun to challenge the tendency
to conceive of this impact on literary modernism in terms of
binary opposition. As Sara Danius puts it, 'the concept of technology invariably appears in the same negatively charged cluster
as science, instrumental reason, and utilitarian thought', as if it
has been seen as the function of the modernist arts to counteract
these deathly influences (*The Senses of Modernism: Technology,*

Perception and Aesthetics, Ithaca, NY, Cornell University Press, 2002). However, in examining Thomas Mann's *The Magic Mountain*, Proust, and James Joyce's *Ulysses*, Danius argues that new technologies of perception, such as the photograph and the X-ray, subtly transform modernist aesthetics and dispel the sense of antithesis. Tim Armstrong's *Modernism, Technology and the Body: A Cultural Study* (Cambridge, Cambridge University Press, 1998), examines the permeability of nature and technology in modernism's preoccupation with changing perceptions of the human body.

- *Magazines.* While the study of modernism has tended to concentrate, understandably enough, on key texts, it is increasingly clear that the actual dissemination of modernist ideas took place via the proliferation of 'little magazines', journals and manifestos. These publications, often on short print runs from very small presses, may seem somewhat ephemeral in comparison to the weighty modernist tomes we now study, yet in their historical context they were at the heart of modernist discourse, sometimes combining print and graphics in innovatory ways. Increasingly these valuable sources are being made available online. The Modernist Journals Project, headed by Robert Scholes at Brown University in conjunction with the University of Tulsa, gives access to *The New Age*, *Blast* and its successor *The Tyro*, *Rhythm* and *Dana*, with more to come in future years (www.modjourn.org). Try looking up the first number of Wyndham Lewis' short-lived but influential British journal *Blast* for a dramatic example of modernist design and mode of address. In the UK, the Modernist Magazines Project has been launched by scholars Peter Brooker and Andrew Thacker (www.cts.dmu.ac.uk/modmags/index. htm).

Beginning Modernism will, throughout, try to operate on either side of the critical debate between 'high' modernism and the new modernist studies. In introducing the reader to the new modernist studies, it will emphasize an increasing pluralism, 'modernisms' rather than modernism. At the same time, however, I want to retain a certain version of 'high' modernism, both as a starting point and as an end point, as is implicit in my opening proposition that *modernism is the moment at which art stops making sense*. The main reason for this approach is that, in my experience, a mixture of surprise, bafflement, bewilderment, and perhaps exasperation, continues to be a common, initial student response to the texts and images of modernism, as if the particular challenges of the modernist artefact have not been assuaged by the lapse of a century or so. One extreme version of this response is what I sometimes call, after Hans Christian Andersen, the 'Emperor's New Clothes' narrative of modernism, according to which it can be claimed that modernism's difficulty is a kind of trick, played on an unsuspecting public, which can be exposed only by a young innocent child's ability to cut through the atmosphere of sycophancy that surrounds the subject. So a key aim of the book, in helping to avoid the easy trap of the Emperor's New Clothes narrative, is also to present various rationales for the difficulty of the modernist artwork (whether it be written or painted, sculpted or composed of musical notes), based on the historical circumstances of thinkers and artists. There is an inspiring sense of intellectual ambition and adventure in modernism, of which difficulty is a primary expression, and which, I believe, obliges us to constantly re-examine and reinvigorate the definition of 'high' modernism. Chapter 9 sketches out a concluding case for this, based on the work of two contemporary (early twenty-first century) artists.

Beginning Modernism will, then, begin with an extended response to the question: how and why does modernism stop making sense? This will be the main aim of the next chapter, which sets up the visual arts as a platform for further debate. It is not quite the same, however, as saying that modernism will be made easy to understand; the book will not seek to explain modernism *away*, because to dispel the difficulty of modernism would be to un-modernize it, and to rob it of its distinctiveness. It will, however, seek to *demystify* modernism in two main ways. First, it will attempt to account for the origin of the Emperor's New Clothes narrative – that is, the fear that modernism is a kind of confidence trick, attempting to dupe an unsuspecting reader, viewer or audience – in the context of modernism's specific, strategic response to a complex set of changing cultural conditions. These would include the rise of literacy, 'mass' production and 'mass' society, and the impact of technologies

– industrialized printing, photography and film, electronic communications, for example – which raised new questions about
what 'art' in the modern world should or might be. In such circumstances, we can perhaps understand how artists might want to
retain for art what the critic Walter Benjamin called a certain 'aura',
or a certain sense of art as a highly specialized human activity,
'arrogant', as the French architect Le Corbusier provocatively puts
it, to the extent that it performs its 'proper functions' only when
addressing itself to 'the chosen few' (*Towards a New Architecture*,
trans. Frederick Etchells (1927), London, Architectural Press,
1970, p. 96). To thus demystify the modernist text is not, however,
simply to debunk its seriousness of origin and intent by suggesting
instead some kind of calculating elitism. *Beginning Modernism* will
also demystify by helping to reveal the complex and revolutionary ideas that often informed modernist artefacts – ideas, drawn
as much from the sciences as from philosophy and the arts, which
highlighted the limitations of what had ordinarily been taken as
'common sense'.

Second, my recurrent emphasis on the close reading of modernist artefacts seeks to show that the difficulty of modernist texts need
never be a condition of *unreadability*. Confronting the difficulty at
close quarters is a way of grasping the nature of modernist techniques, and of appreciating the multiplicity of interpretations that
the modernist text can generate. We could easily erect difficulty as
an artificial barrier to understanding, failing thus to see how modernists texts might call for the dismantling of established habits or
protocols of reading and for the creation of new ones. As Gertrude
Stein noted of the later writings of James Joyce, people tended to
like him precisely because of his incomprehensibility; Joyce's difficulty is, for Stein, a levelling factor, placing all readers in the same
democratically open space, confronting the challenges and pleasures
of generating readings of his work. This, then, is a paradoxical view
of modernist difficulty, situated at the opposite end of the spectrum
from Le Corbusier's explicit elitism and from the fears embedded in
the Emperor's New Clothes narrative: it suggests that modernism is
the entirely appropriate, potentially popular aesthetic for a century
of unprecedented and often unpredictable change.

The structure of *Beginning Modernism* is designed to reflect this

combination of older and newer approaches in modernist studies. Poetry and fiction are dealt with in chapters 6 and 7, marking the continuing importance of these traditional genres within
modernism. Other chapters, however, aim to give a sense of the
interconnections and parallels that we need to grasp in the study of
modernism. You will find that the third traditional literary genre,
drama, is examined in chapter 8 under the rubric of modernist
'performance', alongside music, film and dance, suggesting that the
cross-fertilization of these forms begins to transcend their individual significance. Chapter 2 is an extended introduction to modernist
visual art, taking the visual arts as a case study in rich interdiscipli-
narity, and suggesting how visual artefacts might be read as exem-
plars of a broader modernism. Chapters 3 and 4 aim to establish a
set of key concepts and historical contexts that inform a wide range
of modernist practices. Chapter 5 aims to convey the importance to
modernism of particular *uses* of place and space, bringing together a
study of the metropolis, architecture and sculpture; in other words,
modernism requires us to think in terms of *events* (performances
and exhibitions, for example), geographical *locations* (cities or colonies, for example), and social *groupings* of various kinds, as much as
of individual writers and works. Finally, as I have already indicated,
chapter 9 opens out the question of the legacies, continuities and
discontinuities that might be at stake in any discussion of what lies
beyond modernism.

Key terms: modernism, modernity, postmodernism

An essential requisite for beginning modernism is to establish some
distinctions between the set of closely related terms 'modernism',
'modernity' and 'postmodernism'. Let us reiterate that 'modernism' usually refers to a revolutionary movement in the art and
thought of the early twentieth century. It is a retrospective term,
which became established in American academia of the 1950s,
encompassing an array of cultural phenomena. *The moment at which
art stops making sense*, my opening gambit for an understanding of
modernism, could be said to be clearly elaborated by Eugene Lunn
(*Marxism and Modernism*, London, Verso, 1982, pp. 34–7) under
the following four headings:

1. *Aesthetic self-consciousness or reflexivity*: the tendency of the artwork to draw attention to its own constituent materials and to the issues or problems raised in the processes of its own construction.
2. *Simultaneity, juxtaposition or 'montage'*: the tendency towards 'spatial' rather than 'temporal' form; a movement, in other words, away from the idea of time as a linear succession of moments or movements, and the narrative structures that go with this idea ('once upon a time this happened . . . and then this happened . . . and then this happened . . . '), and towards the idea that different moments or perspectives might be experienced or organized *simultaneously* within the space of the artwork. Examples of this might be the technique of *montage* in film or visual art, or the illustration of *epiphany* in fiction (see the analysis of the opening passage of Virginia Woolf's *Mrs Dalloway* in chapter 7).
3. *Paradox, ambiguity and uncertainty*: the tendency to embody a sense of the provisional and contradictory in forms such as multiple or shifting perspective in painting and unreliable or multiple narration and open rather than closed endings in fiction, for example.
4. *'Dehumanization', or the demise of the integrated humanist self*: in the depiction of human character, the tendency to undermine any sense of harmony or wholeness in favour of a *dissolution* of the self into a congeries of conflicting and discontinuous drives.

I want to sound a note of caution about the use of lists of characteristics such as this: to use them as a checklist against which to measure the modernist credentials of an artefact would be to put the cart before the horse, because 'modernism' does not exist anywhere except in the infinitely varied forms which have given rise to it only as a subsequent general description. Nevertheless, something *did* happen there in the early twentieth century to warrant the emergence of the term 'modernism', and Lunn's list gives a good sense of modernism as a relatively precise cultural phenomenon occurring within the much broader historical movement known as 'modernity'.

'Modernity' should always be used in distinction from modernism, even though the two terms are importantly related. While

modernism refers to the *cultural* forms of a specific period, modernity refers to the much broader *historical* process of transformation within which modernism occurred. Modernism is thus a
relatively small episode within the much more extensive time span
of 'modernity', which refers to a long historical process of becoming 'modern'. To remember that historians use the phrase 'early
modern' to refer to the sixteenth century is to realize how wide is
the remit of modernity in historical discourse. Here then are three
principal historical reference points for the term 'modernity':

1. The main feature of the transition to modernity as this is generally understood is the shift from *feudalism to capitalism* as the
   organizing mode of economic and social life. In its accelerated
   form we might identify this, for example in British history, with
   the agricultural and industrial revolutions of the eighteenth and
   nineteenth centuries. Historians argue however that its origins
   lie much farther back, for example in the rise of commerce and
   the European towns and cities (see ed. Rodney Hilton, *The
   Transition from Feudalism to Capitalism*, London, Verso, 1976).
   The transition cannot be confined to some separate 'economic'
   sphere, but involves fundamental changes in all areas of human
   life. Some of these changes, which resonate within or shape the
   contexts of modernism, are as follows:
   (a) The migration of people from the country to the city, from
       rural to urban ways of life. Thus, the accompanying develop-
       ment of towns and cities, and of the emergence of forms of
       human culture and consciousness specific to these. From the
       later nineteenth century onwards, with nation states turning
       to imperialist, colonial expansion in order to develop their
       markets and resources, inter-national migration begins to
       grow. The imperial centres become the 'metropolis', devel-
       oping increasingly varied populations in which the encoun-
       ter between different ideas and languages fuels the rise of
       modernist art.
   (b) The development of a money economy, and within it the
       concepts of capital (accumulated labour) and the commod-
       ity. Use-value (the valuing of a thing in terms of what it
       can actually do for you) is displaced by exchange-value (the

valuing of a thing in terms of the amount of money it can
be exchanged for). Capital, the commodity, and exchange-
value, are said to introduce a sense of the *abstraction* of things
and people from their actual contexts.

(c) Changes in the nature of work, introduced first by the
discipline of the factory and other industrial locations, and
later by the development of the retail and service industries
necessary for rapidly expanding market economies. Both
involve the domination of the clock over preceding ways of
organizing working life, such as the time it takes to complete
a task, the amount of light in a day, or the conditions of the
seasons. Although it deals with pre-twentieth-century history, E.P. Thompson's essay 'Time, Work–Discipline, and
Industrial Capitalism' (*Past and Present* 38 (Dec. 1967), pp.
56–97) is an illuminating account of the emergence of clock-
time in everyday life, which can feed into your studies of
modernism.

(d) The Enlightenment. This key term in cultural and intellectual
history refers to an eighteenth-century movement characterized by a belief in the emancipatory powers of reason and logic
over superstition, and to the formation of what we now largely
take for granted as a scientific attitude to the world. Originating
in the late seventeenth-century thought of René Descartes
(1596–1650) ('I think, therefore I am'), and in the optics and
physics of Isaac Newton (1643–1727), Enlightenment frames
the eighteenth century as an age, in George Rudé's words, of
'outstanding intellectual vigour' extending into all areas of
human knowledge. Enlightenment gives rise to the assumption that modernity is about gradual linear improvement,
'progress' or 'development', enshrined in the ability of reason
to discover the laws of nature and thus gradually master or
subdue the material world. When at the service or in combination with capitalism, therefore, it can lead to the instrumental
treatment of the world as an object, relatively passive or inert
in comparison with the human subject, and as a 'resource' to
be exploited for the purposes of profit.

2. The French Revolution: 1789. In its overthrow of absolute
monarchy and of the principle of the Divine Right of Kings, the

Revolution of 1789 might be seen as the political corollary of Enlightenment philosophy. Secular government was installed in France following the execution of King Louis XVI in 1793, based on the democratic principles of liberty, equality and fraternity, and thus committed, like the Enlightenment, to the ability of humans to take control of their own history, freeing themselves from ignorance and superstition.

3. The year 1848. Less familiar as a date than 1789, 1848 is nevertheless seen as pivotal in the formation of modernity. It was a year of uprisings and revolution across Europe (Italy, Austria-Hungary, France, Switzerland and Germany, with significant social unrest also in Belgium and Britain), distinguished by the emergence of working class or proletarian movements as the agents of political radicalism. In France, following the abdication of Louis Philippe, the installation of the Second Republic also saw the suppression of the June rising and the installation of the militaristic Louis Napoleon as president. The bourgeoisie or commercial and property-owning middle classes – the prime movers of revolution in 1789 – now became identified as defenders of the status quo against the insurgent demands of mass organized labour: 'the age which began in 1848', proclaims A.J.P. Taylor, 'was the age of the masses' (*Europe: Grandeur and Decline*, Harmondsworth, Penguin, 1974, p. 58). Art, in France and beyond, begins to reflect and interpret these complex changes in hegemony and class formation.

4. The First World War: 1914–18. Precipitated by the Serbian assassination of the Austrian Archduke Franz Ferdinand in Sarajevo on 28 June 1914, this war had nevertheless been anticipated by the European powers for some time. It can be seen as the inevitable result of the conflicting, imperialist–expansionist designs of the European powers in their search for new markets. Unprecedented in its use of machinery for the purposes of destruction, the war involved a vast and senseless loss of human life. In this sense, while undoubtedly a landmark in modernity, the Great War also for many heralded the end of modernity as a narrative of progress and enlightenment. Alternatively, the war pointed up the peculiarly paradoxical character of modernity itself, characterized by Marshall Berman (following Marx and

Engels' lead in the 1848 *Communist Manifesto*) as a process of 'creative destruction'. In its pursuit of change and innovation, modernity must also ceaselessly dissolve that which it creates: the instruments of enlightenment can at the same time be the instruments of barbarism and annihilation.

The relationship between modernism and modernity is the subject of continuing debate in modernist studies. What, for example, is the relationship between modernism and the project of Enlightenment rationality? The famous dictum of the French architect Le Corbusier, 'a house is a machine for living in', aptly encapsulates the combination of technology, modernity and utopia in his work. It would be difficult, of course, to imagine a dystopian architecture! Le Corbusier's scientific and idealistic spirit connects with much of the activity of the Bauhaus School in Weimar Germany in the years 1919–33, or of Russian Constructivism (roughly 1917–27), both movements making bold innovations in the fields of visual and graphic art, photography, sculpture and design. On the other hand, it is equally common to see certain strands of modernism as, precisely, a reaction *away* from Enlightenment modernity. Such reactions could take a variety of forms. In his essay 'Romanticism and Classicism' (1914), the Imagist poet and critic T.E. Hulme (1883–1917) characterized modernism as a *classical* mode of restraint and precision, reacting explicitly against the sloppy 'spilt religion' of Romanticism but also, implicitly, against the frenetic creative–destructive paradox of modernity. A considerably more complex reaction is to be found in the thought of Theodor Adorno (1903–69) as a representative of the Frankfurt School of Critical Theory (or Institute for Social Research), founded in 1923. While endorsing a strongly rationalistic sense of progressive experimentation in modernist music (see chapter 8), Adorno argued that the imposition of Enlightenment reason and values in modernity could only lead, paradoxically, to their totalitarian domination, a fate to be avoided only through the rigorous pursuit of an art which is to be justified only on its own, extra-rationalistic terms.

A sense therefore that the exercise of Enlightenment reason might lead not only to the erosion of older superstitions, but also to an undermining of the conditions of its own possibility, informs a fundamental strain of *irrationalism* in modernism. As we shall see in chapter 4, in key instances such as Charles Darwin's theory of natural selection, or Sigmund Freud's theory of the unconscious, the triumphs of modern scientific thought seem also to bring a renewed awareness of the necessary limitations of thinking. For Darwin, the human being is not a separate and divinely ordained species, but simply part of an evolutionary continuum with the rest of nature; for Freud, human identity is largely determined not by the conscious mind, which is like the tip of an iceberg, but by the unconscious, the mass of the iceberg below the surface of conscious rationality and, by definition, inaccessible to it except in indirect ways. Each theory seems to render increasingly problematic the concept of knowledge, since neither seems to allow for the distance between subject or knower, and object or known, upon which objectivity is predicated.

The fiction of D.H. Lawrence, the paintings of Paul Gauguin or the philosophy of Friedrich Nietzsche, might thus be included in the category of irrationalist modernisms, as if to insist that to be modernist is to question the project of Enlightenment modernity. Nietzsche's work is an important influence in the philosophy of existentialism, emphasizing that the definition or conceptualization of human identity must always be secondary to the prior, onto-logical and meaningless *fact* of existence itself. The development of Surrealism in the 1920s could be seen as the most extensive elabora-tion of a modernist commitment to the irrational, though differing greatly in its orientation from earlier irrationalists such as Lawrence and Gauguin.

Faced then with the often contradictory relationship between modernity and modernism, and with existentialism as an instance of modernist thought, it may be helpful here to focus on another key distinction between terms, this time between modernism and 'postmodernism'. Postmodernism is comprehensively covered by another book in this series, *Beginning Postmodernism* by Tim Woods (2009), and I do not wish to reproduce here the details of Woods' excellent account, which include his own broad-brush outline of modernism (2nd edn, *Beginning Postmodernism*, pp. 6–10). Debates about the relationship between modernism and postmodernism are as wide and varied as those concerning modernism and modernity, and, as Woods notes, it is the meaning of the prefix 'post' that is often at issue. First, we can at least establish that postmodernism designates a later period than modernism, stretching from the early 1960s through to the present. The term is still often used to denote a condition of contemporary culture, of where we are now. But how does the 'post' function? Does it mean that modernism has been superseded, or that it has been extended?

It may help to return here to modernism's complex relationship to rationality. Whether extending the Enlightenment project, or challenging its limitations, modernists tended to exemplify a preoccupation with the possibilities of human expression and knowledge. Where these possibilities appear to be rendered problematic, and Enlightenment progress and development turns against itself, this is often experienced as a *crisis* in meaning or knowledge, even as it produces works of art of startling originality and strangeness. The First World War might be taken as a major exemplar of Enlightenment self-contradiction, its devastating effect on many artists and thinkers following from the realization that this wholesale mechanized destruction of human life was the *result* of a century or more of intellectual and industrial 'progress' and growing technological sophistication. The modernist response might be seen as a scream or howl at this loss of meaning, in a secular world where existing belief systems have been dismantled. A very familiar, anticipatory expression of this condition, and one which became a paradigm of an artistic movement known as Expressionism, is a painting by the Norwegian artist, Edvard Munch, *The Scream* (1893) (this is such a well-known image that I have chosen not to reproduce it here). The distressed and emaciated human figure seems isolated or alienated from those around him, pressured inwards by the lines of force surrounding him. He seems a stranger both to the natural and to the social worlds, such a disconnection suggesting a breakdown in our understanding of these realms as well as in our sense of self.

Munch's *The Scream* epitomizes modernism as a deeply felt response to a crisis of meaning. We can now, however, regularly encounter a postmodernized form of the painting. In 1995, *The Scream* was adopted as a brand image by a chain of British pubs; you may be familiar with this, as the pubs tended to be established in student areas! The transformation of the image into a marketing device is consistent with other ways in which *The Scream* has become commodified: you can also, for example, buy *The Scream* balloons or inflatables. These appropriations of an image of modernist angst can still be read in terms of a crisis of meaning: Munch's anguished figure is now a sign in a system of exchange and consumption, as if to displace a model of depth and authenticity with one of surfaces and interchangeability. Where modernism responds to the crisis through revolt and the search for restoration, however, postmodernism tends towards an acceptance, perhaps even an ironic celebration, of the fact that meaning takes place in systems of signs or surfaces which refer to nothing beyond themselves.

Different critical positions can be taken up in relation to this postmodernism: we could read the transformation of Munch's image as a kind of trivialization, and an invitation to irrationalism, embodying a loss of value consequent upon the reduction of the concept of value to the question of what something can be bought and sold for. Fredric Jameson, a very important commentator, defines postmodernism as 'the cultural logic of late capitalism'. Alternatively, postmodernism can be read as a rational starting point for an analysis of how the conditions of 'truth' are created by human beings alone, and not by metaphysical or supernatural sources. 'The truth of an idea', argued the American psychologist and philosopher William James, 'is not a stagnant property inherent within it. Truth *happens* to an idea' (*Principles of Psychology*, London, Macmillan, 1890). James is in many ways a key *modernist* thinker, but the codification of truth in terms of what *works*, rather than in terms of absolute meaning or value, becomes, in the philosophy of *pragmatism*, an important feature of postmodern thinking. Thus Richard Rorty, a prominent postmodernist philosopher and a successor to James, expresses an even broader historical lineage to postmodernism when he begins his essay 'The Contingency of Language' with the statement that, '(a)bout two hundred years ago, the idea that truth was made rather than found began to take hold of the imagination of Europe' (*Contingency, Irony, and Solidarity*, Cambridge, Cambridge University Press, 1989).

I have used an illustrative comparison to suggest at least one important way of making the distinction between modernism and postmodernism, mainly because I am wary of producing an abstract list of features against which an artefact might be checked either for its modernist or postmodernist credentials. Should you wish to consult such a list, one notable and much-anthologized example is provided by Ihab Hassan in his book *The Postmodern Turn* (1987), which you will find reproduced in Tim Woods' book in this series (p. 72). In the present book, there are a number of points at which I will be reopening the critical dialogue between modernism and postmodernism, and effectively questioning any watertight distinction between the two. A final, useful example with which to end this discussion, derives from the critic Brian McHale. In an influential formulation, McHale identified modernism as preoccupied with an *epistemological* problematic – in other words, with problems of *knowing* – and postmodernism as concerned with questions of *ontology*, in other words questions of *being*. While the modernist asks, what is this world, and how do I know it?, the postmodernist asks: 'Which world is this? What is to be done in it? Which of my selves is to do it?' (*Postmodernist Fiction*, New York and London, Methuen, 1987, p. 10). This goes some way towards reinforcing the sense that, while postmodernism accepts a crisis in the understanding of meaning and truth, to the extent that it posits a kind of cultural relativity in which people simply inhabit different knowledge- or language-worlds, modernism – perhaps heroically, perhaps absurdly, or perhaps in a complex fusion of the two – continues to address and search for ways to resolve the crisis. The next chapter shows how modernists in the visual arts went about this task.

Selected reading

Ardis, Ann, *Modernism and Cultural Conflict 1880–1922* (Cambridge, Cambridge University Press, 2002)
    Good example, like Rainey, of the new modernist studies, sceptical of the self-mythologizing of high modernism.
Armstrong, Tim, *Modernism: A Cultural History* (London, Polity, 2005)
    Eclectic and wide ranging in its references to non-canonical texts and sources. See for example chapter 4, 'Reform! Bodies, Selves, Politics, Aesthetics', and chapter 6, 'The Vibrating World: Science, Spiritualism, Technology'.

Berman, Marshall, *All That Is Solid Melts Into Air: The Experience of Modernity* (London, Verso, 1982)

Distinctive for its (a) affirmative, celebratory account of the 'experience of modernity' and (b) emphasis upon nineteenth-century 'modernism' – Marx, Baudelaire, Gogol, Dostoevsky, Nietzsche. For a fascinating review/riposte by the critic Perry Anderson, and Berman's counter-response, see *New Left Review* 144 (Mar./Apr. 1984, pp. 96–123).

Bradbury, Malcolm, and James McFarlane (eds), *Modernism: A Guide to European Literature 1890–1930* (Harmondsworth, Penguin, 1991)

Second edition of a seminal guide first published in 1976, but still of enormous value as a wide-ranging collection of essays.

Bradshaw, David (ed.), *A Concise Companion to Modernism* (Oxford, Blackwell, 2003)

Comparable to Armstrong in its cultural–historical approach, with distinctively thematic essays on for example, eugenics, technology, the concept of the state and modernist publishing.

DiBattista, Maria, and Lucy McDiarmid (eds), *High and Low Moderns: Literature and Culture, 1889–1939* (New York and Oxford, Oxford University Press, 1996)

Pioneering comparative approach to the blurring of literary and popular modernisms, with interesting material on figures such as Florence Farr, Lady Gregory and Rudyard Kipling.

Gilbert, Sandra, and Susan Gubar, *No Man's Land: The Place of the Woman Writer in the Twentieth Century* (3 vols; New Haven, Yale University Press, 1988–94)

Crucial work of reclamation through feminist scholarship.

Harvey, David, *The Condition of Postmodernity: An Enquiry into the Origins of Cultural Change* (Oxford, Blackwell, 1990)

Although apparently focused on postmodernism, this contains some of the best introductory material on the economics of early twentieth-century modernity, and on the significance of changes in the nature of capitalism in this period.

Kolocotroni, Vassiliki, Jane Goldman and Olga Taxidou (eds), *Modernism: An Anthology of Sources and Documents* (Edinburgh, Edinburgh University Press, 1998)

An excellent anthology of sources, to which I often refer in the course of this book.

Levenson, Michael (ed.), *The Cambridge Companion to Modernism* (Cambridge, Cambridge University Press, 1999)

A good collection of essays.

Lunn, Eugene, *Marxism and Modernism* (London, 1985)

A clear and thorough survey, though with the emphasis on modernism as alienation.

Mao, Douglas, and Rebecca L. Walkowitz, *Bad Modernisms* (Durham, NC and London, Duke University Press, 2006)

An eclectic and thought-provoking volume of essays.

Nicholls, Peter, *Modernisms: A Literary Guide* (Basingstoke, Macmillan, 1995)

More of a monograph than an introduction, but outstanding on poetry, Symbolism and its after effects.

Rainey, Lawrence, *Institutions of Modernism: Literary Elites and Public Culture* (New Haven, Yale University Press, 1998)

A landmark text in new modernist studies, exploring the cultural and economic construction of modernism as a distinctive and 'elite' discourse.

Scott, Bonnie Kime (ed.), *The Gender of Modernism: A Critical Anthology* (Bloomington, Indiana University Press, 1990)

An important anthology, unearthing a range of interesting materials by neglected modernist women writers.

Scott, Bonnie Kime, *Refiguring Modernism* (two vols; Bloomington, Indiana University Press, 1995)

First volume, 'The Women of 1928', sets a context for searching close readings of Woolf, West and Barnes in the second volume, from post-modern and contemporary feminist perspectives.

Scott, Bonnie Kime, *Gender in Modernism: New Geographies, Complex Intersections* (Urbana and Chicago, University of Illinois Press, 2007)

Broader anthology than *The Gender of Modernism*, reflecting the new modernist studies.

Wilk, Christopher (ed.), *Modernism 1914–1939: Designing a New World* (London, V&A Publications, 2006)

Illuminating accompanying text to the highly successful exhibition on design modernism.

Williams, Raymond, *The Politics of Modernism: Against the New Conformists*, ed. Tony Pinkney (London, Verso, 1989)

A collection of Williams' essays on and around modernism from a cultural materialist standpoint.

2
Modernism and the visual arts

Figure 2 Glen Baxter, 'It Was Tom's First Brush with Modernism' (2001)

Narrating modernist art

'Today', wrote the Swiss–French architect Le Corbusier in 1921, 'painting has outsped the other arts. It is the first to have attained attunement with the epoch' (*Towards a New Architecture*, trans. F. Etchells, London, Architectural Press, 1970, p. 23). Attunement to the epoch perhaps, but both painting and the epoch seem to have outsped Glen Baxter's cowboy Tom (Figure 2). What kinds of idea about modernism is Baxter's drawing playing with? Tom encounters an extreme form of *abstraction*, in which the idea no longer obtains that the painting is either referential or figurative (that is, refers to or represents something outside of itself). In different ways, key movements within modernist visual art, such as Cubism, Expressionism or Surrealism, also seem to challenge the assumption that art might re-present an objective world that we can recognize, or that its success might be measured in these terms. Tom's first brush with abstract modernism is a startling and disconcerting experience; it is as if the canvas meets his gaze with the proposition that a new *kind* of gaze, a new way of looking, is required.

Painting, so pre-eminent for Corbusier within modernism, could be said to present the most graphic and immediate evidence of the unmaking of sense in modernism. This extended chapter therefore asks: how do we begin to understand the revolution in visual art that posed such a challenge to familiarity and referentiality? At one level there is a very simple way to answer this. Historically, expectations of referentiality are only a fairly recent phenomenon, relating to a period between the seventeenth and nineteenth centuries during which a certain concept of 'realism' in art became strongly influential. Visual art had not always been about realism (think of the function of stained glass in church windows), and would seem to depart from it again with the arrival of modernism. If, instead of Tom, a visitor from outer space were to encounter the modernist canvas, they might simply see it as an example of what human art is, without realizing that for some people it was failing to do what it was supposed to do. But *realism* itself is a very complex concept within modernism, and as this chapter unfolds the discussion will raise issues which resonate across *Beginning Modernism*. What is the relationship between art and modern life? How important is the question of realism to this relationship? What is the meaning of the tendency towards abstraction in modernist art? And how is art affected by new technologies of visual reproduction, such as the photograph and the film? Developments in modernist painting from 1850s France to 1940s America demonstrate a complex, varied response to modernity. Our aim will be to begin to grasp the conditions and motivations of these responses, not in a purely art-historical sense, but in terms of their parallels and interactions with other modernist forms and with broader historical phenomena.

Before we look more closely at some modernist paintings, a further preliminary question is obliquely raised by Tom's first brush with modernism: how do we tell the story of modernist art? Modernist images have led to debates, not only about ways of looking, but about what *kind* of art history or narrative can best frame and interpret those images. Maps or diagrams have often been used to make sense of the bewildering variety of modernist movements, styles and individual painters, the prototype of this approach stemming from Alfred Barr, early director of the first museum dedicated to visual modernism, the Museum of Modern Art (MoMA) in New York. In 1936 Barr produced an explanatory chart as the cover of a catalogue for the exhibition 'Cubism and Abstract Art', showing a number of interconnecting vectors, beginning in the 1890s and culminating, in 1935, in two forms of abstract art, the 'geometrical' and the 'non-geometrical'.

But is it right to see modernist painting as a linear progress towards the final disappearance of the object, in abstraction? Barr's interpretation was reinforced in a way by the work of the American critic Clement Greenberg (1909–94), who in the 1950s and 1960s established an influential definition of modernist painting as the reflexive development or gradual refinement of its own formal techniques. In the landmark essay 'Modernist Painting' (1960), Greenberg saw visual modernism using 'the characteristic methods of a discipline to criticize the discipline itself – not in order to subvert it, but to entrench it more firmly in its area of competence' (quoted in eds C. Harrison and P. Wood, *Art in Theory 1900–1990: An Anthology of Changing Ideas*, 2nd edn, Oxford, Blackwell, 2003, p. 774). This definition became so closely associated with modernist art that it now tends to be referred to as 'modernist criticism';

its logic, sometimes also referred to as *formalism*, is exemplified in the view of one recent critic that Paul Cézanne's still-life paintings 'pointed the way (though this was hardly Cézanne's intention) to the ultimate disappearance of objects altogether in purely abstract art' (Glen Macleod, 'The Visual Arts', in Levenson, *Cambridge Companion to Modernism*, p. 195).

There are alternative, dissenting voices to this model of modernist art history. One is T.J. Clark, who, in works such as *The Painting of Modern Life: Paris in the Art of Manet and His Followers* (1990, revised 1999) and *Farewell to an Idea: Episodes from a History of Modernism* (1999), has insisted upon the engagement of modernist painting with historical modernity. Despite his excitement at reading formalist critics such as Greenberg, Herbert Read and Michael Fried in the 1950s and 1960s, Clark writes that it became 'chilling' to see Greenberg's views become an orthodoxy: 'What was deadly . . . was the picture of artistic continuity and self-sufficiency built into so much modernist writing: the idea that modern art could be studied as a passing-on of the same old artistic flame . . . from Manet to Monet to Seurat to Matisse to Miro' (*Farewell to an Idea*, New Haven and London, Yale University Press, 1999, p. 175). Another, more recent challenge to this issue idea of the 'same old' modernist artistic flame is made by *Art Since 1900: Modernism, Antimodernism, Postmodernism* (2004), a voluminous text co-written by Hal Foster, Rosalind Krauss, Yve-Alain Bois and Benjamin Buchloh. While aspiring to make it 'straightforward' for the reader to follow the 'development' of art from the beginning of the twentieth century up to the present day, the book also contains a wealth of additional materials which disrupt the linearity of the structure and allow the reader to read laterally, constructing alternative histories of twentieth-century art which might be organized, for example, along national, transnational or thematic lines. Current curatorial practice also shows that debate continues to revolve around these issues of narrative structure. When the Tate Modern gallery opened in London in 2000, controversy abounded at the decision to organize its permanent exhibits thematically rather than chronologically – a decision clearly differentiating the Tate from its counterpart in New York, MoMA. Yet T.J. Clark, sceptical of the Greenbergian evolutionary narrative, nevertheless confesses that he could learn more in an afternoon among MoMA's historical continuities than he could from reading fifty essays criticizing their exclusions. Moreover, the decision was recently taken to rehang the Tate Modern collection along more overtly historical lines, and if you visit, you will now see a long horizontal mural map of modernism, similar to Barr's, as you travel on the escalators.

STOP and THINK

- Consider the kind of instruction you might receive, in an average educational experience, in the history and techniques of painting. How far does this prepare us for an understanding of, or sympathy with, the concerns of modernist painting? How and why should our educational system address the significance of visual art, and modernism along with it?

- Imagine a whiteboard in a physics classroom, covered in complex equations. We might express incomprehension, but we would be unlikely to say 'I don't like that'. Conversely, there is nothing to stop anyone expressing approval or dislike – we feel we are 'entitled' to do so – regarding an abstract painting upon which an artist might have worked for some time. But who are 'we' here? (The French modernist composer Erik Satie, for example, referred ironically to 'the good folk who "know what they like"' as a deeply conservative force, upholding the status quo and resisting 'Progress in all its shapes and forms' (see Satie's 'Some Notes on Modern Music', quoted in Kolocotroni et al., Modernism, p. 199)).

- How are the activities of the physicist and the artist different? Is it possible to argue that the artist's endeavour is just as complex, technical and specialized as that of the physicist, and that we require just as much education in order for it to become appreciable? If not, what does this say about the way we define 'art', and the way we distinguish it from science? Is it enough, for example, to say that science is 'knowledge' whereas art is 'expression'?

- The sociologist Pierre Bourdieu argues that an individual's capacity for artistic 'taste' is likely to be directly related to high levels of educational experience and/or a social class background in which the 'cultural capital' of an appreciation of art is inculcated from the earliest stages of family life. Regular attendance at art museums has become 'almost the exclusive domain of cultivated classes' (quoted by Randal Johnson, introduction to Pierre Bourdieu, *The Field of Cultural Production: Essays on Art and Literature*, London, Polity, 1993, p. 22). Consider how this situation might affect the reception of modernist art.

With these debates and provisos in mind, let us now explore modernist visual art from the perspective of four key critical issues: realism versus abstraction, autonomy, the meaning of the avant-garde and technological change. Some sense of the historical formation of modernist painting will emerge, although you can flesh this out by consulting some of the more specialist guides to modernist art listed in 'Selected reading' at the end of this chapter.

Realism, the 'moment' of Cubism, and abstraction

If we limit ourselves to exact reproduction, we halt the evolution of the spirit.

(Constantin Brancusi)

Robert Hughes' popular book *The Shock of the New* (1991) exemplifies that way of telling the story of modernist art as a challenge to *mimesis*, the Aristotelian principle by which the function of art is to imitate some aspect of external reality. Optical metaphors have often been used to describe this mimetic effect: either a painting holds a mirror up to the world, or it is a window, transparent, through which we gain unmediated access to the real.

To this extent, however, Hughes suggests, concepts of mimesis or realism must be strictly paradoxical. This is because, in order to reproduce the *illusion* of pure reflection or transparency, the painter must be a highly skilled technician deploying a variety of methods for applying paint to canvas. One key technique, perspective, or the ability to suggest a dimension of depth on a flat canvas, was rediscovered, to revelatory effect, by artists of the fifteenth century. It became embodied in the convention of single-point perspective, a vanishing point in the painting which draws the viewer's eye into the distance. Hughes describes this convention, which since the Renaissance 'almost all painting had obeyed', as 'a geometrical system for depicting the illusion of reality'; as such, he then asserts, '*perspective is a form of abstraction*' (my italics) (Robert Hughes, *The Shock of the New: Art and the Century of Change*, London, Thames & Hudson, 1991, pp. 16–17). Our actual vision does not correspond to the kind of vision suggested by a realist painting; perspective 'simplifies' the relationship between eye, brain and object, presenting an 'ideal' view imagined by a god-like spectator or, at least, by a 'one-eyed, motionless person who is clearly detached from what he sees'. If you look at works by the Dutch painter Jan Vermeer (1632–75) such as the *View of Delft*, or Giovanni Canaletto's (1697–1768) images of Venice, you will see this technique at work in the visual equivalent of what literary critics might call a 'classic realist text'.

According to the paradox, then, realism is artifice: it creates a model or illusion of the real, and in this way could be said to be *more* 'abstract' than the blank canvas encountered by Glen Baxter's Tom. An alternative to this approach to realism can be located in the work of the French painter Paul Cézanne (1839–1906), often regarded as the founding figure of modernist painting, who strongly prefigures the development of the movement known as Cubism. Figure 3, a painting of the Mont Sainte-Victoire, shows Cézanne's disregard of the illusion of transparency in two main ways: the paint is applied in heavy brushstrokes or blocks which we can't help seeing; and patches appear as if gaps in the paint are left, through which the canvas shows. Cézanne, it appears, is no longer interested in creating the smooth, mirror-like surface of realist illusion. We realize by contrast how much of the effort of realist painting is invested in persuading the viewer to forget the artifice of painting: the canvas must be covered with paint, so that we are not reminded of its material presence; brushstrokes must be applied in such a way as not to draw attention to themselves. As Rosen and Zerner put it of the French academic painter Meissonier, 'the eye goes right through the surface of a Meissonier painting into a world of fantasy' (Charles Rosen and Henri Zerner, *Romanticism and Realism: The Mythology of Nineteenth Century Art*, London, Faber & Faber, 1984, p. 151).

Figure 3 Paul Cézanne, *Mont St-Victoire* (1902-4)

By comparison, Cézanne's painting appears unfinished, provisional; the brushstrokes and the glimpses of canvas have a blurring effect, arresting the eye, as if the painting is shimmering in motion. Neither the viewer's perspective, nor the artistic process, is settled.

What happens to our conception of realism in the course of this comparison? Robert Hughes' account of Renaissance perspective suggests that real*ism* does not *realistically* reflect how or what we see. 'Look at an object', suggests Hughes: 'your eye is never still. It flickers, involuntarily restless, from side to side. Nor is your head still in relation to the object; every moment brings a fractional shift in its position, which results in a miniscule difference of aspect . . . Any sight is a sum of different glimpses' (p. 17). Would not a truly *realistic* realism, then, build a recognition of the *act* of painting into the painting itself? On this view 'reality, in short', as Hughes puts it, 'is interaction'. Cézanne's painting does not completely renounce the idea of *representing* a reality external to the observer, but it builds interaction into that representation. Cézanne realized, writes the

Figure 4 Pablo Picasso, *Weeping Woman* (1937)

critic John Berger, that the bodily senses through which he appre-
hended the Mont Sainte-Victoire (a scene that Cézanne returned
to paint on many occasions, from different angles and in different
atmospheric conditions) were 'no less part of the material world
than the light on the mountain' ('Problems of Socialist Art', in ed.
Lee Baxandall, *Radical Perspectives in the Arts*, Harmondsworth,
Penguin, 1972, p. 213). In Pablo Picasso's series of portraits of
weeping women of the 1930s (for example Figure 4), the apparent

facial distortions result from the simultaneous representation of the face from various angles, embodying the principle of sight as a 'sum of different glimpses'.

Could modernist art therefore claim to be more realist than realism? Could 'realism', in the sense in which we have used it so far, simply mean a general cultural habit, largely unquestioned, of associating a certain kind of painting with the 'real'? Underlining this are the words of Cézanne which are said to have informed the concept of Cubism. 'Treat nature by means of the cylinder, the sphere, the cone', he states; 'nature for us men is more depth than surface' (letter to Emile Bernard, 15 April 1904, in Harrison and Wood, *Art in Theory*, p. 37). It is as if Cézanne is here recommending us to look beyond the surface appearance of things and at the deeper structures that lie below. The architect Le Corbusier was later to find such forms, as the archetypes of beauty, displayed in the industrial architecture of American and Canadian grain elevators: 'cubes, cones, spheres, cylinders or pyramids are the great primary forms which light reveals to advantage', he wrote in 1923; while for the writer D.H. Lawrence, in his idiosyncratic commentary on Cézanne's still-life paintings, modern French art under Cézanne 'made its first tiny step back to real substance', the apples being 'the first real sign that man has made for thousands of years that matter *actually* exists' ('Introduction to these Paintings', in *Phoenix: The Posthumous Papers*, ed. E.D. McDonald, Harmondsworth, Penguin, 1980, pp. 567–8). For Lawrence, Cézanne's apples were 'a real attempt to let the apple exist in its own separate entity, without transfusing it with personal emotion'; they embodied a struggle or fight with 'the cliché', exemplified by the gaps in the paint through which, Lawrence maintained, the cliché 'fell into nothingness'.

If Lawrence is right to imply the solidity of 'substance' and 'matter' in Cézanne's apples, it is nevertheless worth observing that the apples (Cézanne painted many such still lifes) are characterized by their broken outlines, as if outlines dissolve where light hits the object: challenging the cliché of a finished roundness, Cézanne seems to realize that apples can have quite straight and angular edges. In this sense, it is as if the 'still-life' tradition is modified by the modern sciences: if something is alive, it cannot, by definition, be still. Ideas of dynamism and unpredictability are, as we glimpsed in chapter 1, crucial to a sense of social and economic modernity, as in Marx and Engels' 'all that is solid melts into air', while in chapter 3 we will see their relevance in the new physics of the modernist period.

If there is a danger in these accounts of modernist painting, it is that we begin to think of a pre-modernistic tradition of realism as naïve or, alternatively, as a catalogue of trickery. The complexity of realism's position within the painting of modernity is indicated by some observations on the work of the French painter Gustave Courbet (1819–77) by Charles Rosen and Henri Zerner. Courbet emerges in the 1850s as a radical pioneer of realism, a voice of modernity in his assault on the romanticism and conservatism of French academic art, as in his earlier involvement as a political radical in the revolution of 1848. The dark, brooding canvases of ordinary life painted in the area of his birthplace, Franche-Comté, convey an uncompromising sense of the real. Yet Rosen and Zerner note that Courbet's mimesis went hand in hand with an unprecedented emphasis on the concrete materiality of the painted surface (anticipated, they also argue, by Rembrandt). In mature paintings such as *A Burial at Ornans* (1850), they write, 'the paint is often laid down with a palette knife rather than a brush, so that it becomes a tangible, built-up crust that arrests the eye'; we are 'forced to remember that we are in front of a solid work of art', albeit one dedicated to imagining or visualizing the real world (Rosen and Zerner, *Romanticism and Realism*, pp. 151–2). In thus closing the gap between art and life, the realism of Courbet and Manet among others could be seen as 'above all an avant-garde movement', in other words leading the way in its experimentalism (Rosen and Zerner, *Romanticism and Realism*, p. 179). In subsequent pages we will reflect more closely on the significance to modernism of the term 'avant-garde'.

At the heart of the realism–abstraction dialectic in modernism is Cubism. There is a general consensus that Cubism is central to any map of modernist painting, and that it constitutes, in the terms of a seminal essay by John Berger, a 'moment' decisively puncturing the modernist timescale. The moment may variously be defined as 1907, with the completion of the painting *Les Demoiselles d'Avignon* (Figure 1, p. 5) by Pablo Picasso, or as 1907–14, the brief period of the major works of Cubism.

Key characteristics of Cubism

- A rejection of imitation and pictorialism in favour of the geo-metrical grid or diagram.
- An emphasis on the two-dimensional picture space instead of the illusion of three-dimensional space, paradoxically enhanc-ing the significance of space. No longer simply the empty vessel into which objects are placed, space becomes a kind of entity in itself – shallower, as if the viewer's eye is detained nearer to the flat surface of the picture, yet also taking a more active role in the dynamic of the painting.
- A diminishing of colour (contrasting with the Fauvism of early Henri Matisse), as if to discourage a sensual reaction in the viewer in favour of an analysis of the relationship between the objects and planes on the canvas.
- An uncertainty about the relative solidity or transparency of objects, as if they are to be defined not as complete in themselves but in terms of their changing relationships with other things.
- Simultaneity, in terms of different perspectives on the same object, and in terms of the coexistence of 'different modes of space and time' (Berger).
- Reference to the forms of non-European or 'primitive' cultural artefacts, as for example in the echo of African tribal masks in Picasso's *Demoiselles*.
- In the second, 'synthetic' phase of Cubism, the adherence of found materials and objects to the surface of the painting: paper, in the form of *papiers collés*, and more diverse materials, in the broader generic term *collage*, of which Picasso's *Still Life with Chair Caning* (1911/12) (Figure 5) is taken to be the first example.

T.J. Clark sees as a 'strong misreading' the tendency to see Paul Cézanne as the initiator of Cubism. While no doubt inspired by the later paintings of Cézanne, for example the sequence of *Les Grandes Baigneuses* (1895–1906), Cubism was essentially the col-laborative work of the Spanish painter, Picasso (1881–1973), and the Frenchman Georges Braque (1882–1963). Once introduced by the ubiquitous French modernist Guillaume Apollinaire, the pair developed a synergy which quickly led to the invention of a whole pictorial language, with a new vocabulary of forms, motifs and

Figure 5 Pablo Picasso, *Still Life with Chair Caning* (1911/12)

syntax. In the famous terms of Braque, it was as if they were 'roped together on a mountain'; as Clark puts it, Cubism in the hands of Braque and Picasso was 'the moment when modernism focused on its means and purposes with a special vengeance' (*Farewell to an Idea*, p. 175).

The first, 'analytic' phase of Cubism typifies this seriousness of endeavour. The declared subjects of these famous paintings – a man leaning on a table, for example, or playing a guitar – recede or are dismantled, with only glimpses of realist codes remaining, to be replaced by compositions of overlapping and interlocking blocks and planes. In Braque's paintings in particular, there is a patient effort to continue Cézanne's experiments into the relation- ship between human cognition and the material world. The analogy with scientific analysis is almost irresistible: the Cubists take apart the elements of what we think we know and recompose them into what Braque called a 'new unity'. Abstraction is thus a means to understanding through defamiliarization, an intellectual effort of problem-solving based on the dismantling of the visual cliché: 'The senses deform, the mind forms', wrote Braque in his 'Thought on Painting' (1917): 'Work to perfect the mind. There is no certainty except in what the mind conceives' (quoted in Harrison and Wood, *Art in Theory*, p. 210).

This does not mean that Braque's muted paintings lack beauty, for the Cubist artwork must still combine analysis with affect, or sensory appeal. It was however in the exuberant work of Picasso that the intellectual drive of Braque's Cubism combined with a dramatic sensual appeal, underlining Picasso's repudiation of 'research' in favour of 'finding'. For John Berger, Picasso was 'essentially an improviser' ('Pablo Picasso', in Berger, *Selected Essays*, p. 31). A restlessness in his various styles and periods denotes a constant open- ness to new stimuli and a refusal to be pigeonholed. *Still Life with Chair Caning* (1912, Figure 5) was the founding work of a second, 'synthetic' phase of Cubism, heralding the concept of *collage*, the importation into painting of hitherto alien, 'found' materials, and with it an element of playful critique of the realist tradition. In this synthetic phase, Cubism made constant reference to the gathering or combinatory activity of the imagination, often through the presence of other forms, textual (such as newspapers) and material (such as the oilcloth). It became 'emblematic', suggesting the human impera- tive to attach meaning to things that are only ever in a state of flux, and in that sense rejuvenating the *transformative* quality inherent in the artistic principles of metaphor and allegory. That is, Picasso's Cubist repudiation of imitation and illusion, and his introduction of heterogeneous materials into painting, renewed the capacity of art to take the familiar and transform its meaning and possibilities.

In its epic proportions and startling and unsettling effects, Picasso's later painting *Guernica* (1937) showed how the trans- formative aspect of modernism might also become overtly political, as in Robert Hughes' description of it as 'the last great history- painting' (Hughes, *Shock of the New*, p. 110). The painting is Picasso's outraged response to the bombing and destruction of the Basque city of Guernica by German aircraft, in conjunction with Nationalist forces, during the Spanish Civil War. Cubist tech- niques of fragmentation are at the service of depicting the literal brutalities of war, in the dismemberment of bodies, both human and animal. The muted tones of black, white and grey, recalling analytic

Cubism, guard against any diversion of the viewer's attention onto sheer sensuality. Yet what makes the canvas compelling is a creative ambivalence: the stark depiction of horror and violence on the one hand, but on the other hand the more abstract sculptural beauty of its figures and the harmonic balancing and interweaving of shapes and shades across the vast two-dimensional surface.

Dare we say that these 'purely' artistic qualities possess a utopian or even redemptive quality to offset in some way the horrors of the historical event that was Guernica? Any complacent assertion of this would surely be extremely problematic. Yet John Berger's view is that Picasso takes the fragments of a period of enormous human and cultural disintegration and shows, 'by the example of his spirit', that 'out of the debris, new ideas, new values, new ways of looking at the world can and will develop' ('Pablo Picasso', in Berger, *Selected Essays*, p. 32).

What emerges in the history of Cubism is a sense of the important and often highly complex relationship between such concepts as realism and abstraction. In Cézanne, abstraction is the necessary adjunct to the pursuit of a deeper realism. In the work of the Russian artist Wassily Kandinsky (1866–1944), by apparent contrast, it became the sign of a progressive spiritualization of visual art. Co-founder in Munich of the group Der Blaue Reiter, and according to modernist mythology the painter of the first abstract or fully non-representational canvas in 1912, Kandinsky published a treatise, *Concerning the Spiritual in Art* (1911), in which he saw the impulse to abstraction as the 'awakening of the soul' of Western humanity after a long period of dormancy. Another key work in this respect was *Abstraction and Empathy: A Contribution to the Psychology of Style* (1908), also published in Munich, by the German thinker Wilhelm Worringer (1881–1965), which linked modernism to so-called primitive art in the latter's expression of an 'artistic volition' towards the tranquility and transcendent, absolute value of objects wrested from the 'unending flux' of the external world.

These apparently contradictory orientations towards abstraction – realism, spirituality – nevertheless inform, and perhaps finally help us to read, two of the 'purer' forms of Cubist-influenced abstraction in visual modernism which emerged virtually in parallel in the 1910s: Suprematism, centring on the work of the Russian artist Kazimir

Malevich (1878–1935), and Neo-plasticism, associated with the Dutch painter Piet Mondrian (1872–1944) and the design journal *De Stijl*, established in 1917 and from that time on to exert a wide influence on European modernism for a decade or more. Malevich's *White on White* canvases of 1918 are a clear reference point for 'Tom's first brush with Modernism'. It is important to note, however, and in relation to Baxter's gentle pun on the word 'brush', that a blank canvas is not what Malevich presents the viewer with. Rather, a white square is painted onto the canvas, and at a slight angle to the square of the canvas, so that there remains a palpable sense of encountering a painting. Malevich claimed that his Suprematism began in 1913; preceding the *White on Whites*, the most iconic of his works is *Black Square*, exhibited at the '0.10' exhibition of Russian Futurist painting in Petrograd in December 1915. The works of Piet Mondrian to which I refer here are those of a fully achieved grid-based abstraction, towards which he had been working in the years 1917–20. These paintings, such as *Composition with Red, Yellow and Blue* (1921) (the cover image of this book) and similar variations in other canvases of 1921–2, also use the square or rectangle, but always asymmetrically arranged in a grid divided up by black lines.

What did each painter make of the Cubist legacy, which in each case was drawn from a rich European intellectual milieu? Let us compare their responses to Cubism, through concepts of realism and spirituality, here: first, from Malevich's pamphlet of 1916, *From Cubism and Futurism to Suprematism* (Harrison and Wood, *Art in Theory*, pages 179, 181):

> In Cubism, the attempt to disfigure the forms of reality and the breaking-up of objects represent the striving of the will towards the independent life of the forms which it has created . . . If for thousands of years past the artist has tried to approach the depiction of an object as closely as possible, to present its essence and meaning, then in our era of Cubism the artist has destroyed objects together with their meaning, essence and purpose.
>
> The new picture has sprung from their fragments.

And then from Mondrian's pamphlet of 1921, *Neo-Plasticism: the General Principle of Plastic Equivalence* (Harrison and Wood, *Art in Theory*, p. 290):

Neo-Plasticism has its roots in Cubism. It can equally be called *Abstract–Real painting* because the *abstract* (just like the mathematical sciences but without attaining the absolute, as they do) can be expressed by plastic reality. In fact, this is the essential characteristic of the New Plastic in painting. It is a composition of rectangular colour planes that expresses the most profound reality. It achieves this by *plastic expression of relationships* and not by natural appearance. It realizes what painting has always sought but could express only in a veiled manner. The coloured planes, as much by position and dimension as by the greater value given to colour, plastically express only *relationships* and not forms.

The New Plastic brings its relationships into *aesthetic equilibrium* and thereby expresses *the new harmony*.

Let us tease out some of the similarities between Malevich and Mondrian under the headings of 'realism' and 'spirituality':

Realism

- While it is generally acknowledged that Picasso and Braque never made a completely abstract painting, Malevich and Mondrian separately held that, for modern painting to become emancipated and emancipatory, it was necessary to abolish all connection with fundamental referents: *objects* and *nature*.
- This 'new realism' for Malevich, therefore consisted in acknowledging what is essential to the art of painting alone (for example: 'Colour and texture in painting are ends in themselves. They are the essence of painting, but this essence has always been destroyed by the subject'). Notice that Malevich fully endorses the evolutionary narrative of progress towards abstraction in modernist painting through Cubism's 'destruction' of objects. He also wrote of freeing art from 'vulgar subject-matter', and satirized the copying of nature as the shared pursuit of primitive and academic art – 'academic realists' were, he wrote, 'the last descendants of the savage'. Once thus freed, painting could attain an 'independent life . . . of forms'.
- Mondrian referred to this same kind of realism as the *plasticity* of art, for example in the phrases 'plastic reality' or 'plastic expression of relationships', where the Dutch version of this word, *beeldung*, adds a sense of active shaping and formation to the English

sense of a material waiting to be activated. Mondrian seeks a rather more scientific legitimacy in locating 'the most profound reality' in painting that is able to 'express' relationships of harmony and balance once freed from the necessity to copy appearances. As in life, such relationships are continually forming and reforming, but are never perfectly symmetrical. In the words of Mondrian's collaborator in De Stijl, Theo van Doesburg (1883–1931), the visual artist could thus leave narratives and myths, not to mention the physical features of human beings and the natural world, to writers, who had traditionally shared this material with the painter: now, the painter must turn to what is only unequivocally painterly – colour, forms, lines and planes.

- Another shared means of drawing attention to the painterly 'real' is the abolition of the distinction between 'figure' and 'ground', the positioning of some 'thing' against a background. This, as Charles Harrison puts it, is to do with a challenge to the idea of inert space, as the painting 'offers no space, either technically or conceptually, which a solid body might be imagined as occupying' (Charles Harrison, Francis Frascina, Gill Perry, *Primitivism, Cubism, Abstraction: The Early Twentieth Century*, Yale University Press/Open University, 1993, p. 201). Mondrian tried to enhance this effect by mounting his paintings outwards, towards the viewer.

Spirituality

- Malevich drew from the heavily mystical tradition of Russian Christianity; the positioning of *Black Square* in the upper corner of the '0.10' exhibition room reproduced that of icons in the domestic interior. Malevich also expressed his work in terms of the 'quest for the zero' or 'absolute zero'; paradoxically, this nihilism can be interpreted as a quest to strip art back to a pure ground or condition of ontological simplicity and integrity.

- Mondrian, like Kandinsky, was partly motivated by an attachment to the ideas of Theosophy, as exemplified by the writings of Helena or 'Madame' Blavatsky or P.D. Ouspensky. This body of thought drew on science to question the concept of *matter* (and with it, nineteenth-century 'materialism'), thereby linking forms of occultism and spiritualism with the apparent findings of modern physics. (For a good account of the overlapping of modernism with interest in psychic phenomena and liminal states, see Tim Armstrong's chapter 'The Vibrating World: Science, Spiritualism, Technology', in *Modernism: A Cultural History*). There is accordingly a *dematerializing* impulse in Mondrian's abstraction, as for example in the sense that the basic elements of his painterly language – straight lines, right angles, primary colours, black and white (grey had been present, but receded) – were a neo-Platonic kernel of ideal forms establishing 'universal' models of harmony and equilibrium.

- If in the senses above both Malevich and Mondrian are *visionary* artists, the term 'spiritual' needs to stretch in order to accommodate politics. Malevich's aesthetics after 1917 were fully bound up with Bolshevik revolution. His belief that art should be 'non-objective' – that is, freed from the representation of objects – can thus be read as a challenge to the principle of the ownership of private property, whether this is found in the subject matter of the still-life tradition, or of the 'fat, playful cupids' populating academic painting, or even of individual human consciousness and feeling. Not that Malevich wished his canvases to be devoid of feeling – he wrote in fact of 'the supremacy of pure feeling in creative art' – but that feeling should be an educated and collective response to the painting rather than the expression of subjective whim or fancy. Malevich saw his Suprematism as at the service of the revolutionary transformation of society. By 1919 he was, with El Lizzitsky, leading the pioneering Soviet UNOVIS school of art in Vitebsk, and turning away from painting in order to devote himself to highly abstract *architectural* models ('planits' or 'architectons') for a utopian communist society of the future. After the death of Lenin in 1924, however, Malevich's abstract work began to attract suspicion as a more literal-minded regime adopted a narrower and more utilitarian 'socialist realist' conception of revolutionary art.

- Mondrian's work has a similarly utopian drive. His search for a 'universal' language in the visual arts, taken up in the development of the International Style of architecture and design in the 1920s and 1930s (see chapter 5), carries an inclusive and democratic impulse. Hierarchy and centrality are displaced by his work, as if to seek for a repository of essential forms available to all. This is a collective politics, based, in the words of the De Stijl manifesto, on the 'war against the domination of individual despotism' (the straight line helped to eradicate this individualism) and on progress towards 'international unity in life, art, culture, either intellectually or materially'.

STOP and THINK

How then might we construct a reading of Mondrian's *Composition with Red, Yellow and Blue*, the cover image of this book? Some considerations are as follows:

- Is there a centre or focal point?
- Is there a pattern to the geometrical shapes, or a lack of pattern, or a combination of the two?
- What is the effect of the placing of colours and the relationship between the colours?
- What kinds of effect do the black lines achieve?

This is the way my own reading took shape:

1. I found the painting restful, yet there is no centre in which the eye can rest. The nearest to this is the third white rectangle up from the bottom, yet it is clearly off-centre on the horizontal axis.
2. There is no regular pattern, but there are glimpses of pattern: repeated rectangles next to each other or positioned at 90°. Again there is a sense of something tenuous and mobile, which cuts against the sense of finality given by the straight lines.
3. I found myself reflecting on the curious positioning of the most vibrant colour, the red. Again something seems to be denied centrality. Yet perhaps the very marginality of the primary colours makes them more alluring?
4. Again there is no regular colour pattern, yet a hint or gesture towards one: the fact that the colours are tentatively balanced at opposite corners.

5. I notice that not all of the black lines extend to the edge of
   the canvas, giving an unfinished effect, and that where this
   happens, the colour blue tends to be there too. Does this
   blue's paleness add to the ambiguity deriving from the lines?

Consider the fact that there is potentially no end to the small,
detailed observations that anyone can make about such a
painting, just as there is (almost!) no end to the different
permutations that the shapes and colours on the canvas could
take. Out of such small observations, you can construct your
own more general reading or theory about the painting's
effect, aided perhaps by what we know about the artist's ideas
and motivations, the historical and cultural context, and so on.
As my own reading took shape, above, I seemed to be focusing
on the compelling relationships in the painting between balance and imbalance, pattern and disorder, stillness and motion,
finality and incompletion. Why would we need an idea of
representation to see significance in these relationships, or to
take pleasure in them? However, if my reading does seem very
'formalistic', remember that we have seen the political importance of abstraction for Malevich and Mondrian: as a denial of
'objectivity' or the possession of things for the one, and as a
universal language of rational reform for the other. For a much
more concrete historical reading of Malevich's work, focusing
on who might actually have looked at the paintings in their
contemporary Russian context, and how, see T.J. Clark's impres-
sive chapter 'God Is Not Cast Down', in *Farewell to an Idea*.

Impressionism and Expressionism: uses of autonomy?

In this section we examine the contribution of two major movements to an overall conception of modernist visual art. These
movements seem, by name, to be diametrically opposite. Put rather
schematically, it could be said that Impressionism was motivated
by an *objective* principle – the need to observe and record both
modern life and the phenomenon of light that allows such observation to take place – while Expressionism was concerned with
recording a more *subjective* response to modernity, sensually and

intellectually. Impressionism is a movement that is strictly ante-
cedent to twentieth-century modernism, taking us back as far as
1860s France. Expressionism is more or less contemporaneous with
Cubism, although one of its key antecedents, Vincent Van Gogh,
painted the bulk of his work between 1888 and his death in 1890.
Without wishing to subscribe to the narrative of abstraction as
inevitable, I will suggest that each of these movements is modernist
insofar as it leads towards a conception of 'autonomy' in visual art.

The founding moment of Impressionism is often taken to be
Déjeuner sur l'herbe (1863) by Edouard Manet (1832–83), a fantasy
scene along the lines of the *fête champêtre* tradition, in which a mixed
group of nude and clothed figures take their ease in a pastoral setting. Manet's painting suggestively places a female nude as focal
point, reclining alongside the dressed figures of two bourgeois males
and a stooping woman in the background. The painting was rejected
in 1863 by the exhibition or Salon of the Ecole des Beaux-Arts,
and a public controversy led to the establishment of an alternative
'Salon des Refusés', showing this and other works which had been
rejected by the official organ of French visual culture. Manet became
the originating figure of Impressionism. What was initially, for the
journalist Leroy, a derogatory term for the merely sketch-like, hasty
and impermanent 'impressions' painted by the group, became the
adopted sign of their commitment to the authentic, naturalistic
recording of immediate visual experience. Following the Salon's
rejection of a number of their paintings in 1873, the first independent
exhibition of Impressionist painting was staged in a studio in Paris
in 1874. Though hardly a critical success, there were seven more
such exhibitions up to 1886. Manet himself kept a distance from the
movement, but his work inspired a group of artists, such as Claude
Monet (1840–1926), Auguste Renoir (1841–1919) and Alfred Sisley
(1839–99), and later Camille Pissaro (1830–1903), Berthe Morisot
(1841–95) and Edgar Degas (1834–1917) among others.

While *Déjeuner* scandalized because of its subject matter, technique was an equally important factor in Manet's rejection by
the academy. In the essay 'Manet and the Institutionalization of
Anomie', Pierre Bourdieu surveys the objections made to Manet's
work through the 1860s and 1870s by the guardians of official
painterly technique. Principal among these were the objections to

'flatness' and to lack of 'finish'. Manet did not observe the rules of perspective and detail; human figures could appear to be robbed of their noses, for example. His bold use of colour was seen by some contemporaries as a means of sidestepping the rigour of line drawing – 'The substitution of colour for drawing has made the career easier to pursue', caustically observed Delécluze (Bourdieu, *The Field of Cultural Production*, p. 247). These factors, together with the general lack of 'finish', the apparent offering of 'sketches' complete with their visible brushwork, was virtually perceived as an affront, a lack of decorum, by the academy, and as a sign that Manet was ignorant of his art.

The innovations arose, however, from a quasi-scientific orientation towards the complex relationship between light and colour in human perception. A key example of this was his pioneering of the technique of complementary colour in shading. Where established practice was to depict shading in terms of a seamless gradation of shades of grey into black, typified by the *chiaroscuro* of artists such as Caravaggio or Rembrandt, colour science was beginning to demonstrate that the condition of shadow, especially in outdoor light, is actually tinged with the colour of reflected light from its surrounding objects. Manet's work depicted shadow in this way, representing what we actually see: the often harsh contrasts created by sunlight, for example.

As in the work of Courbet, so with Manet a complex relationship emerges between realism on the one hand and modernism as, in Clement Greenberg's terms, a reflexive practice, on the other. Is it not contradictory to point to Impressionism as, on the one hand, an outward-looking, scientific determination to record the actual play of light, and, on the other hand, a technique that foregrounds its own artifice? In the view of Charles Harrison, this contradiction has to be faced, and the positions thought through together: modernism-as-Impressionism 'was not to be the mere passive expression of the experience of modernity', but stood rather for 'the attempt to secure some independence of thought and value – some autonomy – in the face of that experience' (*Modernism*, London, Tate Publishing, 1997, p. 27). In this process, Harrison maintains, a 'sceptical' viewer is generated – one increasingly alert to the complex process of painterly composition.

Figure 6 Georges Seurat, *Sunday on the Island of La Grande Jatte*
(1884–6)

The meaning of Harrison's word 'autonomy' is intriguingly developed in Pointillism or, in the preferred term of its main exponent,
Georges Seurat (1859–91), Divisionism, a movement that takes
Impressionist technique to a certain logical 'post-Impressionist'
conclusion. Seurat's *Sunday on the Island of La Grand Jatte* (1884–
6, Figure 6) was shown at the final Impressionist exhibition of 1886.
It exemplifies the technique of a systematic application of tiny dots
of paint which resolve themselves into form, rather in the manner
that a digital television image is composed. It is also a painting of
modernity: middle-class families, taking their weekend ease in the
sun on an island in the Seine near Paris. In an important essay,
Linda Nochlin merges these two factors in a reading of the painting
as an anti-utopian allegory of modernity. Taking up the Marxist
Ernst Bloch's observation on the boredom implicit in Seurat's
scene, 'a great load of joyless leisure', Nochlin argues that this
boredom is inscribed not just in the painting's subject matter and
treatment but also in the painterly technique of Pointillism itself.
In his highly systematic use of colour theory and atomized brushwork, Seurat invokes the mass production techniques of modernity,

and with them the model of a routinized capitalist society of the 'spectacle', in which leisure is commodified and contributes to that generalized condition of alienation known as 'anomie'. Nochlin's reading is subtly nuanced. In the sense that Seurat's technique is a mode of *critique*, it is anti-utopian, yet as well as mimicking modern mechanism, the dots imply a model of autonomy that is democratic and liberating, challenging the romantic Western tradition of painting as the spontaneous expression of individual genius: anyone, as it were, can apply paint systematically to a canvas, as exemplified in the later popular commodity of the painting-by-numbers set (Linda Nochlin, 'Seurat's *La Grande Jatte*: An Anti-Utopian Allegory', in *The Politics of Vision: Essays on Nineteenth-Century Art and Society*, London, Thames & Hudson, 1991).

In 1888, soon after *La Grande Jatte* was painted, the young Dutch artist Vincent Van Gogh wrote from the south of France to his brother Theo that he was beginning to cast off the recent example of the Impressionists, because 'instead of trying to reproduce exactly what I have before my eyes, I use colour more arbitrarily, in order to express myself more forcibly' (quoted in Fred Orton and Griselda Pollock, *Avant-Gardes and Partisans Reviewed*, Manchester, Manchester University Press, 1996, p. 28). The story of Van Gogh's last, prolific two years in the South of France has now attained the status of heroic-tragic myth: the severing of the ear after a dispute with fellow modernist Paul Gauguin; the periods of incarceration in a lunatic asylum; the suicide at the age of 37 (Orton and Pollock, however, provide an important corrective approach to this romantic myth in their essay 'Rooted in the Earth: A Van Gogh Primer', in *Avant-Gardes and Partisians Reviewed*). The legacies of this period include some of the most widely consumed 'poster' images of modernist art: a pair of peasant boots; the interior of his lodging room; sunflowers; a street café under starlight. Detaching Van Gogh's work from these popular accounts, we can see that his reference to an 'arbitrary' use of colour heralds another inflection of painterly autonomy; it signifies the release of colour from the burden of mimetic representation, in order to give it a more independent life in the service of a forceful expression that for Van Gogh was personal and political. He channelled an early radical evangelicalism into a commitment to representing in art the conditions of the lives of the peasantry and the labouring poor, and intense coloration, applied with the heavy brushstrokes of Impressionism and with a distortion of scale and perspective hinting at the Cubism to come, embodies the transformative aspirations of Van Gogh's work.

Although never directly associated with the term, Van Gogh's painting is the model for an 'Expressionism' which was to fan out in a number of directions. The short-lived group Les Fauves revolved, in the first decade of the twentieth century, around Henri Matisse (1869–1954), whose work consistently explored the expressionistic potential of colour and, in his later work especially, of rhythmic shapes and forms from non-Western cultures. Pioneering an adoption of the latter, however, had been Paul Gauguin (1848–1903), who left France for Tahiti in 1891. Gauguin's work is primarily associated with the problematic issue of modernism's relationship with the so-called 'primitive', a subject to which we will return in chapter 4. Technically, Gauguin's paintings of Tahitian native people extended the autonomous or decorative use of colour in the form of flat, juxtaposed areas, and this challenge to conventional realism was also embodied in firm outlining and a neglect of shadow. Gauguin figured largely in the London Post-Impressionist Exhibition (1910–11).

It was, however, in the Germany of the first two decades of the century that Expressionism emerged as the explicit motif of a movement. Ernst Kirchner (1880–1934) had been deeply impressed by an exhibition of Van Gogh's paintings in Dresden in 1905, and in the same year he helped found the association Die Brücke (The Bridge). Appealing for support from young artists, Kirchner made the proposal that 'everyone who reproduces that which drives him to creation with directness and authenticity belongs to us' (Harrison and Wood, *Art in Theory*, p. 68). Kirchner's own development underlines, however, the danger of mistaking Expressionism for mere *personal* 'expressivity', as Peter Nicholls puts it (*Modernisms: A Literary Guide*, Basingstoke, Macmillan, 1995, p. 142). His early work in Dresden revolved around vigorously stylized, primitivist female nudes and depictions of cabaret and circus scenes, reflecting the idealized communal lifestyles which formed part of the culture of Die Brücke. Moving to Berlin in 1911, Kirchner's painting assumed the form of an explicit critique of the mechanism and impersonality of the modern metropolis; in some of his most memorable canvases, such as *Potsdamer Platz* or *Friedrichstrasse* (both 1914), prostitutes are depicted in lines of jaggedly repetitive angularity, their impassive mask-like faces and bodies surrounded by the distorted shapes of an urban modernity characterized by violence and speed.

German Expressionism thus becomes an art of the city, enclosing the struggle for individuality and expression within a sense of collective urban identity. The year 1911 also saw the formation, in Munich, of the second key Expressionist group, Blaue Reiter (Blue Rider), whose reaction to the violent and 'infernal nature of the city' (Nicholls) was to turn towards the serenity of abstraction. The group was initiated by the widely travelled Russian painter Wassily Kandinsky, along with Franz Marc (1880–1916), and is later joined by the Swiss painter Paul Klee (1879–1940). As we have already seen, in his treatise *Concerning the Spiritual in Art* (1911), Kandinsky argues that the autonomous quality of art is intimately tied to a *spiritual* effect; colour, if appropriately released from realist representation in order to explore its expressive possibilities, may be tasted, smelled and heard as well as seen (a principle of sense-transfer known as 'synaesthesia', deriving from Symbolist poetics which we will encounter again in chapter 6), and composed in such a way as to create states of sensual and psychic harmony. A painting in this sense might be organized according to a musical rather than a pictorial logic, a 'colour music'.

In this section we have explored the seeming paradox that Expressionism and Impressionism, both resolute in their break with painterly tradition, and both intent on capturing the reality of modern life, whether subjective or objective, also promote a certain autonomy in the act of painting. Autonomy is therefore not simply the preserve of the Cubist-inspired abstraction examined in the previous section. An intriguing combination of these tendencies is literally presented by a final and perhaps ultimate of Expressionism, the movement in America known as Abstract Expressionism, which originates in the 1940s with paintings by Jackson Pollock (1912–56) such as *Full Fathom Five* (1947, Figure 7). Pollock's decisive break with the artistic past was the technique of *drip painting*, variously re-described in terms such as 'Action painting' or 'Process art'. The

Figure 7 Jackson Pollock (1912–16): *Full Fathom Five* (1947)

canvas, often huge, is laid horizontally on the floor; Pollock's activity then is to drip, squeeze, splash or pour paint onto the canvas, adding at times various other forms of the 'debris of everyday life' (the phase is T.J. Clark's, who notes that *Full Fathom Five* includes 'nails of various sizes, a disintegrating cigarette, tops off paint tubes, a button, thumbtacks, matches, a key, pushpins, pennies' – *Farewell to an Idea*, p. 300). Thus densely textured, when seen from a distance the materials take the form of rich and swirling patterns, their sense of intense dynamism – part chaos, part rhythm – transmitted by the energetic, even athletic movements of the painter around the canvas.

STOP and THINK

What new kinds of challenge does Pollock's work pose to the act of interpretation? As thoroughly as Malevich or Mondrian, it abolishes the object and the three-dimensional space of figure and ground, shifting attention onto the resources of painting itself. The value of the work, however, has been seen to lie in an Expressionism *par excellence*: not in the nature of the image itself, but in the existential physical act of painting, within which, as the critic Harold Rosenberg put it, the artist 'grasps authentic being'. We might think of Kirchner here, calling for 'directness and authenticity' of creativity. Pollock himself was interested in the links between art and the unconscious, where the latter might be seen as a deep expression of self, and his techniques might be related to the idea of 'automatic painting' pioneered in Surrealism (see the following section). Yet, in a radio interview of 1950, he could seem to turn Rosenberg's theory of action painting on its head, declaring that, 'naturally, the result is the thing – and – it doesn't make much difference how the paint is put on as long as something has been said. Technique is just a means of arriving at a statement'. To the question of what a layperson should 'look for' in a Pollock painting, the artist argues for a position of pure receptivity, untainted by assumptions: 'I think they should not look for, but look passively – and try to receive what the painting has to offer and not bring a subject matter or preconceived idea of what they are looking for' (Harrison and Wood, *Art in Theory*, pp. 575–8). Pollock thus takes us back to the pleasures and problems of the image, as if to detach it from a painterly technique which in his case was so extremely physical. Such pleasure can be found in T.J. Clark's account of Pollock in *Farewell to an Idea*, where Clark communicates a sense of joyous wonderment at the 'metaphysical dance' of Pollock's work, and at what he sees as a visual 're-enchantment' of the modern world. Do you think these terms are an appropriate response to Pollock's painting?

Finally, is Pollock's physical painting the ultimate example of rebellion and non-conformism in visual modernism? If so, how strange that initial noises of disdain quickly changed to enthusiastic acceptance within the American art establishment of the 1940s to 1950s, and that in this post-war, Cold War context, abstract expressionism became emblematic of the liberal freedom of expression and exploratory frontier mentality of official American ideology. This rapid assimilation into the mainstream pointedly raises the question of what the relationship between modernism and the concept of the 'avant-garde' might signify – a question we will take up in the next section.

The question of the avant-garde: Futurism, Dada, Surrealism

The term 'avant-garde' originally designated those who march into battle ahead of an army unit; its first use as a cultural term is associated with the French utopian socialist Henri de Saint-Simon (1760–1825), who saw artists as crucial members of the elites that would lead societies into future transformation. The idea, which gained ground in the nineteenth century, gave rise to an expectation that innovation in art went hand in hand with a challenge to the values of the establishment, and this was easily assimilated into a history of the radical experimentations of modernism. A key intervention in such debates, however, has been Peter Bürger's *Theory of the Avant-Garde* (1980), in which Bürger insisted that what he calls a 'historical avant-garde' in the early twentieth century needs to be clearly distinguished from 'modernism' as such, by virtue of the former's determination to undermine the *institution* of art per se.

In the course of his argument Bürger therefore brings a slightly different emphasis to the concept of modernist 'autonomy' as we have discussed this so far. Instead of constituting a radical break with the past, the growth of an autonomous or abstract principle in modernist art is held to be perfectly consistent with a bourgeois–capitalist society predicated upon division of labour. To consolidate artistic autonomy by increasingly identifying form itself as the content of the artwork is not, Bürger argues, to challenge the damaging divisions in bourgeois society but rather to typify them; modernism may thus seek to negate the artistic styles of the past and to give birth to the radically 'new', but these aims remain firmly embedded within the bourgeois institution of art as typified by ideas of individual genius or style and the organic integrity of the artwork. By contrast, the historical avant-garde seeks to merge art with the praxis of life, thereby challenging the status of art in its entirety and promising to 'organize a new life practice from a basis in art' (Bürger, *Theory of the Avant-Garde*, trans. Michael Shaw, Minneapolis, University of Minnesota Press, 1984, p. 49). It does not, Bürger claims, bring new 'styles' into existence, but uses techniques such as collage and montage to introduce an inorganic principle which disrupts the very idea of style. This avant-garde is defined principally in terms of the movements known as Dada and Surrealism (especially in the latter's earlier manifestations), Russian experimental art after the October revolution of 1917, and to a lesser extent, and with some severe reservations as to its politics, Italian Futurism, the earliest of these movements to emerge.

Futurists, Dadaists and Surrealists characteristically used manifestos and polemics to signal their merged artistic and political motivations, and in each case the medium of painting was only one element in a diversity of activities. In his founding manifesto of Italian Futurism, the poet F.T. Marinetti (1876–1944), recommended violence and revolt in the poetry of the new, 'the racer's stride, the mortal leap, the punch and the slap', celebrating the 'new beauty' of mechanized speed as embodied in the racing car, and scandalously glorifying warfare and the destruction of museums, libraries and 'academies of every kind' (*Futurist Manifestos*, ed., U. Apollonio, London, Thames & Hudson, 1973, pp. 21–2). Two manifestos of Futurist painting followed in 1910, with contributions from the painters Umberto Boccioni, Carlo Carra, Luigi Russolo, Giacomo Balla and Gino Severini, echoing a contempt for the 'cult of the past' and 'academic formalism', and urging artists to consider only 'our whirling life of steel'.

The paintings that accompanied the shrill polemics of Futurism are charged with a dynamism, as one might expect from a group that felt it had discovered, as if for the first time, though with the help of modern science and technology, the perpetual movement of matter. Balla's *Dynamism of a Dog on a Leash* (1912), for example, seems to present a report on scientific knowledge: the pet dog, its leash, and the feet of its bourgeois female owner are a blur of activity, yet as if each successive position in the act of motion is at the same time broken down and recorded. Such a painting perhaps also betrays a debt to the work of the British photographer Eadweard Muybridge in the 1880s, whose sequences of human and animal movement, arrested frame by frame, revealed previously unimagined postures.

Such a principle of reduction through scientific analysis could, of course, be seen at work in Seurat's earlier Pointillisme, just as the Impressionists' preoccupation with the play of light could be said to be revisited in the Futurist declaration that 'movement and light destroy the materiality of bodies' (Apollonio, *Futurist Manifestos*, p. 30). Despite the rhetoric of a complete break with the past, then, Italian Futurism was intimately linked to a closer modernist history, and nowhere more so than in its relation with analytic Cubism. Ideas and artists flowed between Futurist Italy and the France of Braque and Picasso, and the Futurists staged an exhibition of their work in Paris in 1912, at the height of the Cubist period. In paintings such as Carra's *The Red Horseman* (1913) or Boccioni's *Dynamism of a Woman* (1914), a shared Cubist vocabulary of abstract planes, blocks and angular lines is clearly in evidence. Another distinctive feature of Futurist pictorial space, the drawing of the viewer into the centre of the painting, as if sucked in by a 'vortex' of forces (this term was taken up by the English Vorticist group of 1914), can easily be related to the Cubists' abandonment of a single-point Renaissance perspective which left the ideal viewer stranded outside of the frame. The Futurists nevertheless insisted on the difference that in their work, this vocabulary was at the service of rendering movement rather than underlying structure. In explaining 'what divides us from Cubism', in a manifesto of 1914, Boccioni could characterize Picasso's work as 'lifeless' in comparison with Futurist dynamism.

Marshall Berman criticizes the Italian Futurists' narrowly uncritical 'romance of machines' (*All That Is Solid Melts Into Air*, pp. 24–6). More pointedly, in their open glorification of war ('the world's only hygiene'), militarism and nationalism, Futurist goals entered into alliance with right-wing politics and, specifically, the rise of fascism in Mussolini's Italy. At the end of this chapter (see pp. 71–2), I return to Walter Benjamin's famous definition of this fascism in terms of an 'aestheticization of politics'; for an account of the complexities of this relationship between modernist aesthetics and politics, particularly in relation to Marinetti, see Andrew Hewitt's *Fascist Modernism: Aesthetics, Politics and the Avant-Garde* (Stanford, Stanford University Press, 1993). Ironically, the outbreak of war in 1914 heralded the break-up of Italian Futurism as a coherent group; Boccioni was soon to be killed, and Marinetti wounded, in action. But the urgent activist posture of Futurism, and their acknowledgement of the machine as an irreversible feature of modernity, continued to resonate as artists in Europe scattered and regrouped, and in more markedly left-wing formations. Russian Futurism or 'Cubo-Futurism' was established in the years 1907–13 through the work of the painters Mikhail Larionov (1881–1964) and Natalia Goncharova (1881–1962), and led to the radical experiments of *zaum* poetry, detaching 'pure' sound from rational sense, in the work of writers such as Kruchenikh, Mayakovsky, Khlebnikov and Guro. Mayakovsky's lecture title 'A slap in the face of public taste' became a slogan of modernist anti-bourgeois non-conformity. Russian Futurism was, however, little influenced by the machine aesthetic of its Italian counterpart, and arguably the Italian spirit of avant-garde confrontation, irreverence and anti-humanism was more effectively continued, though with an antithetical political orientation, in the European and American movement known as Dada.

'Dada' began as a specific event, an evening of entertainment at the Cabaret Voltaire on 5 February 1916 in the neutral city of Zurich. It was organized by the German writer Hugo Ball and performed by a group of international refugee figures including the French artist Jean (Hans) Arp (1887–1966), who had been influenced by Picasso and Braque in Paris, and the Romanian, Tristan Tzara, who retained strong links with Marinetti. The nonsense word 'Dada' exemplifies the group's revolutionary aspirations, which were to disrupt and undermine the artistic establishment, its discourses and its institutions, per se. Dada thus best typified the modernist tendency (though far more, Bürger argues, than the 'modernists' themselves) to excoriate the appropriation of art by middle-class cultures (a process which might be traced back to 1848 France), using tactics of shock and transgression to jolt the bourgeoisie out of its complacent proprietorship. In Dada, then, we are at some remove from painting as such, and much closer to a political conception of the *event* which was to inform the later emergence of Guy Debord's Situationist movement in the turbulent streets of late-1960s Paris. An evening at the Zurich Cabaret Voltaire might contain Ball's 'sound poems', simultaneous poetry, 'Negro' noise-music, and absurd theatrical sketches performed in 'African' masks. Principles of spontaneity, a return to childhood, absurdity, violence, irreverent laughter and the breaking of taboos informed this varied work: a combination, as Ball put it, of 'a buffoonery' with 'a requiem mass', designed to short-circuit any attempt at semantics or interpretation, and to question the conception of art per se. A crucial principle of *performance* is at work here, to which we will return in chapter 8.

Modernist 'autonomy' in Dada therefore took yet another paradoxical turn: its shock value derived precisely from its insertion into the everyday and familiar, precisely *because* the concept of art as a separate and transcendent sphere had been challenged. Picasso, along with Marinetti, had contributed to the 1916 publication *Cabaret Voltaire*, and the movement spread as an international network of ideas and practice. From 1915, at the forefront of 'New York Dada', Marcel Duchamp (1887–1968) and Francis Picabia (1879–1953) worked in a more painterly tradition, though in a parallel spirit, under the patronage of Alfred Stieglitz. Duchamp's *Nude Descending a Staircase*, combining Cubist geometrics and Futurist energy, made a dramatic impact at the seminal Armory Show of modern art in New York (February–March 1913); his *The Bride Stripped Bare by Her Bachelors, Even* began to attain a mythic status when it was left unfinished in 1923 after eight years' work. *Bride* is a droll allegory of human sexual relations, drawing on Picabia's satirical undercutting of the functionality of machines, and demonstrating Dada's highly playful and irreverent inflection of the Futurist machine aesthetic. Even in these paintings there is a sense that Duchamp's Dadaist gesture consists essentially in the subversion of painting itself, as in the provocative titles. Accordingly, Duchamp is best remembered for his presentation of a public urinal as a 'readymade', *Fountain*, for an exhibition in 1917, and for *LHOOQ* (1919), a satirical remaking of Leonardo's iconic *Mona Lisa* complete with moustache and goatee. The first phase of Dada peaked around 1920, a year of Dada events and festivals in Paris and elsewhere. It could not, by definition, have sustained itself as a cogent movement; Picabia's wife Gabrielle Buffet insisted that 'his activity was utterly gratuitous and spontaneous' and 'never had any programme, method, or articles of faith' (quoted in ed. Harold Osborne, *The Oxford Companion to Art*, London, BCA, p. 866). It therefore seems inevitable that this anarchic energy should be adopted for more programmatic causes.

Since the end of the war, Dada in Berlin had taken a more political turn, exemplified by the technique of *photomontage*, a development of collage using photographic press cuttings in particular. This began with a group of artists whose opening 'Fair' in 1920 revealed a heavily ironic and politicized extension of the Zurich Dada of 1916: Raoul Hausmann (1886–1971), Hannah Hoch (1889–1978), John Heartfield (originally Helmut Herzfelde, 1891–1968) and George Grosz (1893–1959). Photography in this technique is the illustrative material, drawn from magazines, newspapers and advertisements, which distinguishes *montage* from the Cubist technique of *collage*, the pasting and combination of found pictorial materials onto a single ground, though both are clearly based on an aesthetic of juxtaposition. In its early years the most striking practitioner was Hoch, with works such as *Cut with the Kitchen Knife through the Beer Belly of the Weimar Republic* (1919) and *Pretty Woman* (1920, Figure 8). In the latter, barely more than a foot square, Hoch combines images of female sexuality with the parts of a BMW (Bavarian Motor Company) car, exploiting comparisons between sexual and mechanical performance and highlighting the processes of commodification into which, it could be said, photography itself had

Figure 8 Hannah Hoch, *Pretty Woman* (1920)

already been absorbed. The composite image opens out surgically, as if to expose the capitalist system that evaluates women and cars together. Heartfield, an active member of the German Communist Party since its formation in 1919, developed a powerful body of work through the 1920s and 1930s, sardonically rejecting what he saw as the mere aestheticism of Expressionism, Cubism and early Dada. Here photography combined with newsprint fragments to create some of the most polemical and memorable instances of anti-Nazi satire: Heartfield's deployment of Hitler images formed a central part of a strategy of 'communicative action' designed to aid the formation of a 'proletarian public sphere' in pre-1939 Germany (see Foster *et al.*, *Art Since 1900*, pp. 168–73).

The main transmutation of Dada was into Surrealism, a movement whose codification and coherence was largely the work of the French writer André Breton (1896–1966). Surrealism proposed that art might actively represent the involuntary and irrational processes of the unconscious. Like Futurism, it began as literature: Breton and Philippe Soupault borrowed the term from the ubiquitous Guillaume Apollinaire, as a way of describing a mode of spontaneous or automatic writing championed in their journal *Litterature*, founded in 1919. Breton had glimpsed in the Freudian idea of the talking cure a strategy for unlocking psychic mechanisms in the name of aesthetic creativity. By 1922, Dada artists in Paris were being courted by Breton, and in 1924 the First Surrealist Manifesto was published, declaring 'psychic automatism in its pure state' to be the means of expressing the 'actual functioning of thought'; Freud's notion of the unconscious became the basis of a renewed concept of the 'imagination', which 'is perhaps on the point of reasserting itself, of reclaiming its rights' (quoted in eds Kolocotroni *et al.*, *Modernism*, pp. 307–11).

If surrealism thus presents yet another inflection of modernist autonomy – for what could be more autonomous than an art which is automatic, over which we have no control? – we can see how far removed this is from the highly self-conscious, problem-solving autonomy of Cubism. In surrealist painting, the automatic processes of the unconscious could either take the form of direct physical embodiment, or of indirect representation. In the former case, for example, Max Ernst pioneered the techniques of *frottage*, by which impressions are taken from various surfaces with charcoal on paper, and *decalcomania*, by which blobs or smears of paint or ink are folded or transferred, in each case using the products as a stimulus for further work. The Spanish painter Joan Miró (1893–1983) used similarly chance circumstances, such as the roughening of paper, to stimulate composition; his often beautifully fragile, abstract canvases, characteristically combining organic or amoebic and geometric forms, have become some of the most popular and serviceable of surrealist images.

Two relatively independent figures of the early 1920s prepare the ground for a slightly different inflection of surrealism, the representation or symbolization of the irruption of the unconscious into everyday life. Giorgio de Chirico (1888–1978), who had known Picasso since the Cubist period and signed a Dada manifesto of 1920, painted hauntingly minimalist canvases whose signature was the faceless mannequin figure. Marc Chagall (1889–1985), drawing on Cubism and Russian folklore, created dreamlike, vibrantly coloured compositions, often juxtaposing humans and animals, as if floating free of the exigencies of life. Dream – or nightmare – was for Freud the arena in which the unconscious acted out its repressed contents; *sur-* or 'super' realism claimed to present an amalgam of unconscious and conscious realities. By far the most famous exponent of this art became Salvador Dalí (1904–89), who used all the techniques of illusionist painting, with a sometimes alluring glossiness of finish, yet combined his subject matter with the often-eroticized events of the unconscious.

The case of Dalí, however, points to a history of tensions within surrealism, and perhaps within modernism as a whole. In a very useful retrospect on surrealist art first published in 1942, Breton coldly distanced himself from Dalí, whom he accused of having 'insinuated himself' into the surrealist movement in 1929, of adopting an 'ultra-retrograde technique' characterized by 'borrowings and juxtapositions', and finally of 'sinking into academicism'. By comparison, in *Surrealism and Painting* (1928), Breton had 'emphatically' claimed Picasso as 'one of us', identifying Picasso's work as decisive in the revolutionary break from a model of art as imitating an exterior world to a *'purely interior model'*. Dalí, Breton implies, is an opportunist, taking what is radically subversive in surrealism yet presenting it in a way that is easily assimilable to the status quo; Picasso represents the genuine, avant-garde aspiration to throw bourgeois values into disarray and crisis. Such an aspiration points to the limits of Breton's embrace of psychoanalysis, for example: he could not share Freud's therapeutic goals, through which the analyst might work to restore the (usually bourgeois) subject to a stable position within the social order. By contrast, in 1925 Breton took surrealism into a sometimes-uneasy alliance with the revolutionary politics of the Communist Party. However, the unorthodox critic and thinker Georges Bataille (1897–1962) detected in Breton himself an all-too-familiar collusion with bourgeois values of construction and progress. The prefix *sur*, argued Bataille, demonstrated surrealism's determination to *transcend* its 'low' subject matter, 'the unconscious, sexuality, filthy language etc', by giving it higher 'ethereal' value (*Visions of Excess: Selected Writings 1927–1939*, trans. A. Stoekl, with C.R. Lovitt and D.M. Leslie Jr., Minneapolis, University of Minnesota Press, 1985, p. 39). Such stuff, he insisted, should not be elevated, but should remain as 'heterogeneous matter'; Bataille's reading of Dalí's painting *The*

Lugubrious Game along these lines in 1927 earned for him, from
Breton, the tag of 'excremental philosopher'.

STOP and THINK

What is at stake in such debates, which continue to inform and
enliven modernist studies? The relationship between modernism and the avant-garde as formulated by Peter Bürger appears,
I suggest, to be one overarching feature. What is the role of art
within class-based societies based on inequalities of wealth? Is
it necessary or possible for that role to be truly oppositional?
Modernist defamiliarization seems to promise to deliver such
opposition, yet counterbalancing this is the history of ownership (literal and metaphorical) of art by the middle and upper
classes, and the capacity of modern capitalist societies to assimi-
late 'revolutionary' art, in part by turning it into commodity
form. Leon Trotsky, one of the leaders of the Bolshevik revolution as well as a theorist of art and literature, wrote in *Literature
and Revolution* (1924) that 'art cannot live and cannot develop
without a flexible atmosphere of sympathy around it', and
that to reject art, simply because it had been appropriated in
recent history by the bourgeois class, would be for revolution to
deprive itself of its 'most important weapon' in the building of
a new future (Harrison and Wood, *Art in Theory*, pp. 428–30).
The British critic Herbert Read made a similar argument in distinguishing between Surrealism as a 'negative' and 'destructive'
art with only a temporary role in revolution, and the abstract
artists, true revolutionaries whom 'every Communist should
learn to respect and encourage' because they kept 'inviolate,
until such time as society will once more be ready to make use
of them, the universal qualities of art' ('What is Revolutionary
Art?', 1935, in Kolocotroni *et al.*, *Modernism*, pp. 527–8). We
might note that each of these communist perspectives continues to adhere to 'art' as a privileged category, while the logic
of the avant-garde was that art could only be truly oppositional
by undermining its own status as 'art' and erasing the boundary between art and life. In this light, to what extent do you
think avant-garde modernism has made an impact on everyday

life (notice here that I am not completely accepting Bürger's distinction, choosing instead to include the avant-garde *within* a broader concept of modernism)? Can the images we regularly encounter be related in any way to the principles of Futurism, Dada or Surrealism? The extent to which the new technology of photography was able to effect change, by disrupting the concept of visual art itself and to propose instead a broader concept of visual culture, is the subject of the next section.

Photography: from visual art to visual culture

The implication that the course of painting is decisively changed by the advent of photography is a recurrent feature in the history of modernist visual art. The oldest known photograph is a 'heliograph', taken via an eight-hour exposure from a window in the French town of Gras by Joseph Nicéphore Niépce in 1826. In 1839, to acclaim and some consternation, Louis-Jacques-Mandé Daguerre announced the invention of the daguerreotype process, prompting the painter Delacroix's response, 'from this day, painting is dead' (quoted in Graham Clarke, *The Photograph*, Oxford, Oxford University Press, 1997, p. 13), while in 1859 Charles Baudelaire declared photography to be the 'mortal enemy of art'.

However, the subsequent explosion of modernist painting gives the lie to the predictions of Delacroix and Baudelaire. Theodor Adorno later claimed that the 'liberation of modern painting from objectivity' occurred precisely through 'the defensive against the mechanized art commodity – above all, photography' (*Philosophy of Modern Music*, 1958, trans. Anne G. Mitchell and Wesley G. Blomster, New York, Continuum, 2003, p. 5). Crucial stages in the entwined commercialization and mechanization process to which Adorno refers were: in 1888, the invention of the cheap portable Kodak box camera, pioneered by George Eastman in the US; in 1900, also in the US, the production of the famous Brownie, retailing for $1, and establishing the camera as the epitome of cultural democratization; and in Germany in 1925, the production of the Leica, whose 35mm film technology and miniature design revolutionized photographic art by enabling clandestine use and the production of prints of publishable quality.

Peter Childs observes that '(T)he Kodak camera had made it possible to do what the painter had often been asked to do, that is, to give a lifelike representation of any chosen object. As a consequence, artists needed to assert an alternative, non-representational approach that differed from that of the camera' (*Modernism*, London, Routledge, 2000, p. 108). However, the historical relationship between painting, photography and modernity is more complex than this suggests. It is clear, for example, that painting was the dominant paradigm into which early photographers felt obliged to insert their work. Henry Fox Talbot's published collection *The Pencil of Nature* (1844), including renowned images such as 'The Open Door', clearly reveal a debt to the principles of painterly composition. Only with the Pictorialist movement, first established in England in the 1880s and America in the 1890s, did photography begin to develop an aesthetic based on its own distinctive technology, though even here, as Anne Hammond has argued, the same kinds of argument, for example between the claims of Symbolism and Naturalism, were being played out as were in evidence in the emergence of modernist painting ('Naturalistic Vision and Symbolist Image: the pictorial impulse', in ed. Michel Frizot, *A New History of Photography*, Cologne, Konemann, 1994, pp. 293–309).

Another feature of photography's convergence with artistic modernism was the importance of the collective: camera clubs, galleries, exhibitions and magazines. In 1891, the first international exhibition of photography was mounted by the Kamera-Club of Vienna, followed by events of similar ambition and scale in Hamburg (1893) and Paris (1894). Fred Holland Day's exhibition of the 'New School of American Photography' was shown at the Royal Photographic Society in London in 1900, and at the Photo-Club de Paris in 1901. In the American School promoted by the exhibition, a key figure as both artist and entrepreneur was Alfred Stieglitz (1864–1946). German-Jewish and educated in Berlin, Stieglitz's photographic work in New York in the 1890s gained rapid recognition; his haunting images of the Flatiron building have, for example, become identified with New York on the cusp of a modernity which was about to find expression in the rise of the skyscraper. In 1902, Stieglitz created a breakaway group or 'secession' from the Camera Club of New

York, founding the seminal magazine *Camera Work*, and in 1905 the group found a home as the Little Galleries of the Photo-Secession at 291 Fifth Avenue, Manhattan (from 1908, simply '291'). The remit of the gallery was immediately wider than that of photography: before the famous Armory Show took place in New York in 1913, it had already staged three exhibitions of Henri Matisse and one of Picasso.

Stieglitz, however, occupied an ambiguous position in relation to modernism, and in examining this position we can begin to see how photography pulls modernism towards a broader culture of the visual than was possible in the established dispensation of painterly art. First, Stieglitz sought to distance himself from the potential of the camera to become, in itself, the vehicle of a popular and democratic modernism at the services of journalism and report-age. Initially aligning himself with the Pictorialists because of their commitment to innovation, he nevertheless sought a less manipula-tive, 'straight' photography, more in tune with American puritan values, yet at the same time maintaining the distance and integrity of art. His images of New York are in this sense comparable with the work of Eugène Atget (1857–1927) in Paris in the same period, where photography captures the sense of modernity in these two great centres, Atget's emphasis falling on the remnants of the old, Stieglitz on the construction of the new.

Stieglitz' version of photographic modernism was, then, based on qualities of purity and abstraction in the image, seeking to reflect the integrity of the medium as he saw it. This is strikingly evident in his famous image *The Steerage* (1907, Figure 9), taken on the first-class deck of a liner bound for Europe, and looking down into the steerage area, where would-be immigrants to America, refused entry at customs, were being sent back. Despite the ostensibly sharp social commentary on a class divide, Stieglitz' treatment diverts attention away from this and onto the purely formalistic qualities of a 'picture of shapes'. He found similar qualities in the work, which he strongly endorsed, of Paul Strand (1890–1976), whose sparse and eerily beautiful photographs of New York, manufactured objects and machinery seem, as Graham Clarke suggests, to typify abstraction: although Strand 'always sought to place his concerns in an active world of human movement and meaning', his images 'have

Figure 9 Alfred Stieglitz, *The Steerage* (1907)

about them a deep and often immutable presence which resists any attempt to reduce them to paraphrase' (*The Photograph*, p. 175).

In contrast to this version of modernism as idealism, purity and transcendence, however, an alternative modernism was for photography to embrace the manipulations and impurities of a post-Cubist aesthetic, promising a 'culture' of the visual in which the claims of painting and photography to autonomous 'artistic' status become less significant than their new, joint, hybrid possibilities. For this alternative, we need to turn back to Europe: post-war, post-Bolshevik revolution; post-Dada. The following key trends and movements can be identified:

- *Photomontage*. See above, pp. 60–1.
- *Constructivism*. In Russia and Germany in particular, photography became a crucial element in the ethos of Constructivism, whereby the utopian rebuilding of society was to be pursued, culturally, through a futuristic alliance between art and the machine. After 1917 in Russia, 'easelism' was condemned as a bourgeois illusionist practice, and it was declared that the 'last painting' had been painted. Photography was seen as a way of raising consciousness about the social construction of the natural order of things, and of closing the gap between 'art' and the production of useful materials. This increasing alignment between art and industry in the new Soviet Russia was from 1921 termed 'productivism'. Key practitioners were El Lissitsky (1890–1941) and Alexandr Rodchenko (1891–1956), a painter who had also practised photomontage. Far from hiding the artistic means of production, Constructivists practised a highly manipulative photography, typified by the superimposition of images and typographies within a single frame, or by the choice of unusual angles.
- *The New Photography*. In 1922, a group of Soviet constructivists migrated to Berlin in the newly emergent socialist 'Weimar' Republic of Germany. In 1923, Walter Gropius announced a change of orientation at the Bauhaus Institute, from the earlier 'arts and crafts' emphasis to technology (a fuller account of the Bauhaus will follow in the next chapter). The Hungarian László Moholy-Nagy (1895–1946) began work there. Moholy-Nagy was strongly influenced by Constructivism, announcing the latter as the 'socialism of vision', and this radical concept of the visual became incorporated within the 'New Photography', a broad term with which he became principally associated, covering a range of avant-garde photography in the mid–late 1920s. Moholy-Nagy influenced a distinctive photographic language, ranging from street scenes at acute and vertiginous angles to playful and

Figure 10 Umbo (Otto Umbehr), *Mystery of the Street* (1928)

haunting portraits of the group and abstract still-life compositions (Figure 10). While much of this work was designed to reveal
unacknowledged aspects of everyday life, it also possessed the
enigmatic quality of autonomy to be found in Moholy-Nagy's
earlier *photograms*, cameraless photographs using objects and
light-sensitive paper. In this respect the New Photography had
some parallels with Surrealism, particularly in the work of the
Russian-American Man Ray (1890–1976), whose 'Rayograms'
extended the mysterious other-worldly effects of the photograms.
Moholy-Nagy's book *Painting Photography Film*, published by
the Bauhaus in 1925, is a key work in the theory of the New
Photography, while the culmination of the movement's work was
in the great 1929 'Film und Foto' exhibition in Stuttgart.
• *The New Objectivity* (*Neue Sachlichkeit*). 'Neue Sachlichkeit'
was the name of an exhibition of new realist painting held in
Mannheim in 1925. The term extended, however, to certain

developments in New Photography which reopened the debate
about photography's vexed relation to the 'real'. Albert Renger-
Patzsch's *Die Welt is schön* (The World is Beautiful) and Karl
Blossfeldt's *Urformen der Kunst* (Archetypes of Art) were published in 1928; Renger-Patzsch had earlier written about photography as the perfect 'tool' to capture realistic and non-artistic
'impressions' both of nature and of new technology. While these
views seemed almost oblivious to the intense debates around
visual culture in Constructivism and New Photography, it is
ironic that the sheer objectivity of the Neue Sachlichkeit – for
example, Blossfeldt's images of wrought ironwork or magnified
plant pictures – attained a quality of serene aesthetic abstraction.
Painting within the movement began to take on this photographic
purity, bringing the wheel, in a sense, full circle.

Let us conclude this discussion of the relationship between photography and modernism with reference to the great German critic
Walter Benjamin. Benjamin had written a review, 'A Short History
of Photography', in 1931, but in 1936 published the landmark essay
'The Work of Art in the Age of Mechanical Reproduction'; both
texts include the statement: 'a different nature opens itself to the
camera than opens to the naked eye'. Benjamin argued that any
form of mechanical reproduction threatens the 'aura' of the singular
and authentic work of art; new mass societies increasingly insist
on this eradication of aesthetic distance and on 'getting hold' of
the aesthetic in cheap, reproduction commodity forms, a process
which promises to 'emancipate the work of art from its parasitical
dependence on ritual' (Benjamin, *Illuminations*, ed. Hannah Arendt,
London, Fontana, 1982, p. 226). The invention of photography –
and by extension, film and the cinema industry – had 'transformed
the very nature of art'. We return, therefore, to the question with
which we began this section – how is painting affected by the
advent of photography? – but from an altered perspective, stressing the effect of the photograph on the social idea and standing of
the painting rather than on the technique of painting. The unique
and non-reproducible status of the painting is challenged, while the
camera opens out the previously unseen, an 'unconscious optics',
in the same way that Freudian psychoanalysis had given access to

the unconscious (we think of Eadweard Muybridge's sequences of human and animal locomotion in the 1870s, revealing unknown positions, or the astonishing effect of X-rays, discovered by Röntgen in 1895). While artists of the radical left, such as the Constructivists, could use such techniques to reveal the politics of modes of vision, the way was equally open for an unparalleled aestheticization of everything, including politics itself. Modernist visual culture, according to this logic, thus provided fascism with the means to divert the masses through entertainment and even self-expression, whilst leaving the whole system of power and property relations under central political control: in Benjamin's key formulation, fascism was effectively the aestheticization of politics. As a model of how the artistic and visual cultures of modernism might imply a direct but complex relationship with their historical and political circumstances, Benjamin's analysis leads us in to our next chapter.

Selected reading

Apollonio, Umbro (ed.), *Futurist Manifestos* (London, Thames & Hudson, 1973)

   Valuable anthology of Futurist writing.

Berger, John, 'The Moment of Cubism', in *Selected Essays*, ed. Geoff Dyer (Vintage: New York, 2003)

   Excellent account of the revolutionary impact of Cubism, published in 1969 but still fresh and very readable.

Breton, André, *What is Surrealism? Selected Writings*, ed. Franklin Rosemont (London, Pluto, 1978)

   Another valuable anthology of original sources.

Clark, T.J., *The Painting of Modern Life: Paris in the Art of Manet and His Followers* (London, Thames & Hudson, 1985)

   A definitive materialist account of Impressionism and the struggle to depict 'modern life'.

Clark, T.J., *Farewell to an Idea: Episodes from a History of Modernism* (New Haven and London, Yale University Press, 1999)

   Highly original and inspirational essays, principally on Pissaro, Cézanne, Picasso, Malevich and Pollock, in which Clark explores modernism's heroic failure to realize its ideals.

Clarke, Graham, *The Photograph* (Oxford, Oxford University Press, 1997)

   A good survey.

Fer, Bryony, *On Abstract Art* (New Haven and London, Yale University Press, 1997)

Stimulating study addressing the question of how to find a language for the aesthetic appeal of abstraction. Excellent chapter on interpreting Mondrian, and reclaims the women Suprematist painters Lyubov Popova and Olga Rozanova.

Foster, Hal, Rosalind Krauss, Yve-Alain Bois and Benjamin H.D. Buchloh, *Art Since 1900: Modernism, Antimodernism, Postmodernism* (London: Thames & Hudson, 2004)

Large, comprehensive textbook that tries to break the mould of conventional modernist art history.

Frascina, Francis, chapter 2, 'Realism and Ideology: An Introduction to Semiotics and Cubism', in eds Charles Harrison, Francis Frascina and Gill Perry, *Primitivism, Cubism, Abstraction: The Early Twentieth Century* (New Haven and London, Yale University Press/Open University, 1993)

A good commentary on the issues of the realism and Cubism discussed in the first section of this chapter.

Fry, Edward F., *Cubism* (London: Thames & Hudson, 1966)

Useful introduction followed by an extensive anthology of documents.

Harrison, Charles, *Modernism* (London, Tate Publishing, 1997)

Useful brief survey of critical issues in modernist visual art.

Harrison, Charles, and Paul Wood (eds), *Art in Theory 1900–1990: An Anthology of Changing Ideas* (2nd edn, Oxford and Cambridge, MA, Blackwell, 2003)

Invaluable anthology to sit alongside Kolocotroni *et al.* (some overlaps), with an emphasis on aesthetics and politics.

Hughes, Robert, *The Shock of the New: Art and the Century of Change* (London, Thames & Hudson, 1991)

Racy, entertaining narrative of the modernist revolution in visual and plastic arts, to accompany the BBC series of the same name. Enjoy, but with a pinch of salt!

McLeod, Glen, 'The visual arts', in ed. Michael Levenson, *The Cambridge Companion to Modernism* (Cambridge, Cambridge University Press, 1999)

A useful survey.

North, Michael, *Camera Works: Photography and the Twentieth-Century Word* (Oxford, Oxford University Press, 2005)

Very thoughtful study of the complex impact of photography and film on visual and literary modernism.

Orton, Fred, and Griselda Pollock, 'Rooted in the Earth: A Van Gogh

Primer', in *Avant-Gardes and Partisans Reviewed* (Manchester, Manchester University Press, 1996)

Marxist–materialist revision of Van Gogh.

Read, Herbert, *A Concise History of Modern Painting* (London, Thames & Hudson, 1974)

Clear and chronological, interestingly tinged by Read's revolutionary socialism.

West, Shearer, *The Visual Arts in Germany 1890–1937: Utopia and Despair* (Manchester, Manchester University Press, 2000)

Good historical survey from Jugendstil and Expressionism through the Weimar years to Hitler's Munich exhibition of 'degenerate art' in 1937.

3

History and the politics of modernism

How do we understand the relationship of modernism to the history and politics of its period? In addressing this question, we should immediately beware of constructing a model of history as a 'back-ground' against which artistic movements are played out. As the last chapter implied, intimate aspects of practice in modernist visual art – the application of paint to canvas, or the taking of a photograph – are themselves fully historical phenomena. Nevertheless, it has become commonplace to observe that modernism coincides with a period of cataclysm and incredibly rapid change in world history: a year before his death at the battle of the Marne in 1914, the French poet Charles Péguy wrote that the world had changed less since the time of Christ than it had in the previous thirty years. To encourage you to move beyond such generalizations, and in the spirit of modernism's fight against the cliché, this chapter sets modernism in the light of certain selected historical phenomena, and introduces some of the important critical issues in modernism's relation to the politics of modernity.

If there is a special edge to this historical perspective in the case of modernism, it is perhaps because modernism has been consistently vulnerable to the charge of having *disavowed* history through the turn towards formalism. A key example of this charge occurs in George Orwell's essay of 1940, 'Inside the Whale'.

> About 1928, in one of the three genuinely funny jokes that *Punch* has produced since the Great War, an intolerable youth is pictured informing his aunt that he intends to 'write'. 'And what are you going to write about, dear?' asks the aunt. 'My dear aunt,' says the youth

crushingly, 'one doesn't write *about* anything, one just *writes*.' (*Inside the Whale and Other Essays*, Harmondsworth, Penguin, 1983, p. 28)

This caricature of an 'intolerable youth' reflects Orwell's dim view of an English literary modernism which 'was supposed to consist solely in the manipulation of words', and in which the content of the writing was unmentionable. In English modernism, he notes, there is no attention to 'the urgent problems of the moment, above all no politics in a narrower sense'; writers direct our attention 'everywhere except the places where things are actually happening'. In the 1920s, he persists, 'nothing is queerer than the way in which every important event in Europe escaped the notice of the English intelligentsia'. The Hungarian Marxist Georg Lukács implied a similar retreat from history as the 'ideology of modernism' (that is, through modernist fiction's eschewal of the techniques of nineteenth-century realism – see *The Meaning of Contemporary Realism*, London, Merlin Press, 1962), while Clement Greenburg's famous definition of painterly modernism in terms of an elaboration of its own techniques and materials (see chapter 2) can be seen in a comparably ahistoricist light.

My general premise in this chapter is to take issue with such readings, on the grounds that they tend to underestimate and even misconstrue the ways in which the 'difficult', defamiliarizing forms of modernism might relate to their historical and political contexts. The chapter begins with a discussion of three key events in the history of the modernist period: the First World War (1914–18); the Russian Bolshevik Revolution (1917); and the emergence of the German Weimar Republic and Bauhaus Institute (1919–33). It then considers four phenomena more akin to processes than events: Empire and colonialism; Fordist capitalism and consumer culture; the rise of new technologies; and new discourses on sexuality. In each case the aim is not to provide a 'factual' historical account (the 'Selected reading' provides some sources for your own reading track in this respect), but instead to suggest approaches to the intertwining of history and modernist cultures, informed where possible by recent work from within contemporary modernist studies. The chapter ends with a section, 'The politics of modernism', which poses some key questions that will continue to resurface throughout the book.

The First World War

The Great War of 1914 to 1918 lies at the heart of the modernist period. The origins of the war and the aims of its participants are notoriously difficult to disentangle, as J.M. Roberts' description 'a complex of wars' indicates, and as historiography continues to show (see *Europe 1880–1945*, London, Longman, 1977, ch. IX, 'The Great War'). At least from the beginning of the century, Britain and Germany had been caught up in a naval arms race in the context of an intensifying competition for overseas markets and colonial territories. Europe was also politically divided between the Franco-Russian alliance on the one hand, and that of the Central Powers (Austria-Hungary, Germany) on the other. The assassination of the Austro–Hungarian Archduke Franz Ferdinand by a Serbian dissident in Sarajevo on 28 June 1914 precipitated the actual conflict, while Britain and France's declaration of war against Germany on 4 August closely followed the German invasion of a defenceless Belgium. Although long anticipated, the war became by no means inevitable until these late events. It was split between two 'theatres': the Western front, established quickly by the allies to halt the German advance across France and stretching from the Belgian coast in the North to the Swiss border in the South; and the Eastern front, more reluctantly engaged by the Allies, but necessitated by the Turkish Ottoman Empire's alliance with Germany and threat to Russia from the Black Sea, and characterized by the wasteful and inconclusive Dardanelles campaign of 1915.

Early modernism – including the phase of analytic Cubism, and the earlier writings of Gertrude Stein or Joseph Conrad, for example – was already established by 1914. One familiar structure of interpretation is to see the war as a watershed in modernist cultures, working a devastating effect on artistic imagination. The 'horror' of the war, foreshadowed perhaps in the dying phrase of the prophetic figure of Kurtz in Conrad's *Heart of Darkness* (1899/1902), might be defined in terms of a ghoulishly absurd encounter between traditional methods of warfare and the killing machines of technological modernity. While British officers were instructed to sharpen their swords, and French soldiers wore red trousers (which enabled them to be picked off with ease), new technologies soon came to dominate the conflict: the magazine rifle, the machine-gun, the quick-firing artillery gun and the submarine, followed by the introduction of poison gas and the tank (Roberts, *Europe*, p. 267). In July 1916, Britain sustained 57,000 casualties on the first day of the battle of the Somme, including 20,000 dead.

In 1915 the poet Hilda Doolittle ('H.D.') lost her first child through, she claimed, 'shock and repercussions of war news broken to me in a rather brutal fashion' (*Tribute to Freud*, Oxford, Carcanet, 1971, p. 46). In the same year, 'out of sheer rage' at the war's 'colossal idiocy', D.H. Lawrence began his *Study of Thomas Hardy*, which ended up not simply as an essay on a literary figure but as a wide-ranging Nietzschean philosophical excursus on, or stocktaking of, a whole civilization's health. Many modernist artists were lost in wartime service, while many others, such as May Sinclair, Ernest Hemingway and John Dos Passos, joined support services such as the ambulance corps in Belgium and France. The war also saw a significant geographical redistribution within modernism, as artists migrated away from the centres of conflict and towards neutral countries such as Switzerland.

In literary history, the writings of the British soldier poets, Wilfred Owen, Siegfried Sassoon, Edmund Blunden, Rupert Brooke, and others, still constitute the most powerful body of work to record the war and the ensuing general cultural pattern of rapid disillusionment with nationalistic ideals. The question of the relationship of this work to the simultaneous emergence of literary *modernism* – say, to the Imagist poetry movement, established in London in 1912 – might be seen to focus on the appropriateness of poetic forms to an unprecedented experience. Were the conventional forms deployed, though often significantly modified, by the war poets – the sonnet, the ballad – adequate to this experience? Or had the war rendered language itself, in all its recognized forms, inadequate? 'In the Somme Valley', writes Robert Hughes, perhaps melodramatically, 'the back of language broke. It could no longer carry its former meanings' (*The Shock of the New*, p. 57). The great German-Jewish Marxist writer, Walter Benjamin, had pushed this kind of interpretation into an even more radical shape: it was not that language was now inadequate to experience, but that the value of experience itself had been diminished by a modernity exemplified by the war. Men returned from the battlefield, Benjamin argues, 'grown silent – not richer, but poorer in communicable experience':

> For never has experience been contradicted more thoroughly than strategic experience by tactical warfare, economic experience by inflation, bodily experience by mechanical warfare, moral experience by those in power. A generation that had gone to school in a horse-drawn streetcar now stood under an open sky in a countryside in which nothing remained but the clouds, and beneath these clouds, in a field of force of destructive torrents and explosions, was the tiny, fragile human body. ('The Storyteller', in *Illuminations*, p. 84)

Returning for a moment to Orwell's 'intolerable youth', this satire was no doubt also informed by the apparent tension between the brutal realities of war, and modernist aesthetic autonomy. Claude Monet's paintings of lily ponds were painted in his garden in Giverny in northern France, near enough for the guns of the Western front to be heard. As Charles Harrison notes, 'no shadow of a relevant history could be said to fall in figurative form' across the pictures (*Modernism*, pp. 62–3). Yet this absence might be read, not as simple escapism, but as modernism standing out for a model of aesthetic integrity in the face of an unfolding barbaric history. *Women in Love* (1920) is the novel of Lawrence's appalled response to the war; yet it contains no mention of war, nor any historical specificity other than an implicit sense that the context is the Europe of the early twentieth century. Instead, Lawrence makes the novel a searching examination of all the values and institutions through which we define ourselves as human, such as love, friendship, sexuality, marriage, art, race, education, language and the treatment and representation of animals. The latter theme also informs a highly condensed and displaced reading of the war in an image from *Nightwood* (1936), Djuna Barnes' allusive and hallucinatory fiction of sexually dissident counterculture in 1920s Paris. 'I was in the war once myself', offers the garrulous, transgressive figure of Dr. Matthew O'Connor. 'In', however, transpires here to be a cellar in a small unnamed town during a bombing raid, in the company of a person from Dublin and an old Breton woman with a cow. The terrified beast intensifies the collective fear and a sense of the disruption of known boundaries, O'Connor finding, in her trembling, evidence that 'the tragedy of the beast can be two legs more awful than a man's'. Barnes however pushes the image into even more unfamiliar territory, O'Connor deducing that 'there are directions and speeds that no-one has calculated, for believe it or not that cow had gone somewhere very fast that we didn't know of, and yet was still standing there' (*Nightwood*, London, Faber, 1985, pp. 40–1). The trauma of war is given historical specificity by its association with the modernist intuition of unexplored time–space co-ordinates, as if the cow and the technology of bombing combine to place the human in the midst of unknowable dimensions.

In instances such as these, modernism could be said to continue, but give a distinctive inflection to, the broadly post-Romantic status of art as a guardian of human value against social, political and economic dehumanization: it is precisely in the formal imperative to 'make it new' that modernism figures human possibility in terms of freedom and tolerance. By 1945, however, a second war, and the Nazi extermination of the Jews, had cast a long shadow over this view of art as an inherent bulwark against barbarism. One of the key advocates of modernist autonomy, Theodor Adorno, reflected scep-tically upon the very possibility of poetry in the wake of Auschwitz, after it had become evident that the administrators of the death camps were not necessarily opponents of classical humanist civiliza-tion, but often rather its products and champions. Nevertheless, before the full horror of the Holocaust was revealed, the Second World War had produced key long poems of later modernism, such as H.D.'s *Trilogy* (1944–6) and T.S. Eliot's *Four Quartets* (1939–44), in each of which a more openly accessible voice, and an implicit defence of the role writer or 'scribe' (H.D.) in articulating humane values, was found.

Perhaps reflecting this scepticism about the inherent value of 'high' modernism, therefore, contemporary modernist studies has tended to find more nuanced or ambiguous responses to the First World War, within a framework of cultural history in which modernism blends into war writing in a more general sense. One recurrent emphasis here is on changing meanings and perceptions of the body and its vulnerability, 'tiny and fragile' as Benjamin had put it. Much work has accumulated around the condition of shell-shock and associated 'male hysteria', first diagnosed and

treated by pioneering psychologist W.H.R. Rivers at Craiglockhart
Military Hospital, Edinburgh, in a way which indirectly helped
to present Freudian ideas about repressed unconscious forces to a
hostile and empirically minded British psychological establishment.
Texts such as Rebecca West's *The Return of the Soldier* (1918) and
Virginia Woolf's *Mrs. Dalloway* (1925), as well as the more recent
Regeneration trilogy by Pat Barker, have informed a range of work
dealing with the disruption to accepted notions of femininity and
masculinity emanating from the war and from shell-shock, by critics such as Paul Fussell, Elaine Showalter, William Greenslade
and, most recently, Michèle Barrett. The mutilation of the body
in warfare, taken to horrific new dimensions by the technologies
of the Great War, and as frequently evidenced by survivors of the
trenches, has also been the subject of sophisticated new readings.
The motif of the wounded soldier appears frequently in the post-
1915 works of D.H. Lawrence. More unusually, a case has been
made by Alison Light for a 'conservative modernism' in the novels
of Agatha Christie, whose stylized fictional treatment of the murdered body can be seen as a complex restorative response to the
shattered and dispersed body of the battlefield (*Forever England:
Femininity, literature and conservatism between the wars*, London
and New York, Routledge, 1991). In *Modernism, History and the
First World War* (Manchester, Manchester University Press, 1998),
Trudi Tate sees a dissolving boundary between 'modernism' and
'war writing', and focuses on the shared concerns of how to bear
witness to the war, and of the effects of the literal and symbolic dis-
membering of bodies, drawing interpretations from psychoanalytic
theories of abjection in the work of Julia Kristeva, and imaginary
violence between young children and parents in that of Melanie
Klein. Chapters on the cultural symbolism of the tank, and on the
suppressed presence in Woolf's *Mrs Dalloway* of a debate around
the Turkish extermination of Armenians, demonstrate the ana-
lytical advantage gained from placing modernist responses within
a broader cultural history of the war. More recently, Alex Goody's
*Modernist Articulations: A cultural study of Djuna Barnes, Mina Loy
and Gertrude Stein* (Basingstoke, Palgrave, 2007) offers an alternative to the hysterical/melancholic male modernist response to the
traumatic crisis of masculinity of the war. For Goody, the fact that

the Great War 'cracks open the speaking subject of the lyric and annihilates the stable, signifying capacity of language and gender' proves to be an enabling condition for the love poetry of both Mina Loy and Gertrude Stein, which articulates unthought-of fields of female desire (*Modernist Articulations*, p. 84). This is one way of affirming Stein's arresting assertion in 1926 that the war had helped art and artists to become more contemporary, creating 'the completed recognition of the contemporary composition' (*Look at Me Now and Here I Am: Writings and Lectures 1911–45*, ed. Patricia Meyerowitz, Harmondsworth, Penguin, 1971, p. 28).

The Bolshevik Revolution

> The Bolshevist Revolution of October, 1917, did not overthrow the Kerensky government alone, it overthrew the whole social system that was based on private property. This system has its own culture and its own official literature, and its collapse could not but be the collapse of pre-revolutionary literature.

So begins *Literature and Revolution* (1924) by Leon Trotsky. When the Bolsheviks seized power from the Provisional Government in October 1917, the most significant Socialist uprising since the Paris Commune of 1871 was enacted. The Russian imperial system had already begun to crumble, with the abdication of the Romanovs in the February Revolution of 1917, and thus Russia far surpassed 1871 France in establishing the first modern state to be based on Karl Marx's communist principles of the abolition of private property and the common ownership of the means of production.

As we have seen in the previous chapter, Russia was already a crucible of modernist experimentation, with international and metropolitan dimensions. From 1907 to 1910, 'Moscow became a meeting place for the most revolutionary movements in European art' (Camilla Gray, *The Russian Experiment in Art, 1863–1922*, London, Thames & Hudson, 1962, p. 93), and became a 'truly international centre' in the years leading up to 1914. Its post-1907 Futurist movement was characterized by the work of visual artists such as Mikhail Larionov (1881–1964) and Natalia Goncharova (1881–1962), followed by Olga Rosanova, Lyubov Popova and Kasimir Malevich, and poets such as Aleksei Kruchenikh, Velimir

Khlebnikov, Elena Guro and, pre-eminently, the poet, playwright and painter Vladimir Mayakovsky (1893–1930). The Revolution further provided the perfect context for a key modernist principle: utopianism. What connections might there be between a political system that claims to start everything afresh, and modernism's rupture with tradition? What kinds of literature and culture follow in the wake of what Trotsky, Lenin's second-in-command and advocate of 'permanent revolution', called the collapse of the 'pre-revolutionary'? Could experimental art be at the service of revolution, or must it preserve its own autonomy? And can a revolutionary experimental art at the same time be an art of 'the people'?

These debates in post-1917 Russia can be exemplified by setting the project of Constructivism, as represented by Vladimir Tatlin (1885–1953), in the context of our discussion in chapter 2 of Kasimir Malevich's Suprematism. Malevich, we remember, had hailed Cubism and Futurism as anticipating in art the economic principles of Bolshevism, but despite his own fervour for the revolution, he continued to insist on art's separation as a field of activity, crystallized in the *White on White* canvases of (1918–19), of which he wrote, 'I have broken the blue shade of colour boundaries and come out into white. Behind me comrade pilots swim in the whiteness. I have established the semaphore of Suprematism' (quoted in Gray, *Russian Experiment in Art*, p. 240).

Compare this with the commissioning in 1919 of Vladimir Tatlin's *Monument to the Third Communist International*, the model of which (Figure 11), exhibited in 1920, became the keynote of the Constructivist movement. The 9-metre wooden model foreshadowed a colossal iron and glass structure to be erected in Petrograd, at 400 metres, a third higher than that previous symbol of modernity, the Eiffel Tower, and clearly seeking comparison with its predecessor in bourgeois Paris. The superstructure was a strong diagonal spar continuing the angle of the earth's axis, supporting two spirals tapering upwards, and enclosing four geometrical structures housing departments of the Comintern and rotating at various speeds. Despite its abstract appearance, it might be said that the symbolic values of the monument were relatively straightforward: the various 'revolutions' representing the coordinated dynamism of the Revolution, the upward trajectory representing progress, and

Figure 11 Vladimir Tatlin, *Monument to the Third Communist
International*

the glass representing the transparency of Bolshevik politics and
government.

   Tatlin's monument was never built, leaving it with the curious perennial status of a kind of unrealized eighth wonder of the
world. But it also came to symbolize the gradual ascendancy of
the Constructivist version of modernism in the Soviet Institute
of Artistic Culture or *Inkhuk* over Malevich and Kandinsky as

representatives of abstraction, especially after 1921 when civil war in Soviet Russia subsided. Easel painting was condemned as a practice redolent of bourgeois individualism, and instead Tatlin and artists such as Otto Brik, Alexei Gan, Varvara Stepanova, Lyubov Popova and Alexander Rodchenko pursued the interconnection of art and modern technology, the informing scientific knowledge of materials, and the practical intervention of art in everyday life.

It is perhaps not difficult to see how this version of modernism might prevail when the success of revolution depends upon the technological modernization of a vast and largely agricultural country (Lenin's bold announcement in 1920, for example, promised the electrification of the entire Soviet Union). Yet Malevich equally committed his abstraction to the practical cause of modernity, and produced quasi-Platonic designs for the ideal form of everyday domestic objects such as cups and saucers.

STOP and THINK

In *Literature and Revolution* (Michigan, Michigan University Press, 1960/1971) Trotsky's comparison of the Tatlin monument with the Eiffel Tower is not favourable. Beauty, he argues, is linked to rationality of function: if we know what something is *for*, it is likely to be more aesthetically perfect. If the Eiffel Tower was then 'not a building, but an exercise', this is even more true of Tatlin's monument. Its superstructure, he claims, is as ugly and heavy as 'unremoved scaffolding'; it supports a cylinder designed to hold meetings, but 'meetings are not necessarily held in a cylinder and the cylinder does not necessarily have to rotate' – quite apart from the fact that the cylinder looks like 'a beer bottle'! While managing to sound very utilitarian here, Trotsky at the same time preserves a sense of separate aesthetic principles which must combine with practicality in any design; thus, for example, he writes:

> To make an 'ideal' knife, one must have, besides the knowledge of the properties of the material and the methods of its use, both imagination and taste. In accord with the entire tendency of industrial culture, we think that the artistic imagination in creating material objects will be directed towards working out the

ideal form of a thing, as a thing, and not towards the embellish-
ment of the thing as an aesthetic premium to itself. If this is true
for penknives, it will be truer still for wearing apparel, furniture,
theatre and cities. (p. 250)

Trotsky's rather sniffy response to Tatlin's Monument typifies
the complexity of debates within Soviet Russia around the relationship between modernist art and utopian politics.

- Whose art, Malevich or Tatlin, is most 'revolutionary'? Are
  'aesthetic imagination' and 'industrial culture' fundamentally different things, or can they be reconciled? Is aesthetic
  value necessarily enhanced by functionality or is it best characterized as functionless?
- There is a structure in the Municipal Bus Station in Bridgend,
  South Wales, far from the context of Bolshevik Russia, which
  suggests to me that the architect must have been aware of
  the designs for Tatlin's monument! Is it the fate of modernist
  design that its revolutionary impact must always be absorbed
  into the mainstream?

Weimar and Bauhaus

As the defeated aggressor, Germany had punishing financial repa-
rations imposed upon it by the allied powers in the aftermath of
the war and the 1919 Treaty of Versailles. However, neither the
national fabric nor industrial strength of Germany had been entirely
crushed: it had not, for example, been invaded and occupied by the
victors. Instead, Germany itself was to partake in, if not to lead,
the rehabilitation of democratic forms and national identities that
followed the armistice. Coinciding with the abdication of Wilhelm
II, socialist revolution occurred in 1918, potentially mirroring the
Bolshevik revolution of the previous year: the sailors of Kiel helped
form a Soviet which was then reproduced across Germany; a republic was declared in Munich, and provisional government in Berlin.
The new assembly of the Weimar Republic met for the first time on
6 February 1919, drawing up a paper constitution exemplary in its
statement of the principles of inclusive and institutionalized state
democracy. This, however, was at the expense of the suppression

by the Social Democratic socialists of the Leninist and ultra-leftist Spartacists, whose leaders Rosa Luxemberg, Karl Liebknecht and Leo Jogiches were murdered – an uneasy premonition, perhaps, of the Republic's transmutation and eventual demise with the appointment of Adolf Hitler as German Chancellor in 1933.

As is evident in an enduring interdisciplinary account such as John Willett's *The New Sobriety: Art and Politics in the Weimar Period 1917–33* (London, Thames & Hudson, 1978), the Weimar Republic created conditions of democratic optimism, particularly in the brief period of economic prosperity between 1924 and 1929, within which avant-garde culture could flourish. Two key instances were: the development of experimental working-class theatre in the work of dramatists such as Erwin Piscator (1893–1966), Ernst Toller (1893–1939) and Bertolt Brecht (1898–1956), which we will examine later, in chapter 8; and the history of the Bauhaus Institute (1919–33). A common feature of these developments was their treatment of a legacy of German Expressionism. The history of the Bauhaus Institute is co-extensive with that of the Weimar Republic itself (1919–33). Paralleling the utopian collectivism of Bolshevik Russia, the Institute aspired to use the arts to help 'build' a new socialist society of the future. Under its first director, Walter Gropius (1883–1969), the Institute declared an initial debt to the late nineteenth-century English Arts and Crafts movement of John Ruskin and William Morris in its insistence that '*we must all return to crafts . . . a foundation in handicraft is essential for every artist*'. 'Let us together desire, conceive and create the new building of the future', the programme of 1919 continues, 'which will combine everything – architecture and sculpture *and* painting – in a *single* form which will one day rise towards the heavens from the hands of a million workers as the crystalline symbol of a new and coming faith'. The mystic and spiritual side of this aspiration was itself 'crystallized' in the wood-cut image of the 'Cathedral of Socialism' by Lyonel Feininger, a thrustingly angular building seemingly hewn out of ice and combining aspects of Cubist and Futurist technique, yet whose three shining stars on the apex of each spire add an almost sentimental touch of optimism. Similarly, the first teacher of the *Vorkurs* preliminary course, Johannes Itten, sought to transcend the inert copying methods of the traditional art schools through engaging his students in a

more active understanding of the nature of materials, primary forms
and colours. 'Rhythm' and 'intuition' were key concepts in Itten's
teaching, suggesting a subjective, holistic approach to the objects
of study: as Magdalena Droste notes, this might be described as an
Expressionist phase of the Bauhaus in that 'it was dominated by a
preoccupation with the individual and his cosmic integration. Social
concerns were less real' (*Bauhaus 1919–33*, Berlin, Taschen, 1990,
p. 51). The products of this phase, from Itten's self-styled monastic
robe to multiform and multi-coloured tapestries and stained glass,
or the beautiful stylized timber slats and zig-zag internal patterns of
the Sommerfeld house (Berlin 1920–1), combined natural materials
with a simple mysticism. In pursuit of their own particular spiritual-
ized versions of abstraction, both Paul Klee and Wassily Kandinsky
were drawn to the Bauhaus in the early 1920s.

This might be contrasted with a famous image of the Hungarian
artist László Moholy-Nagy in 1925, two years after taking over from
Itten as head of the *Vorkurs*: red workman's overalls, neat necktie and
white shirt, oiled hair and a determined focus on something outside
the frame, his body framed against a pure white plane. While still
under the directorship of Gropius, the Bauhaus underwent profound change as the German republic entered its period of relative
prosperity in 1924 (aided by the American-sponsored Dawes Plan),
and in so doing seems to encapsulate one of the enigmas of aesthetic
modernism whenever its utopian drive brings about contact with
modernity's interest in technological progress and mastery. The
emphasis on handicrafts and the implicit backward glance to medi-
evalism is discarded, and replaced by a machine-driven functionalism of design for the purposes of industry, under the slogan of 'Art
and Technology: A New Unity'. Moholy-Nagy, in his garb, is both
technical worker and professional 'white collar' manager.

Economics and aesthetics are intertwined in this complex mutation. In part, Gropius sought to free the Institute from state subsidy
and to allow it to compete in the marketplace, at a fragile moment
when the republic was still subject to rampant inflation; in part,
its direction was changed by the gravitation to Weimar of the
likes of Theo van Doesburg (De Stijl abstraction) and the Russian
Constructivist El Lizzitsky (the Bolsheviks began to look eagerly
towards Taylorism in America for a model of productive efficiency,

Figure 12 Marcel Breuer, Wassily Club Chair (1925)

as if to de- and re-politicize this blueprint of late capitalism). Moholy-Nagy expanded and transformed the *Vorkurs*: the analysis of materials was extended, visits to industry were staged, while at the same time the practice of drawing was so diminished as to inevitably call to mind the Constructivist rejection of easel painting as a bourgeois error. Yet tellingly, perhaps, Moholy-Nagy ushered in a phase that produced some of the most memorable associations with the word 'Bauhaus' in the popular imagination: the angular font that you can now find on your computer software; the Marcel Breuer club chair of 1925 (Figure 12); minimalist domestic interiors with tubular steel furniture; and whitewashed, angular buildings with flat roofs and horizontal windows, typified by the Gropius building which became the new centre of the Institute when it moved to Dessau in 1925.

From this point until the demise of the Bauhaus in 1933, a new emphasis on architecture gave rise to one of the fundamental paradoxes in the politics of the modernist movement. Gropius gave way to the Swiss architect Hannes Meyer in 1928, but not before he had pioneered the application of the machine aesthetic to the desperate social need for new, low-cost housing in Weimar Germany. At Torten, south of Dessau, Gropius built an estate of 316 two-storey, modular and prefabricated houses whose essential construction components were breezeblock and concrete beams. Of this development Gropius wrote, 'It is high time to enter the stage of sober calculation and precise analysis of practical experience . . . Building means shaping the different processes of living. Most individuals have the same living requirements', while Meyer insisted that 'the new house, being prefabricated, is an industrial product and accordingly a job for specialists: economists, statisticians, hygiene experts, climatologists, industrial consultants, experts on standards, heating technicians . . . as for the architect? . . . from being an artist he becomes a specialist in organisation! The new house is a social work' (quoted in Willett, *The New Sobriety*, p. 121). Meyer saw this austere functionalism as a means of achieving communist utopia, fulfilling collective human needs on a vast scale, and modernist housing spread extremely rapidly across many German cities in the late 1920s, filtering into the work of a range of less-celebrated architects in conjunction with the municipal authorities. But it is clear that the same attitude and its uncompromising idealism could be seen to embody forces of dehumanization – an imposition of uniformity by a new dominant class of 'expert' and 'specialist' social engineers. What it might be like for human beings to live in such environments was a question that was yet to be answered; questions of elegance, ornament and aesthetic beauty had been laid aside in the name of functionalism, despite the fact that in other areas of modernist art it was precisely the *functionless* quality of autonomy that was seen to carry an emancipatory charge. Later in the century, 'functionalism' was sometimes to be replaced by the term 'brutalism', and the visions of the Bauhaus architects condemned for their impracticalities as well as for their soullessness. In John Willett's account of Weimar Germany, the growing sobriety (Gropius' 'sober calculation') of this cultural phase typified the way in which a radical, democratically socialistic modernism carefully prepared the ground for its antithesis, a rationally organized fascism, in which Hitler's regime transferred Bauhaus principles of functional efficiency to the construction and operation of the death camps.

STOP and THINK

In 2006, the exhibition 'Modernism: Designing a New World 1914–39' was held at the Victoria and Albert Museum in London, sponsored by the retailer Habitat. Acknowledging the influence of modernist design on Habitat products over four decades, Jens Nordahl cites in particular 'the Modernist belief that our daily lives can be improved through good-quality design', and also claims that 'Modernist ideals and aesthetics have timeless appeal' (ed. Christopher Wilk, *Modernism: Designing a New World 1914–39*, London, V&A Publications, 2006, p. 6).

• How enduring, do you think, is the modernist belief that the everyday can be improved by good-quality design? Does this signify the same collapsing of the distinction between art and life which, for Peter Bürger, characterizes the work of the modernist avant-garde? And is it true that the distinctive designs of the Bauhaus Institute, for example, have transcended history to develop 'timeless appeal', or are they still subject to the shifting dictates of taste and fashion?

Empire and colonialism

The beginnings of modernism in the late nineteenth century coincide with a period of intense imperialist expansionism among the European nations and America. With the consolidation of the idea of the modern nation-state, and the exhaustion of domestic markets for capitalism, the industrialized nations began to look overseas for new markets and raw materials. The Berlin Congress of 1884 crystallized what became known as the 'scramble for Africa', by which the already extensive incursions of Leopold of Belgium were ratified in the formation of the Belgian Congo, and Central Africa was carved up between the European powers. The British Empire was at its height: this was also the era of the 'discovery' and exploration of Africa, as typified by the expeditions and colonizations of explorers such as Stanley and de Brazza. As Edward Said's study *Orientalism* (1978) showed in relation to British dominance in India and the project of the map-making Indian Survey, an inextricable linking of politics and knowledge is crucial to the imperialist–colonialist enterprise: to 'know' a territory is to exert power over it.

Artistic modernism has a profoundly ambivalent relationship with the politics of what Eric Hobsbawm calls this 'Age of Empire'. Undoubtedly, modernism is fed and enriched by the processes of cultural exchange set in train by colonialism: as artefacts and ideas flowed from the new 'peripheries' of empire into the museums and universities of the Western metropolises, an awed reassessment and integration of the so-called 'primitive' took place in experimental art. I deal with this in greater detail in the section on 'primitivism' in chapter 4. A landmark gesture such as Pablo Picasso's use of African tribal masks in *Les Demoiselles d'Avignon* (1907) could thus be consolidated by Wilhelm Worringer's theory that abstraction is a quality shared by primitive and by advanced modernist art, and that the bourgeois aesthetic of the reproduction of organic beauty in art leaves us 'helpless' to understand the art of many other non-Western cultures. In explaining that the primitive urge to abstraction expressed a deep spiritual dread of empty space, Worringer also subtly reinforced imperialist notions of the intellectual inferiority of the non-Western. Nevertheless, the general tendency in Worringer's thesis and in artistic modernism is increasingly seen to be a resistance to and critique of Western cultural supremacy.

So Edward Said, in the later work *Culture and Imperialism* (London, Vintage, 1994), argues that 'many of the most prominent characteristics of modernist culture . . . include a response to the external pressures on culture from the *imperium*', and that the 'pervasive irony', self-consciousness and discontinuity of modernist writings register the growing vulnerability of Europe and its imperialist triumphalism (pp. 227–9). In Thomas Mann's novella *Death in Venice* (1912), the pre-war fragility of imperial cultures is figured in the German 'master' composer Gustave Aschenbach, whose sojourn in Venice, a traditional gateway to the East, exposes him to the perils of transgressive desire in the shape of the beautiful young Polish boy, Tadzio. Said identifies the Asiatic cholera that kills Aschenbach as a complex trope threatening the contamination of the West by its colonial Other in a way that combines 'dread and promise . . . degeneration and desire'. Thus critics have come increasingly to argue that the fear of degenerationism prevalent in some modernism (see the section 'Evolution and entropy' in chapter 4 for a further discussion of this term) is also an admission of the permeability of the border between the imperial centre and its periphery, if not an undermining of that border's very existence.

Such a debate is staged in Rod Edmond's essay 'Degeneration in Imperialist and Modernist Discourse' (2000), where Edmond takes issue with Fredric Jameson's essay 'Modernism and Imperialism' (1990). Jameson's essay makes clear distinctions both between popular imperialist and modernist writing, and between the modern metropolis or imperial centres and the colonies, newly constituted as peripheral to those centres. Jameson argues the 'radical otherness' of colonial life could not be assimilated into metropolitan consciousness, such that the forms of modernist texts bear the traces of imperialism in their own inability to represent the colonial Other ('Modernism and Imperialism', in eds S. Deane, F. Jameson, T. Eagleton and E. Said, *Nationalism, Colonialism and Literature*, Minneapolis, University of Minnesota Press, 1990, pp. 43–68). Edmond however disputes such antitheses as oversimplifications, in that they ignore the 'process of shuttling, displacement and substitution in which the metropolis and the colony were in constant interaction' ('Degeneration in Imperialist and Modernist Discourse', in eds Howard J. Booth and Nigel Rigby, *Modernism and Empire*, Manchester, Manchester University Press, pp. 39–63; 57). For example, as émigré artists such as Joseph Conrad (born in Poland) and Katherine Mansfield (a New Zealander) knew only too well, colonies had their own cities and metropolitan experience. Where Edmond and Jameson coincide is in identifying James Joyce's *Ulysses* (1922) as a text that celebrates cultural difference and disdains the degenerationist anxieties associated with Conrad and T.S. Eliot for example. This may be a reflection of the highly ambivalent relation of Joyce's Dublin to the British Empire, combining in itself the features of metropolis and colony, centre and periphery.

The resulting hybrid and unhierarchical vision is what the American critic James Clifford is also able to trace in a poetic sequence taken from the 'dada treatise on the imagination', *Spring & All* (1923) by William Carlos Williams. The sequence reflects upon Elsie, Williams' home help with a 'dash of Indian blood', whose presence bespeaks the unsettling of racial and cultural boundaries such that, in its opening words, 'The pure products of America/go crazy'. This characteristic predicament of an 'ethnographic modernity' consists in being 'off-centered' among 'scattered traditions' and 'distinct meaning systems'. In accounts such as those of Edmond and Clifford, we derive a sense that modernism has already anticipated that 'post'-modernist condition that often goes under the name of the 'postcolonial' in later twentieth century culture: the periphery has already begun to speak and write back to the imperial centre. For a further discussion of how such issues are inflected in the modernist text, see the section on Primitivism in chapter 4, where I examine Chinua Achebe's discussion of a *locus classicus* of modernism and empire, Joseph Conrad's *Heart of Darkness* (1899/1902).

Technology

In his essay 'The Double Image', Alan Bullock enumerates key factors in an international 'technological revolution' of the 1890s and 1900s:

- the internal combustion engine, the diesel engine and the steam turbine
- electricity, oil and petroleum as the new sources of power
- the automobile, the motor bus – the first London motor buses appeared in 1905 – the tractor and the aeroplane
- the telephone, the typewriter and the tape machine, the foundation of modern office organization
- the production by the chemical industry of synthetic materials – dyes, man-made fibres and plastics. (Bradbury and McFarlane, *Modernism: A Guide to European Literature 1890–1930*, p. 59)

This has often been seen to constitute a 'second industrial revolution', and from our current perspective it is tempting to characterize the implied historical process in terms of a spectrum of literal and metaphorical 'weight'. The 'heavy' industries and technologies of the nineteenth century were, as Hobsbawm puts it, highly visible and audible, typified in Britain by 'the 100,000 railway locomotives (200–450 horse power), pulling their almost 2.75 million carriages and wagons in long trains under banners of smoke' (*Age of Empire*, p. 27). At the other end of this spectrum, our twenty-first century digital 'revolution' deploys forms of ineffable lightness and invisibility, reproducing a pattern that has been seen, for example in the history of money, as a gradual dissolution of materiality (from coins to notes, cheques, plastic and numbers on computer screens).

Modernist technologies seem poised between these moments, on the one hand still representing an onward march of technology and in an increasingly interventionist way in ordinary lives, yet on the other hand signalling a transition towards the smaller, the cleaner, the more intimate and insubstantial. The *significances* of modernist technologies might therefore accompany Bullock's list as follows:

- invisible forces – electricity, X-rays and radiation;
- more obtrusion into the fabric of *everyday* life – streets, shops, the home – rather than simply being confined to industrial locations such as factories;
- more personalized uses and applications – motor car, telephone, telegraph, radio, household gadgets – consistent with the economic shift from production to consumption;
- more application to methods of communication and the storage of data; and
- the possibility of mass communication and therefore of new forms of collective experience – radio, cinema.

Virginia Woolf's novel *Mrs Dalloway* (1925) is set on a single day in London in June 1923. In the early stages of the novel, Woolf dramatizes the complex effects of two new forms of transport technology. A car backfires as it draws up to a shop in Westminster where Clarissa Dalloway is buying flowers. Although blinds in the car are drawn, rumour spreads that it contains the Prime Minister or a member of royalty. This combination of 'violent explosion' and rumour has a profound effect: 'Everything had come to a standstill. The throb of the motor engines sounded like a pulse irregularly drumming through an entire body' (*Mrs Dalloway*, Harmondsworth, Penguin Popular Classics, p. 17). Characteristically, Woolf subtly conflates objective truth with subjective experience: 'The sun became extraordinarily hot because the motor car had stopped outside Mulberry's shop window'.

> The car had gone, but it had left a slight ripple which flowed though glove shops and hat shops and tailors' shops on both sides of Bond Street. For thirty seconds all heads were inclined the same way – to the window. Choosing a pair of gloves – should they be to the elbow or above it, lemon or pale grey? – ladies stopped; when the sentence was finished something had happened. Something so trifling in single instances that no mathematical instrument, though capable of transmitting shocks in China, could register the vibration; yet in its fullness rather formidable and in its common appeal emotional; for in all the hat shops and tailors' shops strangers looked at each other and thought of the dead; of the flag; of Empire. (p. 21)

However, by the time the car glides through the gates of Buckingham Palace, it passes completely unnoticed by a small crowd, its inconsequentiality registered by parenthesis – '(and the car went in at the gates, and nobody looked at it)' (p. 24). This is because the crowd have now become completely distracted by an aeroplane which is writing an advertising slogan with white smoke in the sky. Partly the plane conveys a kind of intrusive threat: it 'bored ominously into the ears of the crowd' and at one point drops 'dead down', an effect curiously mirrored in Mrs Coates' baby lying 'stiff and white' and 'gazing straight up' in its mother's arms. Partly too, however, what the shell-shocked male hysteric figure of Septimus Smith sees as 'exquisite beauty' is mirrored in the responses of the crowd, who gaze awestruck at the plane's breathtaking movements in an atmosphere, which it has created, of 'extraordinary silence', 'peace' and 'purity'. Like Septimus, who feels the plane is signalling to him, people in the crowd interpret its writing in subjective ways: '"Blaxo" . . . "Kreemo", "it's toffee"' (p. 24).

What do we glean from this evocative writing about the impact of modern technologies in 1920s Britain? Woolf condenses a number of profound suggestions. Technologies can have an enormous power of mass suggestion, an effect akin to the 'mesmerism' that was often attributed to early cinema; this effect is deeply registered in individual bodies, changing everyday experience; they can disrupt and reshape notions of time and space, emphasizing the relativity of each (see chapter 4); and the effect can be a combination of force and violence with peace, aesthetic appeal and therapeutic value. In addition, traditional hierarchies are unsettled, and in the speed of development one technology or function can soon displace another: despite the modernity of the motor car, in Woolf's scenario it becomes associated with an older world of political and aristocratic privilege, easily upstaged by the aeroplane as the symbol of a new economy of consumption, just as the use of the plane in war, some five years earlier, is here transformed into a commercial function. In an enlightening essay, 'The Island and the Aeroplane: The case of Virginia Woolf', Gillian Beer develops many of these ideas in the light of the 'crucial presence' of the aeroplane in Woolf's writing. Beer shows how, for example in Freud's work between 1900 and 1916, the aeroplane 'rapidly entered the repertoire of dream symbols, with their capacity for expressing erotic politics and desires', and how Woolf used the 'formal reordering of the earth' implicit in airborne perspective – a reordering 'which does away with centrality and very largely with borders' – to express historical changes in the nature of English national consciousness and identity (in ed. Homi K. Bhabha, *Nation and Narration*, London, Routledge, p. 265).

Woolf's emphasis on the intimate and interactive relationship between technology and the human is crucial. While modernism inherits from the nineteenth century its share of dystopian narratives polarizing people against the overpowering threat of the machine (the films *Metropolis* (1926) by Fritz Lang or *Modern Times* (1936) by Charlie Chaplin, for example), and the War consolidated that threat, the exploratory embrace of the machine and the predication of a 'machine modernism' is more typical. Technology was crucial to the utopian social revolutionary thrust of German and Soviet post-war societies, as we have seen. Much valuable work in new modernist studies centres, as I have already highlighted in critics such as Tim Armstrong and Sara Danius (see chapter 1, pp. 10–11), on surprisingly 'soft' interconnections between bodies, technologies and the immaterial, for example in the interests in telepathy and spiritualism within enlightened scientific communities of the early twentieth century. For a sense of how these interests might have been further informed by developments in theoretical physics, see chapter 4.

Fordist capitalism and consumer culture

In what ways might modernism and the ubiquitous Ford motor car be connected? The emergence of the first Model T Ford to roll off the production line in Dearborn, Michigan in 1913 is often taken to be a key symbolic moment of modernism. David Harvey suggests, however, that the truly symbolic moment of what we now call 'Fordism' was 1914, when Henry Ford introduced the standard $5, eight-hour day for workers on his Michigan assembly line. To understand the significance of this – and how a modernism otherwise characterized by artistic enigma and indeterminacy can also be found in highly regulated work practices – we need to grasp the fact that the 'second industrial revolution' also involved a new and distinct phase in the history of advanced capitalism. This phase, stretching roughly from 1870 to 1920, effects a shift of emphasis from *production* to *consumption*; that is, from the satisfaction of basic needs, to the shaping of desires for new and inessential kinds of commodity.

Key features of the new capitalism

- What Hobsbawn calls a 'change of gear' in Western economies, business and international trade booming after a period of Depression which had brought prices low.
- An economy that is increasingly an *international* system, facilitated by new technologies of transport and communication.
- The emergence of monopolies and corporate organizations instead of individual or family businesses – a bakery, for example, that is part of a local or national chain rather than owned by an individual – signalling a strategy to corner or monopolize markets instead of trusting to their 'free hand'.
- 'Mass' production for 'mass' markets: through the means of advertising, modern capitalism increasingly seeks to construct the

desires for non-essential or luxury goods that it will then proceed to satisfy
- The adoption of the 'scientific management' of the workplace, seeking the maximization of production and profit through the streamlining, simplification and acceleration of working practices

Modernism in this context becomes closely if curiously associated with two primary instances of late capitalist culture: the invention of the modern mass-production work environment; and the invention of that cultural activity we now habitually call 'shopping'. In the first case, a founding text is Frederick Winslow Taylor's *The Principles of Scientific Management* (1911). 'Taylorism' became the principle of maximizing efficiency and productivity through the scientific analysis of work processes. This involved, for example, 'time and motion' studies, and the incentivization of the worker, while at the same time isolating workers and subordinating them to the dictates of central management. 'Fordism' carried a more comprehensive vision of a society of mass production and consumption on rational lines, and led to a missionary aspect to Henry Ford's enterprise in America, where the lifestyles of employees were subjected to advice and scrutiny by corporate 'social workers'.

Changing patterns of retail and consumption are implicit in texts such as Thorstein Veblen's *Theory of the Leisure Class* (1899) and Walter Benjamin's *Arcades Project* (1999). Veblen, a sociologist of capitalism, constructs in an almost tongue-in-cheek way a set of connections between earlier 'barbarian' phases of culture and the more competitive, predatory forms of late capitalism. In order to maintain advantage, members of the newly emergent 'leisure class' must be able to display their wealth through what Veblen terms 'conspicuous consumption'. Here, Veblen places this process in the context of modern urban life:

The exigencies of the modern industrial system frequently place individuals and households in juxtaposition between whom there is little contact in any other sense than that of juxtaposition. One's neighbours, mechanically speaking, often are socially not one's neighbours, or even acquaintances; and still their transient good opinion has a high degree of utility. The only practicable means of impressing one's pecuniary ability on these unsympathetic observers of one's everyday life is an unremitting demonstration of ability to pay. In the modern community there is also a more frequent attendance at large gatherings of people to whom one's everyday life is unknown; in such places as churches, theatres, ballrooms, hotels, parks, shops, and the like. In order to impress these transient observers, and to retain one's self-complacency under their observation, the signature of one's pecuniary strength should be written in characters which he who runs may read. (*Theory of the Leisure Class*, Harmondsworth, Penguin, 1994, pp. 86–7)

In contrast to Veblen's formal prose, Walter Benjamin's *Arcades Project* rather resembles a monumental modernist collage; it is a collection of jottings, observations and quotations contributing towards an analysis of the elegant indoor shopping arcades built in Paris largely between 1822 and 1837. Like Veblen, however, Benjamin's concern is a shift in the character of commerce, within cities where the anonymities of the 'mass' coincide with a new kind of individual experience – Veblen's 'leisured gentleman', Benjamin's Baudelairean *'flâneur'*. Benjamin writes:

> Trade and traffic are the two components of the street. Now, in the arcades the second of these has died out: the traffic there is rudimentary. The arcade is a street of lascivious commerce only; it is wholly adapted to arousing desires. Because in this street the juices slow to a standstill, the commodity proliferates along the margins and enters into fantastic combinations, like the tissue in tumours. – The flâneur sabotages the traffic. Moreover, he is no buyer. He is merchandise.
>
> For the first time in history, with the establishment of department stores, consumers begin to consider themselves a mass. (Earlier it was only scarcity that taught them that.) Hence, the circus-like and theatrical element of commerce is quite extraordinarily heightened. (*The Arcades Project*, pp. 42–3)

The late capitalist economics of modernity thus seem to give rise to a central paradox: systems of industrial, automated efficiency and utility, devoted increasingly to the mass production of excess or luxury goods for the relatively affluent Western consumer. Unsurprisingly, and not at all superficially, modernist literary texts begin to pay serious attention to shopping, consumption and the activities of marketing and advertising. Two classic narratives based on a day in the city, James Joyce's *Ulysses* and Woolf's *Mrs*

Dalloway, feature Leopold Bloom and Clarissa Dalloway starting out to shop (for kidneys and soap in Bloom's case, flowers
in Clarissa's). Bloom's stream-of-consciousness excursion in the
'Lotuseaters' chapter, from butchers to post office to chemist, demonstrates a mediated and indirect arousing of 'desire', in Benjamin's
terms, interlaced with his reading of Martha's love letter. Bloom
however is not just a consumer but, in his work, a seller of advertising space – even emptiness has been commodified – and this confirms the sense that commodification of desire is intimately linked
to the *reading* of modernity: Joyce grants epistemological equivalence to Stephen Dedalus' philosophical musings on the beach at
Sandymount Strand, 'signatures of all things I am here to read', and
Bloom's constant reflection on the spaces and language of advertising ('all kinds of places are good for ads'). As in Woolf's sky-writing
plane, such strategies are always open to creative misreading, in a
Freudian model of the straying or displacement of desire.

Closely allied to the attention given to texts and commodity
culture, new modernist studies have also turned to the potential
connections between marketing and modernism itself – artefacts,
images, reputations, celebrity status, careers. This emphasis, flying
somewhat in the face of the established view of the haughtiness of
'high' modernism as a resistance to commercialism, draws on the
dialectical arguments of the likes of Bourdieu and Rainey that difficulty and scarcity are precisely the qualities that confer market
value. Does the commodity relation enter even into the structure
of the artefact itself? On such an argument, for example, the bare,
austere aesthetic of the Imagist poem (see chapter 6) could also constitute the perfect form of a culture based on immediate consumption and gratification; or, in the case of Peter D. McDonald's very
detailed reading of the published contexts of Ezra Pound's poem
In A Station of the Metro, it could be seen to be carefully reshaped
according to different anticipated readerships.

Sex reform and gender relations

'The modern civilized neurotic woman has become a by-word in the
Western world. Why?' Marie Stopes, the campaigner and writer on
human sexual health and founder of a clinical movement addressing

issues of contraception and fertility, offered the answer to her own
question in *Married Love* (1918), thus: 'I am certain that much of
this suffering is caused by the *ignorance* of both men and women
regarding not only the inner physiology, but even the obvious outward expression, of the complete sex-act' (*Married Love: A New
Contribution to the Solution of Sex Difficulties*, London, A.C. Fifield,
1918, p. 64).

The period of artistic modernism coincides with international
movements of 'sex reform', of which Stopes' text is a famous British
product, paralleled in America by the writings of Margaret Sanger.
Married Love opens out an intriguing way of reading the voice of the
neurotic woman as it appears in the second section of T.S. Eliot's
The Waste Land (1922): 'My nerves are bad to-night. Yes, bad. Stay
with me./Speak to me. Why do you never speak. Speak.' While
Eliot's poem presents the woman as an image of the general paralysis and sterility of modernity, an insomniac chess-player 'Pressing
lidless eyes and waiting for a knock upon the door', Stopes' text
might encourage the reader to imagine the more down-to-earth
possibility of the neglectful sexual behaviour of a lover or husband,
forcing himself upon her at inappropriate times or failing to help
her to orgasm. *Married Love* is a curious blend of the practical and
the mystical. The explicitness of the scientific manual, providing
anatomical details of the mechanisms of arousal and coition, and
charts representing the 'Law of Periodicity of Recurrence of desire'
in women, combines with a mythicized discourse more reminiscent
of courtly love, in which human 'souls' seek permanent unions with
their mates and the husband must regard each sex act as needing to
be 'tenderly wooed for and won', only at that point of the month
when welling up in his wife are 'the wonderful tides, scented and
enriched by the myriad experiences of the human race from its
ancient days of leisure and flower-wreathed lovemaking, urging her
to transports and to self-expressions' (p. 20). Overarching the text
is the rather less idealized, firmly political enterprise of serving the
state through the creation of more happy homes, on the grounds
that 'the only secure basis for a present-day State is the welding of
its units in marriage' (p. xi) (for a more detailed treatment of this
scientific discourse of 'eugenics', see chapter 4).

This hardly sounds like a discourse of modernistic emancipation, and the relationship of modernism to sex reform and to two related historical developments, the science of sexology, and the women's suffrage movement, is indeed fascinatingly contradictory. A greater frankness in the artistic treatment of sexuality and bodily functions can certainly be related to the rise of sexology, the application of scientific methods of analysis and classification to sexual behaviour, which emerges in the late nineteenth-century in writers such as Richard von Krafft-Ebing in Germany and Havelock Ellis in Britain. (Sigmund Freud could also be included in this category, though his concepts could in some respects be seen as a challenge to the principles of positivism and empiricism underpinning sexology, as references elsewhere in this book to Freud may suggest.) The individual case study was the main source of data in such work, using first-person accounts of sexual behaviour and neurosis, and therefore releasing an unprecedented amount of intimate sexual confession into the public domain, allied to a freer circulation of technical knowledge. As Tim Armstrong argues, such discourses can be directly linked to 'the exploration of sexual licence in modernist texts . . . for example in the focus on young women which runs from [Theodor] Dreiser's *Sister Carrie* (1900) to [Rebecca] West's *The Day of the Locust* (1939) – novels evoking sexual panics about actresses, prostitution and disease', and to a greater explicitness in the treatment of subjects such as masturbation and excretion, notably in the work of James Joyce (*Modernism: A Cultural History*, p. 70). So, in Alfred Döblin's Joycean, colloquial and cinematic novel *Berlin Alexanderplatz* (1929), the ex-convict Franz Biberkopf's unsuccessful attempt at the spontaneous release of his sexual tension with a prostitute lurches into a playful parody of sexological discourse:

> Sexual potency depends upon the concentered action of 1. The internal secretory system, 2. The nervous system, and 3. The sexual apparatus . . . In this system the spermatic gland preponderates. Through the matter prepared by it, the entire sexual apparatus is charged from the cerebral cortex to the genitals. The erotic impression releases the erotic tension of the cerebral cortex, the current flows as an erotic stimulus from the cerebral cortex to the switch center in the interbrain . . . Not unimpeded, however, for, before leaving the brain, it has to pass the brakes of the inhibitions, those

predominantly psychic inhibitions which play a large role in the form of moral scruples, lack of self-confidence, fear of humiliation, fear of infection and impregnation, and things of this order. (*Berlin Alexanderplatz*, London and New York, Continuum, 2004, pp. 20–1)

In British culture, Havelock Ellis (1859–1939), author of the six-volume *Studies of the Psychology of Sex* from 1897 onwards, was widely influential. Despite the transparency of approach, however, Ellis' work continued to encode a traditionally active principle in male sexuality and a passive principle in female sexuality. *Love and Pain* (1913), for example, presented this in terms of woman's pleasure at experiencing pain (for example in the lovebite, or in the male use of appliances on the penis) during sex play and intercourse. No doubt conscious of how far the suffrage campaign at this time was driven by outrage at the prevalence of male sexual violence against women, Ellis insisted that the pain principle applied only in the specific circumstances of the sexual relation, and could invoke Nietzsche in arguing that the 'psychic dynamics' of pain took the issue beyond conventional morality and into the central place of cruelty in human life: 'One ought to learn anew about cruelty', he quotes from Nietzsche's *Beyond Good and Evil*, 'and open one's eyes. Almost everything that we call "higher culture" is based upon the spiritualizing and intensifying of *cruelty* . . .' ('Love and Pain', in ed. Sheila Jeffreys, *The Sexuality Debates*, New York and London, Routledge & Kegan Paul, 1987, p. 521).

It clearly emerges that such an idea could inform the transgressively amoral experimentalism of Antonin Artaud's 'Theatre of Cruelty' in 1930s France. Yet the women's movements of the early twentieth century were not, on the whole, to be convinced either by Ellis' disclaimers (for example that the pain issue was an empirical fact, and that 'the day for academic discussion concerning "the subjection of women" has gone by' (p. 531)), or by the emancipatory potential of modernism. In Britain, the suffrage campaigns had been led by Millicent Garrett Fawcett's reformist and democratic National Union of Women's Suffrage Societies (1897) and, from 1903, the more sensationalistic and militant face of the Women's Social and Political Union (WSPU), led by the Pankhurst sisters and Emmeline Pethick-Lawrence. The actions of the WSPU could, themselves, be seen as a form of modernist transformation of public space, asserting the changing identity of women in gestures of performative violence: hunger strikes (and subsequent force-feeding), self-chainings, Lillian Fenton's burning of the Kew pavilion in February 1913, followed by Emily Wilding Davison's death under the King's horse at the 1913 Derby, and Mary Richardson's slashing of a classical image of female beauty, the *Rokeby Venus*, in 1914, as well as the countless public meetings and marches. In 1918, 8.5 million women over the age of 30 gained the vote.

The preoccupation of these movements with legislative equality and the campaign against male sexual violence meant that sexuality itself was a subject of far greater reticence, causing tension between the suffragists and radical thinkers who might be more inclined to ally themselves with the greater freedoms of artistic modernism. This led the socialist-feminist thinker and advocate of women's sexual freedom Dora Russell, for example, to the assessment in 1925 that, 'The feminist movement, like one dissentient voice in an excited public meeting, was querulous, hysterical, uncertain of itself. It dared not cry out that women had bodies. Its one hope of success was to prove that women had minds' ('Hypatia or, Woman and Knowledge', in *The Dora Russell Reader*, London, Pandora, 1983, p. 13). More recently, Rachel Potter has shown how the context of modernism led prominent feminist writers and activists such as Emma Goldman (the charismatic anarchist who made a profound impact on American cultural life), Beatrice Hastings (an editor of the British Nietzschean–socialist journal *The New Age* from 1907 to 1914) and Dora Marsden (a founding editor in 1911 of *The Freewoman*, later to be *The New Freewoman* and then *The Egoist*) to distance or dissociate themselves from political feminism, because of their subscription to the ego-philosophies of Nietzsche and Max Stirner which stressed the need for an ontological freedom fundamentally at odds with juridical democracy and lawmaking per se (*Modernism and Democracy: Literary Culture 1900–30*, Oxford, Oxford University Press, 2006). As D.H. Lawrence reflected this view in his 'Study of Thomas Hardy' (1915), the suffragists, 'who are certainly the bravest and, in the old sense, most heroic party amongst us', would undo themselves by winning the vote only in order to make more laws, putting their trust in the State mechanism instead of achieving 'true individuality and . . . a sufficient completeness in ourselves' (*Study of Thomas Hardy and Other Essays*, ed. Bruce Steele, Cambridge, Cambridge University Press, 1985, pp. 14–15).

As Glenda Norquay argues in her literary anthology of the women's suffrage campaign, this newly public role undoubtedly brought concepts of female identity into crisis as the jostling of conflicting representations both of women and of 'the suffragette' within the movements came to prominence. Suffragette poetry and fiction exposed the presence of complex debates; yet they remained within literary forms whose wariness of experimentation seemed to encode a fastidiousness about wider sexual freedoms. In her novel *Tree of Heaven* (1917), May Sinclair, an acknowledged modernist and important theorist of 'stream of consciousness' (see chapter 7), has her militant protagonist Dorothea shrink away from the crowd psychology ('soul of the crowd') of mass modernity apparent at a suffrage rally she attends; yet the gesture is itself made in the name of a Nietzschean–Stirneresque individual egotism:

> The singing had threatened her when it began; so that she felt again her old terror of the collective soul. Its massed emotion threatened her. She longed for her whitewashed prison-cell, for its hardness, its nakedness, its quiet, its visionary peace. She tried to remember. Her soul, in its danger, tried to get back there. But the soul of the crowd in the hall below her swelled and heaved itself towards her, drawn by the Vortex. She felt the rushing of the whirlwind; it sucked at her breath: the Vortex was drawing her too; the powerful, abominable thing almost got her. (Quoted in Glenda Norquay ed., *Voices and Votes: A Literary Anthology of the Women's Suffrage Campaign*, Manchester, Manchester University Press, 1995, p. 272)

'Vortex', the powerful nodal energy against which Dorothea asserts her individuality, would knowingly refer to the Vorticism of the artist Wyndham Lewis, established with the publication of the short-lived but highly important English magazine *BLAST* in 1914. Ironically, then, *BLAST* asserted its own support for the suffragettes, qualifying this only with a 'WORD OF ADVICE' not to destroy any more art (there had been twelve such attacks on paintings in the two months prior to *BLAST*'s publication in June 1914). 'NOUS VOUS AIMONS', *BLAST* declared, 'WE ADMIRE YOUR ENERGY. YOU AND ARTISTS/ARE THE ONLY THINGS (YOU DON'T MIND/BEING CALLED THINGS?)

LEFT IN ENGLAND/WITH A LITTLE LIFE LEFT IN THEM'. Notwithstanding Lewis' rather incoherent politics of revolution, it has been suggested that the Vorticists approved of the suffragists' very innovative uses of advertising, while Janet Lyon, in her study of the significance of manifestoes in modernism, notes parallels between *BLAST* and the language of Christabel Pankhurst's polemical work *The Great Scourge and How to End It* (1913). If the suffrage campaign kept its distance from modernism, modernism was nevertheless able to construe the campaign itself as a modernist phenomenon.

An equally complex and ambivalent relationship existed between modernism, sex reform and same-sex relations. Sexology acknowledged the existence of homosexuality through the classification of a 'third' sex characterized as the 'Urning' by Krafft-Ebing or as the 'intermediate sex' by the English utopian socialist Edward Carpenter. The positivist tendency of sexology could however produce an *essentializing* of the homosexual which was as burdensome as it was liberating A landmark text which both highlights and grapples with this condition is Radclyffe Hall's novel *The Well of Loneliness*, suppressed on its publication in 1928, and the first to deal openly with the dilemmas of the 'manly' lesbian in the character of Stephen Gordon. Conventionally realist in form and based around a series of Stephen's romances, the only mildly experimental passages of prose in the novel deal, significantly enough, with Stephen's experiences as an ambulance driver on the battlefields of France during the war. But the novel resituates Stephen in modernist–bohemian Paris for its poignant later stages, where the impossibility of sustaining a relationship with her lover Mary is set in the context of a decadent subculture in which dissident sexual identities and relationships can be lived out only in the salon.

If Parisian modernism then is the site of alternative sexualities, but hardly a characteristic of Hall's novel itself, it is instructive to compare *The Well of Loneliness* with Virginia Woolf's highly experimental novel of the same year, *Orlando*. Parodying biography, a form which assumes stability and singularity of identity, Woolf's fantasy narrative follows Orlando from his early life as a nobleman in the Elizabethan age to his metamorphosis into a woman in nineteenth-century Britain, and beyond. The fantasy is a vehicle, however, for an essential fluidity in Orlando's sexual identity, which was ambiguous even when 'he' was a man. Woolf thus pursues an interest in androgynous sexuality which had been established with the Clarissa of *Mrs Dalloway*, who in epiphanic moments 'knew what men felt' and had retained a hetero-normatively unthinkable 'virginity' through marriage and childbirth.

As Bonnie Kime Scott suggests, the 1920s saw the rise of metropolitan modernist communities in which women writers could flourish in a context of relative equality and freedom, and in which 'lesbian and gay sexuality was tolerated, sometimes celebrated, and often textualised': around Sylvia Beach, Gertrude Stein or Natalie Barney in Paris, in New York's Greenwich Village or Harlem, or at Peggy Guggenheim's Hayford Hall in England, for example (*The Gender of Modernism*, Bloomington, Indiana University Press, 1990, p. 6). Nevertheless, there is no easy correlation between artistic modernism and freedom of sexual identity; Woolf, whose lectures in *A Room of One's Own* became a formative text in international feminism and whose fictional style became a model of what Hélène Cixous called *écriture féminine*, kept her distance from such groupings, and could as Kime Scott notes be withering about the bold 'modern woman' image of a writer such as the New Zealander Katherine Mansfield. (Considering also the verbal treatment of Mansfield by male modernists such as T.S. Eliot, D.H. Lawrence or her husband the Imagist poet Richard Aldington, it is instructive to note the profound treatment of male sexual repression, and modernist experimentation with style and time-frames, in a short story of Mansfield's such as 'The Man Without a Temperament'). While Parisian modernism gave rise to landmark texts of male homosexual literature in Proust and later in the work of André Gide (the influence of Verlaine and Rimbaud, and of Oscar Wilde, who was buried in Paris, lingered from the perspective of the decadent late 1800s), elsewhere the encoding of a suppressed homoeroticism is a characteristic of some male modernism, such as in the fiction of Ernest Hemingway and D.H. Lawrence. In the latter case, it has taken groundbreaking critical work by Angela Carter and Linda Ruth Williams to reveal that Lawrence's writing is far less 'straight' than earlier critiques of the misogynistic Lawrence (such as that of Kate Millett) could allow.

The politics of modernism

'Avant-garde: left or right?' In approaching this question in his excellent study of Marinetti's Futurism, *Fascist Modernism: Aesthetics, politics and the avant-garde* (1993), Andrew Hewitt shows it to be unanswerable on these simple terms. We often habitually reach for words, like 'revolutionary' or 'emancipatory', which are borrowed from the political sphere and applied to the modernist aesthetic. Yet what I hope this chapter has shown is that we cannot automatically retranslate modernism into the left-leaning, socialist or communist politics that these terms suggest, and which are clearly apparent, for example, in Russian Futurism, Suprematism and Contructivism, Berlin Dada, Weimar culture of the 1920s, or French Surrealism of the same period. There is clear historical evidence that totalitarian regimes are uneasy with the freedoms implicit in experimental art, condemning the 'decadence' that they bring. The exhibition of 'Degenerate Art' in Munich in 1937 confirmed the Nazi view of its German modernist heritage as 'cultural bolshevism' (*Kulturbolschewismus*), while Soviet regimes under Stalin installed an official aesthetic of 'socialist realism' designed to purge Russian culture of the 'bourgeois decadence' of two decades of Futurism and Constructivism. Yet, on the other hand, there are 'fascist modernisms', forms of modernism openly sympathetic to authoritarianism, of various complexions, for example from the support of Filippo Marinetti or Ezra Pound for Mussolini's regime in Italy, through D.H. Lawrence's so-called 'leadership' novels of the 1920s, to the cultural conservatisms of W.B. Yeats and T.S. Eliot, or the totalizing conception of architecture which could be said to link Hitler's Albert Speer with modernist champions of 'clean' and 'pure' design from Adolf Loos and Le Corbusier to Mies van der Rohe. As we shall find in the further course of this book, there are a range of ways in which a conservative or traditionalist *contestation* of the idea of modernity as a condition of inevitable progress and of the expansion of participatory democracy seems to lie at the heart of modernism.

There is, then, no single 'politics' of modernism, but instead the complex and often contradictory involvement of modernism in the sphere of the political. I conclude with two texts that help to frame some of the most prominent issues in the politics of modernism, and which I recommend that you read at some point in your studies. The first is a set of debates about modernism from within Marxist aesthetics in the 1930s, collected in the volume *Aesthetics and Politics* (London, NLB, 1977, new edition 2007) by Rodney Livingstone, Perry Anderson and Francis Mulhern. In these closely woven responses and correspondences between the great Marxist thinkers Ernst Bloch, Georg Lukács, Bertolt Brecht, Walter Benjamin and Theodor Adorno, a non-doctrinaire politics is matched by a range of positions on the political implications of modernist art. Although these debates occur within Marxism, they are more indicative of faultlines in the politics of modernism per se. In the first half of the volume the principal reference point is German Expressionism, and Lukács' contention that all 'modern literary schools of the imperialist era', from Naturalism to Surrealism, are so 'frozen in their own immediacy', emotionally and intellectually, that their art can only remain 'abstract and one-dimensional', denying any reference to 'objective reality'. These are the grounds of Lukács' preference for a literary realism – Thomas Mann over James Joyce or Franz Kafka, or for novelists of the nineteenth-century tradition – which is able to express a social totality, rather than the psychological fragmentation and sense of randomness through which Expressionism simply accommodates itself to bourgeois commodity culture.

At stake here therefore are such questions as: how far was modernism capable of taking up an oppositional stance against a dominant bourgeois culture to whom art – say, after 1848 – seemed to belong? To what extent were the subjectivist techniques of modernist art, such as stream of consciousness and montage, themselves an inherent expression of that dominant order? Bloch, a utopian thinker, and Brecht, both respond with defences of modernist experimentalism. As well as accusing Lukács of referring only to abstract categories rather than engaging with the actual imaginative works of Expressionist painters and writers, Bloch argues that Lukács' totalizing conception of capitalist culture makes the very idea of avant-garde resistance a theoretical impossibility. Brecht mounts a more energetic defence of experimental artistic practice, based on the conviction that historical change requires and calls forth new forms of art. 'Literature', he writes, 'cannot be forbidden to employ skills newly acquired by contemporary man, such as the capacity for simultaneous registration, bold abstraction, or swift combination' (Adorno *et al.*, *Aesthetics and Politics*, p. 75). He therefore claims not to understand the tendency for Lukácsian Marxists to use the term 'formalist' to condemn modernism, and in fact turns the accusation on its head, arguing that it is precisely the proposition to represent twentieth-century modernity by applying to it the forms of nineteenth-century 'realism' that is formalist, in other words that fetishizes outmoded forms. So montage, for example in the films of Eisenstein or the novels of Dos Passos, is perfectly appropriate to the modern displacement of the family by institutions such as the soviet or the factory, where individuals are 'quite literally "assembled"' and where, for example in Moscow or in New York, 'woman is less "formed" by man than in Balzac's Paris; she is less dependent on him' (Adorno *et al.*, *Aesthetics and Politics*, p. 79). In Brecht's radical theory of history, human nature is not essentialized: the proletarian masses in shedding their dehumanization might 'become men again – *but not the same men as before*' (my italics; Adorno *et al.*, *Aesthetics and Politics*, p. 69).

In the second half of the volume the ground of debate, occupied more by Benjamin and Adorno, shifts towards the implications for modernism of the development of mass popular cultural forms. In Adorno's hands this frequently involved a discussion of the concept of artistic autonomy and the vexed relation of this to technology. Referring to Benjamin's essay 'The Work of Art in the Age of Mechanical Reproduction', for example, Adorno objects that the attribution of 'aura' to the autonomous work of art renders it simply 'counter-revolutionary', and he expresses scepticism about Benjamin's faith in new technologies as the basis of a revolutionary conjunction of modernism with the popular sphere. Typically, however, the concept of technology is fluid and subject to nuances of meaning: Adorno adheres to 'the primacy of technology' in the case of music and finds that a fundamental liberation in the music of Arnold Schoenberg comes from a rigid adherence to a certain kind of technicality (see chapter 8); alternatively, he finds the laughter of the cinema audience 'full of the worst bourgeois sadism' and therefore 'anything but good and revolutionary' (Adorno *et al.*, *Aesthetics and Politics*, p. 129). Despite the fact that no key term can ever be

condemned outright in Adorno's constantly shifting dialectics, the
conclusion of the 1962 essay 'Commitment' is that 'today every
phenomenon of culture, even if a model of integrity, is liable to
be suffocated in the cultivation of kitsch' (Adorno *et al.*, *Aesthetics
and Politics*, p. 194), and that as a result it is only the most rigorous
pursuit of aesthetic principles could constitute a viable politics of
resistance for avant-garde modernism.

Adorno's sense of commitment is somewhat at odds with my
second framing text, John Carey's *The Intellectuals and the Masses:
Pride and prejudice among the literary intelligentsia, 1880–1939*
(London, Faber, 1992). The promotional puff on the cover of my
edition by Julie Burchill of the *Mail on Sunday* – 'an incredibly juicy
read' – gives some sense of the book's impact and of the way it has
been marketed. 'The principle around which modernist literature
and culture fashioned themselves', writes Carey, 'was the exclu-
sion of the masses, the defeat of their power, the removal of their
literacy, the denial of their humanity' (p. 21). Carey attributes to a
range of modernist writers in Britain of the early twentieth century
a conspiracy to make their work too difficult for ordinary people
to understand, and an underlying desire for the extermination of
the degenerate modern masses which anticipates Nazism, driven
as he claims they were by a 'fury, loathing and fear' of the masses
derived from eugenic theory and crowd psychology (see chapter 4
of this book for an introduction to these). A range of evidence is
relentlessly compiled to highlight frequent expressions of disdain
and disgust for ordinary people, on the part of writers such as Eliot,
Woolf, Lawrence, Joyce, Wells and Lewis.

The modernists' mistake, Carey maintains, was to be frightened
into thinking that 'the masses' existed; as Raymond Williams had
argued in his conclusion to *Culture and Society* (1958), there is
no such thing as 'masses', only ways of thinking about people *as*
masses. The key concept that Carey himself takes for granted,
repeated mantra-like throughout the book, is the 'intellectual',
which comes to stand both for the modernist and for anyone who
tries to make art or thought too difficult for others to understand,
and it attains an almost self-explanatory status in the argument: 'In
response to the revolt of the masses, intellectuals generated the idea
of a natural aristocracy, consisting of intellectuals' (*Intellectuals*

and the Masses, p. 71). In examining the prevalence of questions in Eliot's poem *Prufrock*, for example, Carey observes that their unanswerability is a deliberatively obstructive strategy: 'The questions are unanswerable because the poem designedly withholds the information needed to answer them. It withdraws itself into indefiniteness, eluding the fact-hungry masses' (*Intellectuals and the Masses*, p. 33). This surprising assumption that the poem might be required to provide readers with answers or information confirms Carey's status as a champion of 'middle-brow' writing (the term 'high brow' is also often used to designate the intellectual): 'the hero of this book', he announces, is the social–realist novelist Arnold Bennett (we will later, in chapter 7, closely examine Bennett's writing alongside that of Virginia Woolf, one of his most trenchant critics).

STOP and THINK

Because of the very direct and polemical way *The Intellectuals and the Masses* is written, it seems impossible not to take a position on Carey's argument. Are you persuaded that the book is a devastating exposé of modernism's elitism and deeply reactionary, anti-democratic nature? Or do you suspect that it is a defensive and ungenerous piece of opportunism whose own fear of the 'intellectual' consists in an inability to appreciate the artistic complexity of modernism? My own view may well be betrayed in the way I have described Carey's book, but I do not apologize for that, because I think that the combative nature of the book calls forth such a response. In your own reading and assessment of this text, and of *Aesthetics and Politics*, you will certainly derive a sense of how passionately the politics of modernism can be debated, and of how the debates may be shaped by the ideological positions of the protagonists.

Selected reading

Adorno, Theodor, Walter Benjamin, Ernst Bloch, Bertolt Brecht and Georg Lukács, *Aesthetics and Politics* (London, Verso, 2007)

An absorbing compilation of writings which stages the critical dialogues between these key Marxist thinkers on the relations between modernist art forms and radical political commitment.

Begam, Richard and Michael Valdez Mozes (eds), *Modernism and Colonialism: British and Irish Art, 1899–1939* (Durham and London, Duke University Press, 2007)

Seeing Jameson's essay 'Modernism and Imperialism' as the springboard of debate in the field, this volume gives a comprehensive overview of developments.

Benjamin, Walter, *Understanding Brecht*, trans. Anna Bostock (London, Verso, 1984)

Essays of profound insight on Brecht and the aesthetics of political theatre in Weimar Germany.

Benjamin, Walter, *The Arcades Project*, trans. Howard Eiland and Kevin Mclaughlin (Cambridge, MA and London, Belknap Harvard, 2002)

A key work for the understanding of metropolitan modernity; notebook/aphoristic style encourages the reader to browse and select.

Booth, Howard J. and Nigel Rigby (eds), *Modernism and Empire* (Manchester, Manchester University Press, 2000)

Stimulating collection of essays focusing on the British colonial experience and questioning the 'imperial heart' of modernist studies from a range of perspectives.

Dettmar, Kevin and Stephen Watts (eds), *Marketing Modernisms: Self-promotion, Canonization, Rereading* (Ann Arbor, University of Michigan Press, 1996)

Good collection of essays on aspects of post-Rainey studies in modernism and the marketplace.

Esty, Jed, *A Shrinking Island: Modernism and National Culture in England* (Princeton, NJ and Oxford, Princeton University Press, 2004)

Esty's interesting account of the coincidence of late modernism with imperial decline in England, giving rise to artistic insularity and cultural holism.

Gay, Peter, *Weimar Culture: The Outsider as Insider* (London, Secker & Warburg, 1968)

Remains a good, accessible introduction.

Griffin, Roger, *Modernism and Fascism: The Sense of a Beginning under Mussolini and Hitler* (Basingstoke, Palgrave, 2007)

Major new contribution to the debates, linking the rise of fascism to modernism's search for transcendence and renewal.

Hewitt, Andrew, *Fascist Modernism: Aesthetics, Politics, and the Avant-Garde* (Stanford, Stanford University Press, 1993)

Takes Marinetti and Italian Futurism as a case study.

Hobsbawm, Eric, *Age of Extremes: The Short Twentieth Century 1914–91* (London, Abacus, 1994)

An excellent survey coloured by Hobsbawm's European communistic perspective.

Jaffe, Aaron, *Modernism and the Culture of Celebrity* (Cambridge, Cambridge University Press, 2005)

Innovative study of the historical overlap and interrelation between the concept of celebrity and artistic modernism.

Lyon, Janet, *Manifestoes: Provocations of the Modern* (Ithaca, Cornell University Press, 1999)

An original work on the diverse influence of manifestoes.

MacKay, Marina, *Modernism and World War II* (Cambridge, Cambridge University Press, 2007)

Considers the work of writers such as Rebecca West, Henry Green, Evelyn Waugh and Eliot's *Four Quartets*, from the perspective of a British modernism 'beyond the Blitz'.

McDonald, Peter D., 'Modernist Publishing: "Nomads and Mapmakers"', in ed. David Bradshaw, *A Concise Companion to Modernism* (Oxford, Blackwell, 2003), pp. 221–42.

Interesting both for its account of Pound's situation-based typographical changes to *In A Station of The Metro*, and for its critique of Lawrence Rainey's influential reading of modernism.

Oxford English Limited, *News from Nowhere* 7 (winter 1989), 'The Politics of Modernism'

Special issue of this journal, with a range of good essays including Peter Bürger on Wyndham Lewis' *Tarr* and Jean Radford on Dorothy Richardson.

Pinkney, Tony, 'Editor's Introduction: Modernism and Cultural Theory', in Raymond Williams, *The Politics of Modernism: Against the New Conformists* (London, Verso, 1989)

A wide-ranging essay which, though the prism of Raymond Williams' essays collected in the volume, challenges many of the commonplaces associated with modernism and its relation to politics.

Sherry, Vincent, *The Great War and the Language of Modernism* (Oxford, Oxford University Press, 2003)

A densely detailed and closely argued study.

Tate, Trudi, *Modernism, History and the First World War* (Manchester, Manchester University Press, 1998)

Excellent example of new historical–cultural studies approach to a broadly defined modernism.

Timms, Edward, and Peter Collier (eds), *Visions and Blueprints: Avant-Garde Culture and Radical Politics in Early Twentieth-Century Europe* (Manchester, Manchester University Press, 1988)

Sharp collection of essays covering a range of approaches to the politics of modernism, prefaced by Raymond Williams.

Trotter, David, 'Modernism and Empire: Reading *The Waste Land*', *Critical Quarterly* 28:1/2 (1986), pp. 143–53

Links Eliot's high-modernist poem to popular imperialist narratives in which the symbolic quest for the 'frontier' represents an antidote to cultural degeneration.

Willett, John, *The New Sobriety: Art and Politics in the Weimar Period 1917–33* (London, Thames & Hudson, 1978)

Lively and impassioned account of all aspects of Weimar culture, arguing for a complex continuity with post-1933 politics.

4
Modernist ideas

The secular

> There will soon be no more priests. Their work is done. They may
> wait a while . . . perhaps a generation or two . . . dropping off by
> degrees. A superior breed shall take their place . . . the gangs of
> kosmos and prophets en masse shall take their place. A new order
> shall arise and they shall be the priests of man, and every man shall be
> his own priest. (Walt Whitman, Preface to *Leaves of Grass*, 1855, in
> Kolocotroni *et al.*, *Modernism*, p. 96)

Walt Whitman's words sound one of the keynotes of modernism: the rise of a secular society. Whitman (1819–92) is one of the
most important precursors of modernist poetry, particularly in his
pioneering of free verse, a mode of composition that eschewed the
structures of rhythm, rhyme and metre. Replacing 'the priests', for
Whitman, would be a robust body of modern democratic people,
their strength deriving both from collectivity, the 'en masse',
and from their distinct individualities within the mass. It may be
noticed, however, that this new dispensation does not so much
exclude the religious, as transfer it to democratic individualism –
every man his own priest.

Against this optimistic vision, it may be more customary to view
the decline of religion in modernity figured in terms of crisis and
loss. From Edvard Munch's iconic study of alienation, *The Scream*
(1893), through to the late 1940s bronze sculpted figures of Alberto
Giacometti (1901–66), some modernist art can be read as depicting
a human condition stripped of the reassuring lineaments of faith.
Giacometti's early attachments were to Cubism and Surrealism,

but after the Second World War his human figures, naked, roughly hewn and skeletal, could be read by Francis Ponge as 'Man – and man alone – reduced to a thread – in the ruinous condition, the misery of the world – who looks for himself – starting from nothing . . . Coming and going with no reason in the crowd' (quoted in Foster *et al.*, *Art Since 1900*, p. 423). They come to be associated (though the sculptor Anthony Gormley has recently contested this association) with a deeply influential twentieth-century philosophy, existentialism, typically found in the French writers Jean-Paul Sartre (1905–80), Simone de Beauvoir (1908–86) and Albert Camus (1913–60), which emphasized the priority of the sheer fact of *existence* over the discredited possibility of human *essence*. On this distinction, we simply *are*; any definition of *what* we are can only be a case of human invention or elaboration.

Each of these perspectives on post-religious humanity can be located in the philosophy of Friedrich Nietzsche (1844–1900), one of the foundational thinkers of modernism. Their coincidence suggests something of the complexity of atheistical modernism, and warns against any glib deployment of the catchphrase with which Nietzsche has now, perhaps unfortunately, become associated: 'God is dead'. In its context, *The Gay Science* (1881), the phrase is uttered by a madman in a fictionalized anecdote, who runs into a marketplace holding a lantern in broad daylight. Mocked by bystanders for his claim to be 'looking for God', he turns to them with the accusation that 'we' have all murdered God; having reasoned away a sense of the divine from the natural world, we are left in the emptiness of cold, infinite space. How, he asks, can we console ourselves for the death of God? How can we purify ourselves, or what kinds of ritual or game must we invent in order to do so? To have performed such a momentous deed, in fact, do we not ourselves assume the status of gods?

The bright morning light, against which the madman's lantern seems a merely futile gesture, invokes the historical movement of Enlightenment, whose secular programme was 'the disenchantment of the world', according to the famous Frankfurt School critique of Theodor Adorno and Max Horkheimer, *Dialectic of Enlightenment* (1947). In Nietzsche's madman, we see how the general cultural tendency to replace magic and religion with the analytic power of reason creates an urgent need which is itself, as it were, God shaped. If this is 'nihilism', the encounter with nothingness or the abyss of meaning after the removal of God as an explanatory principle, then it seems possessed by an urge to compensate for the absence: humans become godlike. Modernism can then emerge to fill the void with various claims to a redemptive power: Henry James writes of the 'sacred office' of the art of fiction, while Virginia Woolf pursues the 'spirit' of life; T.S. Eliot, paraphrasing Stephane Mallarmé, reflects upon 'purifying the dialect of the tribe'; Apollinaire's concept of 'pure painting' takes an explicitly spiritual turn in Kandinsky's abstraction.

It could be said that in this respect, modernism continues the reaction of romanticism, for example in the poetry of Blake and Wordsworth, against the rise of an unreflexive secular reason increasingly at the service of industrial capitalism – a version of rationality described as 'instrumental' by Adorno and Horkheimer. Nietzsche is, however, far from straightforwardly 'irrationalist'. Even as it betrays a sense of loss and emaciation, his philosophy from the outset undertook a rigorously *rationalistic* dismantling of the principles of Christian belief. 'Would anyone care to learn something about the way in which ideals are manufactured?', he asks in the late work, *The Genealogy of Morals* (1887); 'Does anyone have the nerve?' Nietzsche proved his nerve in a breathtaking confrontation with the Christian ideals of love and charity, which he saw as inculcating a 'slave morality', translating weakness into merit and thereby falsifying the natural hierarchy of power relations. It thus made no sense, for Nietzsche, to impose an abstract schema of 'good' and 'evil' on a natural order in which the 'will-to-power' would assert itself willy-nilly.

The Nietzschean concept of the will–to–power, crystallized in the figure of the Superman who must transcend normative morality, has a controversial history. Having been appropriated in reductive and distorted form by the Nazis to help underpin an ideology of Aryan supremacy, it is common to encounter the uninformed view that Nietzsche was, for example, a 'fascist philosopher'. To begin to understand modernism, I recommend some reading of Nietzsche's texts, whose rhetorical, aphoristic unpredictability and dialectical energy will almost certainly dispel the foregoing caricature. In his first work, *The Birth of Tragedy* (1872), a latent concept of will-to-power possesses a specifically aesthetic dimension. Nietzsche takes from the early Greeks a sense of art as always poised between the Apollonian and Dionysiac principles. Apollo, the god of light, symbolizes dream, the mind, contemplation, ideas, the plastic arts, while Dionysus represents darkness, the body, instinct, intoxication and the art of music. The tendency in modern culture for the Apollonian to prevail over the Dionysiac is therefore the tendency for that culture to decline or decay, as it prioritizes the ideal and rational at the expense of the life-giving, darker material forces. In nations, Nietzsche argued, 'secularization' occurs when history replaces myth as a form of self-understanding, where myth represents an 'unconscious metaphysic'. The profound influence of these ideas can be traced in what Michael Bell among others has called the 'mythopoeic' or mythmaking tendency in modernism, in texts such as James Joyce's *Ulysses*, T.S. Eliot's *The Waste Land* or Ezra Pound's *Pisan Cantos*, where a conscious drawing on extant mythic structures – classical literature, or anthropological sources – combines with the desire to configure the modernist text itself as a new form of mythic utterance (see *Literature, Modernism and Myth*, 1997).

There is a further, almost scientific dimension to Nietzsche's critique of Christian ethics, and this might be highlighted by the position of *agnosticism* in secular modernity. The term is attributed to the British scientist and evolutionary theorist T.H. Huxley (1825–95), and designates a condition of active and inquisitive uncertainty about religious belief. Huxley's reputation as a public intellectual in later nineteenth-century British culture was as the champion of the crucial secularizing work of Charles Darwin (1809–82). Darwin's *On the Origin of Species* (1859) established the theory of natural selection, which dealt a blow to the concept of the divine creation of species as separate entities, and in particular to the concept of the human as a uniquely favoured species created in God's image. According to natural selection, any variation in a species that gives it an advantage over similar individuals in the struggle for life will mean that it is more likely than others to successfully reproduce and perpetuate the variation. The strong feature thus being 'selected' over time accounts for the emergence of new species. While the *Origin* focuses almost exclusively on non-human nature, it is everywhere implicit that the creation of the human owes itself to this same purely fortuitous, non-teleological process. The nature of variation itself was to remain unclear, at least until the discovery of Mendelian genetics in the early twentieth century; Darwin however distanced himself, not only from metaphysical speculations on it, but even from the influential theory of Lamarck, which held that learned variations or improvements could be internalized and passed on to succeeding generations in the genetic material. Evolution, including human evolution, occurs through a mechanism of mathematical inevitability: to Darwin's own anguish – 'O you Materialist!', he recorded in his notebooks – the role of a divine artificer in this vision of life became increasingly difficult to place. The congeniality of this theory of blind natural forces to Nietzsche's conception of a vitalistic will-to-power will be evident here. The further resonances of post-Darwinian evolutionary thinking for modernism are the subject of the following section.

Evolution and entropy

Forward, or back? Up, or down? Out of the evolutionary debates of the late nineteenth century, precarious ambivalences around the direction of modernity emerged, confirming Marx's sense of a condition always 'pregnant with its contrary'. Darwin's theory of natural selection provided a new explanatory mechanism not just for the evolution but also for the *extinction* of species, a possibility often previously refuted by Victorian creationist thinkers even when faced with the evidence of the geological record. Against the tendency to see Darwinian evolution in terms of a progression towards complexity and perfection, it was equally claimed that the ruthless mechanism of natural selection rooted out many potential life forms. In *Degeneration, a Chapter in Darwinism* (1880), Edwin Ray Lankester argued for the parasite as an instance of successful evolutionary adaptation, yet one which militated against heterogeneity and towards a simple homogeneity.

Equally apparent in the dystopian tendency were the implications of Lord Kelvin's second law of thermodynamics, according to which the dissipation of energy was an inevitable feature of living systems.

In late Victorian culture, fears abounded about the heat-death of the sun, temporally distant perhaps, yet overshadowing the present with an image of infinitesimally gradual yet inexorable decline. At the same time as the cultural investment in modernity-as-progress continued, an awareness of the fragility of that process also gained momentum. A strong example is the discourse of *degeneration* and its various cognates from the *fin de siècle* through the modernist period. Daniel Pick's *Faces of Degeneration: A European disorder, c.1848–1918* (Cambridge, Cambridge University Press, 1989) traces a 'general shift from notions of the individual degenerate', as embodied in the work on criminal types by Cesare Lombroso, 'towards a bio-medical conception of crowd and mass civilisation as regression' (p. 222). In other words, discourses on mass modernity, on the metropolis and on degeneration coincide. Key works in this field of interrelations between biological science, urban sociology and political reaction include Max Nordau's *Degeneration* (1892, translated from the German in 1895) and Gustave Le Bon's *The Crowd: A Study of the Popular Mind* (1895, translated from the French in 1896). Nordau notoriously bracketed aesthetics within a 'severe mental epidemic' sweeping Europe and characterized, in sub-Nietzschean terms, by an over-stimulation of the intellect and a dislocation of the balance between bodies and society. Hysteria and other nervous diseases, Nordau claimed, were the palpable physical effects of general cultural degeneration. Le Bon's study of the crowd argued the similarly reactionary case that the discrete psychological entity constituted by the crowd, or any such form of gathering, was inherently regressive; as Pick points out, Le Bon was able to conflate all revolutionary movements, including socialism, with qualities of 'femininity' and the associated dangers of feminism, in a somewhat demonic image of modern mass society.

Despite their lurid and unreliable speculations, such works as those of Nordau and Le Bon are increasingly studied in modernist contexts, seen to contribute to a cultural fabric within which 'high' modernist artefacts no longer float free of politics and the popular. Debates around evolutionary downturn and the degeneration of the human 'stock' repeatedly inform modernism, yet have tended, as Anne Fernihough puts it, to be 'bleached out' of histories of modernism-as-formalism. Another way of putting this is to draw attention to the widespread discourse of *eugenics* in the period, a 'science' of racial improvement so pervasive across the cultural and political spectrum that Fernihough describes it as the 'dark underbelly of modernist theory' ('"Go in fear of abstractions"; Modernism and the Spectre of Democracy', *Textual Practice* 14:3, 2000, p. 481). The originator of the term 'eugenics' was the British writer and scientist Francis Galton, whose *Hereditary Genius* (1869) is one of the founding texts of the movement. Galton agreed with the idea of a connection between urban, industrial life and degeneration, and further maintained that the uncontrolled reproduction of the urban working classes would lead to an inevitable, hereditary increase in this degenerative tendency. Set in the historical context of growing commercial and imperial competition between European nation-states, and the apparent rise of militarism in Germany, eugenics in Britain seemed to offer a means of ensuring the health and wealth of the national body politic through the social regulation of individual bodies and their sexual reproduction. Buoyed by the Darwinian parallel between natural selection and the 'artificial' selection processes of breeders of pigeons, for example, eugenicists aspired towards the similar selection of 'fit' human types, and the gradual eradication of the 'weak', as a means of achieving political and economic well-being.

The darkest manifestations of eugenics in the early twentieth century were the policies of compulsory sterilization that emerged in Hitler's Germany. Yet eugenics is also a common currency of political and cultural debate in the modernist period in Britain; a journal such as *The New Age*, which was largely responsible for the initial introduction and dissemination of Nietzschean ideas, consistently demonstrated that the issue of how to produce healthier human beings, and of how this might in turn create stronger and healthier nations, was variously pursued across a spectrum of progressive-left thinking. In the unlikely context of her Futurist-inspired 'Feminist Manifesto' of 1914, the poet Mina Loy asserted that 'every woman of superior intelligence should realize her race-responsibility by producing children in adequate proportion to the unfit or degenerate members of her sex' – this, in a polemic which elsewhere includes the startling proposal that the sexual independence of women should be furthered through '*unconditional* surgical *destruction of virginity'* at puberty (Kolocotroni *et al., Modernism,* p. 260). Fernihough's discussion of the journal shows a continuity between the elaboration of modernist aesthetics and the practical formulation of policy and advice on every aspect of personal and everyday life, from healthy eating to family planning. Birth control is thus a subject that gets caught at the intersection of very different political interests, being the potential vehicle both of a mode of social and racial engineering, and of the emancipation and empowerment of women.

Physics, fields and forces

> That the glass would melt in heat,
> That the water would freeze in cold,
> Show that this object is merely a state,
> One of many, between two poles.
> (from 'The Glass of Water', Wallace Stevens, 1942)

Should we think of phenomena as objects, or as events? Is a glass of water a thing, complete in itself, or is it a temporary stage in a process, made possible by the conditions that prevent the water from freezing or evaporating, and the glass from melting or breaking? Wallace Stevens' poem alludes to radical transformations in the science of physics during the period of modernism, placing an overriding emphasis on the nature of phenomena as events or processes. Recent modernist studies have shown increasing interest in a range of texts through which these ideas were filtered through to thinkers, artists and an enthusiastic reading public: such would include A.N. Whitehead's *Science and the Modern World* (1925), A.S. Eddington's *The Nature of the Physical World* (1928) and Sir James Jeans' *The Mysterious Universe* (1930). These are popular and accessible if challenging texts, and are still strongly recommended as indicators of the impact the new physics might have had on modernist cultures. Emerging from them is a consistent narrative encapsulating the historical pattern of change in physics: what is overthrown is a 'materialist' or 'mechanistic' conception, deriving from Newtonian physics, according to which units or corpuscles of matter act and react on each other according to certain definite laws while located in time–space. Through the course of three centuries since the early seventeenth century, this had attained the status of a 'common-sense' world-view, allowing us to think of scientific 'progress' in terms of predictability – an increasing knowledge of the nature of matter itself and of the laws that determined its movement, such that the more we know, the more we can anticipate what will happen. How was this narrative or conception challenged?

Key characteristics of the new physics

- *Substance.* As characterized by the development of the microscope, we might think of materialist science in terms of *atomism*, the ability to analyse or break matter down into ever smaller units, in the search for the quintessential building blocks of the universe. When this led to Ernest Rutherford's splitting of the nitrogen atom in 1910, however, the result was a challenge to the concept of substance itself. The atom, in what became 'Bohr theory' after the work of Rutherford's co-worker Niels Bohr, consisted of even smaller particles held together in a kind of planetary system by electric charges, the nucleus containing a positive proton and a neutron, orbited by negatively charged electrons. It became possible to think that, when you arrive at the smallest units of matter, what you find is not substance, but a field of forces or energy.
- *Fields.* The concept of the electromagnetic field, combining electricity and magnetism, had been established in the work of J. Clerk Maxwell by the mid-nineteenth century. The decade of the 1890s, however, saw extraordinary developments: the discovery of X-rays by Röntgen in 1895, radioactivity by Becquerel in 1896 and the element radium by the Curies in 1898. In 1900, while studying thermal radiation, the German physicist Max Planck realized that a theory of discrete particles could not account for the way in which energy is transmitted. Because heat consists in vibrations of a certain frequency, Planck concluded that energy could only be transmitted in packets, lumps or 'quanta' of a certain size, a process of discontinuous jumpiness rather than smooth gradation. Planck's 'quantum' theory was then extended by Bohr to the new atomic theory, in order to account for the 'leaping' of electrons which was the basis of all physical and

chemical activity. For Whitehead, in the new physics it became futile to talk about particles as individual entities, because the 'adventures' of electrons and protons are only conceivable within a field of force: 'an electron for us is merely the pattern of its aspects in its environment, so far as those aspects are relevant to the electromagnetic field' (A.N. Whitehead, *Science and the Modern World*, Cambridge, Cambridge University Press, 1927, pp. 192, 165). This constituted a dramatic rethinking of the 'field' itself, which had previously been understood simply as the space within which the movements of matter occurred; as Einstein and Infeld put it, 'in the new field language it is the description of the new field between the two charges, and not the charges themselves, which is essential for an understanding of their action. The recognition of the new concepts grew steadily, *until substance was overshadowed by the field*' (my italics) (Albert Einstein and Leopold Infeld, *The Evolution of Physics: The Growth of Ideas from the Early Concepts to Relativity and Quanta*, Cambridge, Cambridge University Press, 1938, pp. 157–8).

- *Waves/particles.* 'We are beginning to suspect that we live in a universe of waves, and nothing but waves', wrote Sir James Jeans (*The Mysterious Universe*, Cambridge, Cambridge University Press, 1930, p. 44). This again reflects the emphasis of the field theories of physics, but it is nevertheless, strictly, half of the story. In 1905, after experimental work on the photoelectric effect (the bombardment of metals with light in order to release electrons), Einstein applied Planck's quantum theory of wave energy to light: he claimed that a stream of light should be seen as a collection of tiny quanta later termed *photons*. But these photons defied previous ideas of causality and probability by behaving, in a famous experiment, simultaneously as particles (individual entities) and waves (collective entities). This is perhaps the most compelling example of the replacement of an 'either/or' with a 'both/and' epistemology in modernism: the glass of water, in Stevens' poem, is *both* object and process at the same time. In 1923, Louis de Broglie extended this theory to matter, or more precisely to the microscopic level of the behaviour of electrons. In 1926 Max Born concluded that these 'electron waves' could only be interpreted in terms of probability, tallying thus with

Heisenberg's 'Uncertainty Principle' of 1927, insofar as to record accurately the migration of electrons would be inevitably to affect that behaviour with the instruments of recording. The Uncertainty Principle is now regularly invoked, though not always with due care, to signal the modernistic end of a principle of scientific objectivity: 'by 1927', concludes Brian Greene, 'classical innocence had been lost' (*The Elegant Universe*, p. 107).

The question of the actual historical understanding and impact within modernism of these scientific challenges to common sense remains openly debated. As Gillian Beer has speculated, 'it may be that to rebuff common sense itself becomes a "common-sense" move of the time, a counterfactual, sustaining, question-closing communality for literary modernism, under the wing of contemporary physics. Scepticism and credulity become one'. In this essay, Beer's attention to the cultural absorption of field theory focuses on the emergence of radio and the associated conceptual resonances of 'wireless' rather than on the plane of specialized scientific debate ('"Wireless": Popular Physics, Radio and Modernism', in eds Francis Spufford and Jenny Uglow, *Cultural Babbage: Technology, Time and Invention*, London, Faber, 1996, p. 159).

Nevertheless, the new physics struck peculiar resonances with other modernist forms. Freudian psychology was undoubtedly a form of field theory in its emphasis on a dynamic relation of forces in the psyche – ego, id and superego – rather than on a single organic self. Cubist art was equally field-oriented in its reconfiguration of the classical scenario of things arranged in static, three-dimensional space. The formal innovations of James Joyce's *Ulysses* (1922) or of Virginia Woolf's *The Waves* (1931) can be very profitably read afresh as experiments in fictional field theory. Einstein and Infeld are wryly suggestive when they observe that, despite the 'abstraction' attributed to modern physics by Whitehead, 'the electromagnetic field is, for the modern physicist, as real as the chair on which he sits' (p. 158). The material substantiality of the ordinary world had been revealed, arguably, as a kind of illusion; writers were undoubtedly provoked to reconsider that precarious concept known as 'reality', and might sometimes focus the effort on that reimagining of the *literal* furniture of the everyday. In an essay on Franz

Kafka, Walter Benjamin borrowed a passage from Eddington's *The Nature of the Physical World* in which, Benjamin claimed, 'one can virtually hear Kafka speak'. The 'I' of the passage is a scientist about to negotiate the 'complicated business' of entering an ordinary room, given that the human body must shove against an atmosphere of 14 pounds per square inch, and land on a plank of wood travelling at 20 miles per second around the sun:

> The plank has no solidity of substance. To step on it is like stepping on a swarm of flies. Shall I not slip through? No, if I make the venture one of the flies hits me and gives me a boost up again; I fall again and am knocked upwards by another fly; and so on. I may hope that the net result will be that I remain about steady; but if unfortunately I should slip through the floor or be boosted too violently up to the ceiling, the occurrence would be, not a violation of the laws of Nature, but a rare coincidence . . .
>
> Verily, it is easier for a camel to pass through the eye of a needle than for a scientific man to pass through a door.
>
> (Quoted in Benjamin, *Illuminations*, p. 145)

Eddington's scientist insists on the defamiliarization of the commonplace by the new science of physics. Science thus reinforced what, for the Russian Formalist critics of the 1910s, was the role of literary language: to remind us of how 'common sense' gets embedded, and becomes invisible as such, in the languages we habitually use.

Language

> We can no longer take language for granted as a medium of communication. Its transparency has gone. We are like people who for a long time looked out of a window without noticing the glass – and then began to notice this too.
>
> (Iris Murdoch, *Sartre* (1953))

Iris Murdoch here characterizes what has been called the 'linguistic turn' in early twentieth-century thought. The double-take she describes – we think we are looking at a scene, until we realize we are looking at glass, which obtrudes or mediates between us and the scene – might be compared to a modernist awareness, over a range of fields and activities, of the *materiality* of language. Language, in other words, is no longer regarded as an empty vessel into which we pour our previously conceived thoughts and ideas; rather, it is the material *in and through which* these thoughts and ideas are conceived. Instead of speaking and writing language, language speaks and writes *us*. You will recognize here the familiar modernist stamp of the inversion of the accepted, common-sense position. How does this inversion come about?

The first key reference point is the work of Ferdinand de Saussure (1857–1913), the Swiss thinker whose posthumously compiled *Course in General Linguistics* (1915) became the founding work of the modern sciences of structural linguistics (or structuralism) and semiology. Saussure's Course gave a detailed account of that sense in which the individual is unfree in language even as they think themselves most free. All examples of our actual use of language, or *parole*, are determined, Saussure argued, by a pre-existent system of rules, or *la langue*. Language awaits or pre-exists the individual, and the process of language acquisition in childhood consists in entering the system of *la langue* and learning what it is possible to say. In this sense the term 'structure' in structuralism has a quite specific meaning: the world is always-already structured for us *by* language, rather than structured by us *in* language. Certain commonplace assumptions about experience are challenged by this: for example, that our experience of any natural thing, such as a cat, is a purely unique, immediate and physical event. Once we have language, structuralism insists, we can never see the cat as in itself it really is; language embeds the cat in a grid or system of connotations and concepts, which moreover are fully subject to cultural and linguistic differences.

This principle of relativity is inscribed in Saussure's theory of the *arbitrary* nature of the sign. Any sign, such as 'cat', consists of two components: the physical shape and sound of the words, or *signifier*, and the concept, meaning or *signified*. In normal language use the signifier and signified appear to be indissolubly wedded together, like the sides of a sheet of paper: 'cat' cannot call to mind a computer, no matter how hard we try. But at the same time, the relationship between signifier and signified is purely arbitrary: there is nothing in nature to dictate that the letters c-a-t should designate the small furry creature with whiskers. Language, Saussure concluded, is a *system of differences without positive terms*; c-a-t generates its meaning from being different from everything else in the language that isn't 'cat', but has no 'positive' or necessary connection with the thing itself.

A second reference point, closely related to structuralism, is the elaboration of *linguistic relativity* from within the field of anthropology, primarily associated with the work of American anthropologists such as Edward Sapir (1884–1939) and Benjamin Lee Whorf (1897–1934). Whorf's structuralist formula was to say that it is language that 'carves up' nature for us, and that the relativity of language extends far beyond differences of vocabulary and into lived experience itself. From his fieldwork on the Hopi Indian peoples of Arizona in the 1920s and early 1930s, Whorf drew the general conclusion that it would be imprecise to claim that different cultural languages are simply alternative ways of labelling what is essentially the same understanding of the world. Instead, differences of grammatical and syntactic structure inscribe fundamentally different conceptions of the basic co-ordinates of time and space. Whorf claimed, for example, that after detailed study, he could find in the Hopi language 'no words, grammatical forms, constructions or expressions' that refer to what we would call "time", either implicitly or explicitly (*Language, Thought and Reality: Selected Writings*, ed. John B. Carroll, Cambridge, MA, MIT Press, 1982, p. 57). Hence, although the Hopi prefer verbs in contrast to the European linguistic preference for nouns, turning 'our propositions about things into propositions about events', those verbs do not have tenses within which differences of past, present and future could be inscribed (p. 63). Where the grand cosmic forms of European languages are time and space, in Hopi they are, as Whorf describes them, the *manifested* or *objective*, which includes everything of past and present without distinguishing between them, and the *manifesting* or *subjective*, which includes the future, and everything mental or, in Hopi terms, felt in the heart. What in English would be differences of time, in a 'timeless' language such as Hopi are differences of quality or validity.

Perhaps the crucial distinction between Whorf's work and much of the preceding scientific interest in language and culture concerns the question of value. To a nineteenth-century sociologist such as Herbert Spencer, the absence of abstract concepts of time and space in Hopi would be viewed as a failure to evolve or develop. To Whorf, the Hopi world view is not inferior to the modern world-view. 'What surprises most', he writes in 1940 – although such surprise may seem quaintly patronizing in what is now a more emphatically multicultural world – 'is to find that various grand generalizations of the Western world, such as time, velocity and matter, are not essential to the construction of a consistent picture of the universe' (p. 216). Moreover, while Hopi can describe and explain, 'in a pragmatic or operational sense, all observable phenomena of the universe', it is actually seen to be 'better equipped' than 'our latest scientific terminology' to deal what Whorf calls 'vibratile' phenomena – electrical and chemical wave processes and vibrations of the kind that were increasingly crucial to the new physics, as we saw in the previous section.

It is thus possible to have any number of non-Western world-views, or languages, which are equally valid, in that all are situated in and relative to their own circumstances. The single Hopi noun for all things, except birds, that fly, might seem 'too large and inclusive' for 'us', but so would our word 'snow' to an Eskimo (p. 216). The temptation to dismiss the Hopi world-view as 'metaphysical' is countered by Whorf's insistence that a Newtonian view of the universe as homogenous space is equally metaphysical (pp. 58–9). Here, in pointing to the common-sense assumptions of Western thought as 'metaphysical', Whorf interestingly anticipates Jacques Derrida's later twentieth-century critique of logocentrism – that is, of the metaphysics by which it is assumed that meaning and selfhood are fully 'present' in our use of language.

Whorf's ideas have certain clear vulnerabilities: they are open to the accusation of essentializing cultures through their languages, making translation for example theoretically impossible. However, his insight that, through language, 'no individual is free to describe nature with absolute impartiality but is constrained to certain modes of interpretation even while he thinks himself most free', condenses many other strands of thought about language which are crucial to modernism (p. 214). Together, the work of Saussure and Whorf attaches a crucial ambivalence to the *materiality* of language: first, a sense of determinism and necessity – language structures experience for us, so that our 'freedoms' of thought and expression

are at once modified – but second, a precarious and perhaps liberating sense that there is no inevitability to the connection between
language and the world. Language imprisons us, but by the same
token the world might be radically otherwise, through linguistic
change or difference.

In modernist Russia, through Futurism and the literary–
theoretical movement known as Russian Formalism, for a decade
or so after the Bolshevik Revolution of 1917, Saussure's thinking
fed into a newly systematic analysis of the particular nature of literary language, but one which tended to stress this emancipatory
potential. We have already encountered Victor Shklovsky's famous
definition of the function of the literary as that of *ostranenie*, or
defamiliarization, fulfilling the aesthetic goal of increasing 'the difficulty and length of perception', in chapter 1. An important modi-
fication of Saussurean linguistics came through the Bakhtin School
of the 1920s, whose theoretical cornerstone was V.N. Volosinov's
Marxism and the Philosophy of Language (1928). This work held
that Saussure's idea of *la langue* could not account for the realities of linguistic change or the complexities of meaning in actual
speech situations. Rather than being determined by an abstract
system of rules, meaning, Volosinov maintained, was forged anew
in every encounter between an addresser and an addressee; any
word, whether written or spoken, was inherently *dialogical*, half
someone else's. The work of the Bakhtin School in this sense
intersects with the later twentieth-century thought of, for example,
Roland Barthes and Jacques Derrida, under the broad banner of a
post-structuralism. While a sense of the structuring, material power
of language remains in place, the relationship between signifier and
signified has been dislodged, so that the linguistic net in which we
are caught is constantly changing.

Modernist artefacts display a striking awareness of the materiality of their own constitutive languages. As we saw in chapter
2, Cézanne's paintings foreground the paint and the process of
painting; in Cubism, the grammar and vocabulary of painting itself
takes centre stage within the problems that visual art addresses.
Dada and the *zaum* poetry of Russian Futurism both foreground
the physical sound qualities of language and the way these can
be uncoupled from sense. If modernism and structuralism share

the same historical moment, it is fascinating also to note Andreas Huyssen's point that modernist texts and ideas remain central in the later twentieth-century development of French post-structuralism (the work of the Bulgarian-French theorist and writer Julia Kristeva (born 1941) exemplifies this). So, while we might equate the determinism of structuralism with modernism's sense of crisis, and of the imprisonment and alienation of the self within the abstract systems of modernity, there is equally the possibility, as Huyssen puts it, of 'a modernism of playful transgression, of an unlimited weaving of textuality, a modernism all confident in its rejection of representation and reality' and 'quite dogmatic in its rejection of presence and in its unending praise of gaps and absences, deferrals and traces which produce, presumably, not anxiety but, in Roland Barthes' terms, *jouissance*, bliss' (*After the Great Divide: Modernism, Mass Culture, Postmodernism*, Bloomington and Indianapolis, Indiana University Press, 1986, p. 209). The fiction of James Joyce may be seen as the most vivid example of the coincidence of these modernisms, in an œuvre that extends from the early naturalistic fictions of *Dubliners* (1914) to the surrealist linguistic play of *Finnegan's Wake* (1939). Joyce's masterpiece *Ulysses* (1922) is often seen to be as much about the condition of language itself as it is about the lives of its key protagonists, Stephen Dedalus and Leopold Bloom, on a single day in Dublin in June 1904. Much recent work in the enormous critical field of Joyce studies elaborates post-structuralist readings of Joyce, building on the important earlier readings of Cixous and Kristeva, and on the influential work by the British critic Colin McCabe, *James Joyce and the Revolution of the Word* (1979).

STOP and THINK

In the following extract from Joyce's *Portrait of the Artist as a Young Man*, the child (Stephen Dedalus) has just read his own inscription in the flyleaf of his geography book – 'Stephen Dedalus/Class of Elements/Clongowes Wood College/ Sallins/ County Kildare/Ireland/Europe/The World/The Universe':

> What was after the Universe? Nothing. But was there anything round the universe to show where it stopped before the nothing

place began? It could not be a wall; but there could be a thin line there all round everything. It was very big to think of everything and everywhere. Only God could do that. He tried to think what a big thought that must be; but he could only think of God. God was God's name just as his name was Stephen. *Dieu* was the French for God and that was God's name too; and when anyone prayed to God and said *Dieu* then God knew at once that it was a French person that was praying. But, though there were different names for God in all the different languages in the world and God understood what all the people who prayed said in their different languages, still God remained always the same God and God's real name was God. (*A Portrait of the Artist as a Young Man,* 1916, Harmondsworth, Penguin, 1976, p. 16)

- In what ways are these reflections about the universe and God also reflections about language?
- Does Stephen here experience language as an enabling or a restricting medium?
- How is Stephen led to think about the relationship between signifiers and signifieds, in Saussurean terms?
- Does Stephen understand linguistic relativity?

What I love about this passage is the way Joyce playfully captures the child's early attempts to grapple with philosophical profundities. These, however, are conveyed as completely ordinary thought processes, just as the early coming-to-terms with how language shapes and divides up the world for us is also a very ordinary thing. The 'linguistic turn' is in a way no more than an elaboration of these kinds of musings; conversely, we might see the passage as a symbol of modernism's reclamation of the childlike or primitive as highly complex ways of seeing.

The 'linguistic turn' of which modernism was a crucial aspect in early twentieth-century thought can thus be summarized in two main ways. First, it involved a reconfiguration, as *linguistic* problems, of issues previously conceived in other terms. Second, the matter of gaining access through language to absolute or metaphysical truths lying outside of language – what Derrida was to call *logocentrism* – is questioned, opening out a more pragmatic approach to human signifying practices as directed by rules, formal conventions and the principle of *play*. In the field of philosophy, this is typified by the work of the Austrian-born British thinker Ludwig Wittgenstein (1889–1951), who is most readily associated with 'language games', a concept or model for explaining the acquisition of language through praxis. In his earliest work, *Tractatus Logico-Philosophicus* (1921), Wittgenstein had established that '*The limits of my language* mean the limits of my world'; he thus sought to redefine philosophy as the pursuit only of the logical possibility of what can be said. 'Games' in Wittgenstein do not translate into a playful style; the reader of *Tractatus* will find an enigmatically cryptic yet systematic attempt to define these philosophical limits. In the closely related Vienna Circle, whose Logical Positivism took a scientific approach to drawing up the logical parameters of science through Karl Popper's principle of falsifiability, it may be possible to see how some saw this modern movement as a retreat from philosophy's traditional concerns with being and knowledge.

Similar associations might cling to the American movement known as Pragmatism, whose main exponent, William James, had a multifaceted influence on modernism. Truth, James insisted, was not inherent, but something that 'happened to' a word in use. James, however, straddles the fields of philosophy and psychology, and the linguistic turn in psychology leads to a radical expansion rather than contraction of this new science's concerns. The expansion is mirrored in the trajectory of James' own work, which shows a gathering interest in linguistic and cultural problems from the empirical foundations of *Principles of Psychology* (1890) through *The Varieties of Religious Experience* (1902) to *Pragmatism* (1907). It is inevitably, however, in the work of Sigmund Freud (see pp. 150–2), and the emergence of the 'subjective science' of psychoanalysis, that the linguistic turn in psychology comes to the fore. Words for Freud are the clues to the unconscious, and in a variety of ways – the unrestricted 'talking cure' as the basis of analysis, the importance of jokes, and of parapraxis or 'slips of the tongue' – demonstrate the materiality of language and linguistic play in the body's accommodation with culture. Freud's follower Jacques Lacan was to modify further this linguistic turn though the proposal that 'the unconscious is structured like a language'.

Time and space

As we have seen above, the principle of linguistic relativity suggests that even the fundamental concepts of time and space might be thought differently in different languages. Alongside this, however, modernist cultures are heavily influenced by a profound rethinking of time and space from philosophical and scientific perspectives. In essence, the notion of time as a *linear* and *diachronic* entity of homogeneous and measurable quality, as instanced by clock and calendar time, comes under severe scrutiny. Time comes to be conceived as a complex phenomenon composed of different temporalities or speeds, and in which past, present and future interpenetrate. Modernism in literature appears to take upon itself the role of getting behind or beyond common assumptions about time and in this sense rejuvenating our experience of time. This ability to experience time had, it was argued, been diminished by our tendency to *spatialize* time, to translate it into spaces such as the face of a clock. Equally, however, and to some extent contradictorily, modernist artists are themselves involved in a more complex spatialization of time, as if to confirm that what characterizes modernity is a gradual ascendancy of spatial thinking and even, as the philosopher Henri Lefebvre puts it, a 'manifest expulsion of time'. To begin to clarify these issues, we need to pause for some examples.

STOP and THINK

• Imagine you are sitting through a particularly tedious one-hour lecture, and can't wait to be released. Compare this with listening to another lecture that is so riveting and entertaining that the hour is over before it barely seems to have begun. You might say that, in the first case, 'time drags' and that, in the second case, 'time flies'. Do you mean that in these instances time really does slow down or speed up, or are you using the words 'drag' and 'fly' merely as metaphors for our distorted impressions of time in these cases; as if we know that, *really*, an hour is always an hour, as measured by the clock?

  What if it was suggested, however, that the *reality* of time

> was your experience of it, dragging or flying? And that it
> is your view of time as measured by the clock, a uniform
> and consistent medium, that is abstract or metaphorical?
> What if time is, *really*, our varying experience of it?

The effort of adjustment required here is similar to that required
by the concept of *durée*, which inadequately translates as 'duration',
in the work of the French philosopher Henri Bergson (1859–1941).
Across works such as *Time and Free Will* (1889), *Matter and Memory*
(1896) and *Creative Evolution* (1907), Bergson mounted a sustained
critical interrogation of the logics of scientific and rationalistic
thinking, particularly as applied to causality and evolution. In spatializing time, Bergson argued, we intellectualize it, and thereby
lose the palpable experience or quality of time. *Durée* designates that
sense of the real passing of time, or duration, which is overridden by
our spatializing of time as units or commodities (seconds, minutes,
months, and so on). The spatial model of time is also inscribed in
traditional models of causality and predictability; on the basis of
separate categories of past, present and future, we identify patterns in the past and use these to explain the present and predict
the future. Bergson challenged this mode of thinking as vulner-
ably mechanistic, posing instead the question of *becoming*. Here, in
Creative Evolution, Bergson takes the development of personality,
and the painting of a portrait, to illustrate the idea that the logic
of cause and effect can only account retrospectively for the sheer
creativity of becoming:

> Doubtless, my present state is explained by what was in me and by
> what was acting on me a moment ago. In analyzing it I should find no
> other elements. But even a superhuman intelligence would not have
> been able to foresee the simple indivisible form which gives to these
> purely abstract elements their concrete organisation . . .
>
> The finished portrait is explained by the features of the model, by
> the nature of the artist, by the colours spread out on the palate; but,
> even with the knowledge of what explains it, no one, not even the
> artist, could have foreseen exactly what the portrait would be, for to
> predict it would have been to produce it before it was produced – an
> absurd hypothesis which is its own refutation. Even so with regard
> to the moments of our life, of which we are the artisans . . . It is then

right to say that what we do depends on what we are; but it is necessary to add also that we are, to a certain extent, what we do, and that
we are creating ourselves continually. (*Creative Evolution*, trans.
Arthur Mitchell, Lanham, University Press of America, 1983, pp.
6–7)

Self-creation might here be linked to Bergson's notorious 'vitalism',
embodied in the concept of *élan vital*, a life force which is only, in retrospect, reducible to an explanation through cause and effect. In the
middle decades of the twentieth century, Bergson's apparent irrationalism became discredited (see, for example, Bertrand Russell's
rather satirical account in his *History of Western Philosophy*, 1946).
But its recent revival in the form of a 'new Bergsonism', partly due
to the retrieval work of French philosopher Gilles Deleuze, finds
Bergson's work aligned with new discoveries in the fields of genetics and neuroscience, as well as with postmodern philosophies of
the decentred self (see, for example, ed. John Mullarkey, *The New
Bergson*, Manchester, Manchester University Press, 1999).

In the modernist decades of the early twentieth century, Bergson
achieved something akin to celebrity status, and his thinking
was widely debated and influential. Gertrude Stein's construction
of a fictionalized 'continuous present' has clear affiliations with
Bergsonian becoming and self-creation. In the story 'Melanctha',
Stein's heavily repetitive and circular style seems to insist on re-
creating its characters sentence by sentence; despite a strong under-
tow of historical determinism, there is also a sense that nothing of
our prior knowledge can be taken for granted in the development
of character. The strongly repetitive rhythms of a novel like D.H.
Lawrence's *The Rainbow* (1915) might also be connected to what
Lawrence later referred to as the distinctive grammar of the 'emotional mind', with 'its own rhythm, its own commas and colons and
full-stops'. Within such a rhythm, Lawrence argued, time, in the
familiar sense of a sequence, ceases to exist; only afterwards can
you 'deduce the logical sequence and the time sequence, as historians do from the past'. Lawrence's view of scientific analysis as a
'post-mortem' activity, based on the Italian writer D'Annunzio's
assertion that 'anatomy presupposes a corpse', is a strong aesthetic
version of Bergson's critique of temporality and causality.

Lawrence based his assessment of the 'emotional mind' on the novelist Giovanni Verga's depiction of the Sicilian peasantry. In this way, as Terry Eagleton has noted, modernism was able to align the primitive with the most sophisticated developments in modern physics in a joint *exposé* of the deficiencies of conventional time–space thinking. Central to any account of modernist time–space are the special (1905) and general (1916) theories of relativity of Albert Einstein, revealing the nature of time and space to be relative to the state of motion of the particular observer and capable of being warped by the particular configurations of matter and energy. Einsteinian theories of physics operate at unimaginable extremes of physical magnitude: the minute, subatomic level of quantum physics, and the effects obtaining across the seemingly limitless proportions of the universe. Observing and measuring phenomena at these extremes reveals behaviours and principles that are simply imperceptible in day-to-day life; such results oblige us to reassess habitual notions of time and space.

Yet the notion of 'relativity' in Einstein's work is misleading if it is translated as an attack on any 'absolute' scientific knowledge and thus as a complete break with the history of physics ('Revolution in science – new theory of the universe – Newtonian ideas over-thrown', declared *The Times* headline on 7 November 1919, after a verification of Einstein's general theory). In fact, at the root of Einstein's special theory is the establishing of an absolute: that the speed of light is always 670 million miles per hour. Only with this established could Einstein then go on to prove a parallel but apparently contradictory truth: that the speed at which anything appears to happen varies according to the velocity of the observer relative to the thing observed. Thus, while modernist artists and writers explored states of simultaneity, as a way of recording the non-linear complexities of history and experience, Einstein's physics outlawed the possibility of absolute simultaneity, whether at macro or at micro levels (a star seen to be exploding while you eat your sandwich does not happen at the same time, because of the time taken for light from the star to reach earth; two people in a moving railway carriage can make a simultaneous action, but to stationary observers outside, watching the train pass, one action will be marginally ahead of the other).

In the later, general theory of relativity, Einstein extended this thinking into the unresolved nature of Newtonian theories of gravity. Investigating the conditions of accelerating bodies, he concluded that gravity is not a mysterious attractive force but a condition of the warped fabric of space due to the presence of large entities such as planets; the image of space as a stretched sheet, curving when a ball or stone is placed upon it, communicates something of this. The light from a star thus curves, to an infinitesimal degree, before it reaches earth. This requires the rejection of the established Euclidean view of space as a homogeneous vacuum; the idea that space has a quality or fabric, is a material entity, appears confirmed in later 'big-bang' theories of the origin of the universe, where we are similarly challenged to accept that this initial tumultuous explosion does not release the materials of the universe *into* space, but rather *creates* both space and time themselves, as entities dependent upon matter and energy.

How we track the significance of these complex scientific theories within a broader cultural context remains a key methodological issue in the study of modernism. In practical terms, a consideration of the abstract 'influence' of such ideas on modernist artists is less satisfactory than to consider the complex network of sources, such as newspapers, journals and popularizing scientific texts, within which the rethinking of time and space entered circulation. A recent essay by Michael H. Whitworth provides a valuable survey of such sources, and in the process manages to convey a certain scepticism about the extension of first-hand knowledge ('Physics: "A Strange Footprint"', in ed. David Bradshaw, *A Concise Companion to Modernism*, Oxford, Blackwell, 2003, pp. 200–20). It might be equally valuable to return to John Berger's essay 'The Moment of Cubism' (see chapter 2), where Berger claims that in the brief space of seven years (1907–14) Cubism broke with the 'illusionist three-dimensional space' of the Renaissance, undermining the 'habit of centuries' by which discrete objects are seen to float in empty space. Cubism instead projects a pictorial space of relatedness and interaction in which 'the space between objects is part of the same structure as the objects themselves'. In accounting for this 'revolutionary transformation', Berger offers the founding of modern physics as only one factor within a spectrum of the predominantly socio-economic effects of modernity: the new network of world capitalism, and the counterbalancing socialist international; electricity, radio cinema, and mass print circulation; the structural and design possibilities offered by steel, aluminium, chemicals and synthetic materials; the motor-car and the aeroplane. What David Harvey, in another excellent analysis, calls modernist 'time-space compression' is transmitted through the experience of modernity itself, in an extraordinary seven-year 'moment' of convergence which is itself a prime example of time–space compression. It thus seems to follow that commentators are drawn to echo Virginia Woolf's enigmatic attraction to the year 1910; while Berger sees Cubism's decisive shift into non-Euclidean space occurring after 1910, so Henri Lefebvre, the distinguished philosopher of modern 'daily life', writes:

> [A]round 1910 a certain space was shattered. It was the space of common sense, of knowledge (*savoir*), of social practice, of political power, a space hitherto enshrined in everyday discourse, just as in abstract thought, as the environment of and channel for communications; the space, too, of classical perspective and geometry, developed from the Renaissance onwards on the basis of Greek tradition (Euclid, logic) and bodied forth in Western art and philosophy, as in the form of the city and the town. (*The Production of Space*, trans. Donald Nicholson-Smith, Oxford, Blackwell, 1991, p. 25)

Some of the implications of Lefebvre's translation of modernist conceptual space into the very concrete social spaces of modern living – the city, the town – will be explored in chapter 5.

Primitivism

This section is closely connected to the discussion of empire and colonialism in the previous chapter. Modernism's engagement with the so-called 'primitive' involves a central paradox. In the early twentieth century, the term could be applied either to ancient societies, or to contemporary societies perhaps only recently discovered by Western explorers, which were deemed to have been arrested at an earlier point of development. 'Primitive' thus embodied a judgement about hierarchy based on quasi-Darwinian theories of evolutionary development, a kind of natural selection at work in the human world. However, with the eruption of the motif of African tribal masks into Picasso's *Demoiselles d'Avignon*, Paul Gauguin's work in Tahiti, or a new theoretical study such as Wilhelm Worringer's *Abstraction and Empathy* (1908), it is clear that modernism substantially aspired to *invert* this estimation of the 'primitive', embracing and celebrating it as an alternative to an exhausted and self-deluded civilization of 'progress'.

In this sense then, returning to our earlier discussion of the directional ambivalence of modernism, to go back was to go forward. As empire and colonialism brought the primitive into proximity, and artefacts poured into Western societies through a rapidly burgeoning museum culture, the primitive presented the civilized with forms of thought and imagination it had lost or never been able to realize. In modernism, civilization realizes its impoverishment and responds through the deployment of the primitive. One claim was that contemporary advances in art and thought were anticipated by long forgotten or previously unknown primitive forms. On the subject of Bushman folklore, for example, D.H. Lawrence writes:

> The ideographs are so complicated, the sound-groups must convey so many unspeakable, unfeelable meanings, all at once, in a stroke, that it needs myriads of ages to achieve such unbearable concentration. The savages are not simple. It is we who are simple. They are unutterably complicated, every feeling, every term of theirs is untranslatably agglomerate. (Lawrence, *Studies in Classic American Literature*, eds Ezra Greenspan, Lindeth Vasey and John Worthen, Cambridge, Cambridge University Press, 2003, p. 338)

As Wilhelm Worringer argued concerning the correspondence between primitivism and modernist abstraction, 'a causal connection must . . . exist between primitive culture and the highest, purest regular art-form' (Harrison and Wood, *Art in Theory*, p. 71).

However, as Terry Eagleton wryly puts it, 'Whenever one hears admiring talk of the savage, one can be sure that one is in the presence of sophisticates' (*The Idea of Culture*, Oxford, Blackwell, p. 24). While the importance and sincerity of modernism's endorsement of the 'primitive' or 'savage' is not necessarily at issue, this endorsement may also be viewed as a product of the same power structure that fixes the West and its Other in a relationship of superiority to inferiority. The Other is held in place not by denigrating it, but by glamourizing it as 'exotic', beautiful, sensual, instinctive, and

so on. Thus, the gesture by which the modern humbly acknowledges the superiority of the primitive is simultaneously that which
patronizes and exploits it as the necessary means of maintaining a
sense of essential difference. The vexed question of the politics of
modernism's encounter with the primitive, of the extent to which
the uses of the primitive in the cultural sphere might be associated
with processes of Western imperialism and exploitation, continues
to inform major debates within modernist studies. In the visual arts,
Paul Gauguin's migration to the South Sea islands and his pioneering representation of native peoples is often seen to constitute one
example of this relationship (for a thorough discussion, see Gill
Perry, '"The Going Away" – A Preparation For the "Modern"', in
Harrison *et al.*, *Primitivism, Cubism, Abstraction*, pp. 8–34). German
Expressionism also exhibits a crucially ambivalent relationship with
primitivism, crystallized, as Jill Lloyd shows in a detailed study,
in the critical debate between Ernst Bloch and Georg Lukács in
1938. The exchange, Lloyd argues, posed a central question about
modernist primitivism: 'Could the inspiration the Expressionists
drew from non-European and folk art be used as a disruptive
strategy to challenge the norms and values of European culture?
Or was it, as Lukács suggests, merely an appropriate device, reaf-
firming precisely those values it set out to undermine?' (*German
Expressionism: Primitivism and Modernity*, New Haven and London,
Yale University Press, 1991, pp. viii–ix).

In literature, Joseph Conrad's novella *Heart of Darkness* (1902)
has become a particular focus for such questions since the dramatic
critical intervention of the Nigerian novelist Chinua Achebe in his
essay 'An Image of Africa: Racism in Conrad's *Heart of Darkness*'
(in Achebe, *Hopes and Impediments*, New York, Anchor, 1990).
Against the grain of a critical tradition which had established *Heart
of Darkness* as one of the most profound literary meditations upon
modern spiritual crisis, Achebe saw the text as the vehicle of its
author's 'thoroughgoing racism'. *Heart of Darkness* principally
involves the narration of the mariner Marlow, commissioned by a
Belgian trading company to sail up the Congo river to investigate
the fate of the company's chief agent, Kurtz. During his journey,
Marlow encounters the idealism, absurdity, disenchantment and
brutality that characterized the European colonialist exploitation of

Africa. A strong anti-imperialist critique is therefore implicit in the
text; yet Achebe argues that, through the voice of Marlow, racist
postures are perpetuated even in the midst of this political critique.
Among other things, it is the exoticization of the native that is at
issue for Achebe; thus, for example, at an early point in Marlow's
journey, when he begins to feel oppressed by the strangeness and
absurdity of the colonial enterprise, Marlow is reassured by the
sight of some natives in a rowing boat. Conrad writes:

> Now and then a boat from the shore gave one a momentary contact
> with reality. It was paddled by black fellows. You could see from
> afar the white of their eyeballs glistening. They shouted, sang; their
> bodies streamed with perspiration; they had faces like grotesque
> masks – these chaps; but they had bone, muscle, a wild vitality, an
> intense energy of movement, that was as natural and true as the surf
> along their coast. They wanted no excuse for being there. They were
> a great comfort to look at. (*Heart of Darkness*, 1902, Harmondsworth,
> Penguin Popular Classics, pp. 19–20)

Achebe sees in this an instance of the 'comfort' Conrad derives from
keeping savages 'in their place'. We might add that the black men
are admired purely for their physical qualities or 'wild vitality', and
in this gesture so deprived of the human qualities of thought and
speech that they blend into the 'surf along their coast'. There is the
curious anticipation of Picasso's *Demoiselles* in 'faces like grotesque
masks', though here the simile is consistent with the way the narrative deprives the natives of human agency; Conrad never takes the
opportunity, which might be regarded as a fictional prerogative, to
imagine them thinking or speaking.

Of course, Conrad is not identical with his narrator Marlow.
Achebe is more dismissive of this distinction than he might be, and
he does not admit the possibility that in simply allowing the reader
to listen to Marlow's voice, Conrad exposes the contradictions of
modern attitudes to the primitive, showing how it might be possible
to be anti-colonialist and racist at the same time. *Heart of Darkness*
also consistently inverts or undermines the binary oppositions
– light–darkness, civilization–barbarism, rationality–irrationality,
centre–periphery, for example – by which Europe's supposed superiority over Africa is structured, from the highly symbolic opening
scene in which the cruising yawl *Nellie*, which contains Marlow and

four representatives of the masculine professional bourgeoisie, sits becalmed at a moment when it is impossible to make clear distinctions between day and night, past and present, sea and sky, sea and the Thames, upriver and downriver. However, the broader strategic importance of Achebe's essay lay in scandalizing European and American literary criticism into a recognition that this revered work of Western literature might conceivably be racist in orientation or effect, and that literary criticism had colluded in this by ignoring the culturally specific representation of Africa and Africans in *Heart of Darkness*. In this Achebe drew attention to what he elsewhere called 'colonialist criticism', the tendency to dress up the values of the West as 'universal', as if Conrad's fictional Africa were merely the setting for a timeless human dilemma, thus ignoring the extent to which in this move both Africa and Africans are marginalized and dehumanized.

A striking confirmation of these points can be found in *Dreams from My Father* (1995), the memoir by the President of the United States, Barack Obama, in an episode touching on Obama's own experience of reading *Heart of Darkness* as an undergraduate in California in the late 1970s. Challenged by two friends to explain why he is reading what they collectively acknowledge as a racist book, Obama first notes that it was 'assigned', a set text on his course. In addition, however, Obama reveals a more nuanced critical perspective than Achebe. 'If you can keep your distance', he argues, Marlow's narrative, including what is 'said' and what is 'unsaid', teaches him not about Africa or black people but about:

> (T)he man who wrote it. The European. The American. A particular way of looking at the world . . . So I read the book to help me understand just what it is that makes white people so afraid. Their demons. The way ideas get twisted around. It helps me understand how people learn to hate. (*Dreams from My Father*, Edinburgh, Canongate, 2008, p. 103)

Through Obama's perspective, therefore, 'primitivism' is detached from its supposed object and becomes the description of an outsider mindset, leading us to another crucial reappraisal of the primitive in its relation to literary modernism: that is, through the historically specific concept of Negro art and culture in inter-war America, with particular reference to the Harlem Renaissance. It may seem as unthinkable to us now to associate the Harlem writers with the concept of the primitive, as it would be to use the term 'Negro' without racist connotations. Yet within the Harlem discourses of the 1920s 'Negro' underwent a major and extremely positive conceptual revaluation which involved a gradual overhauling of previous primitivist connotations. A key text is the literary anthology *The New Negro* (1925), edited by the African-American scholar Alain Locke (1886–1954). In his introduction to the anthology, Locke identifies the 'New Negro' in terms of an emergent generation still undergoing 'inner' transformation and the acquisition of a 'new mentality'. If a conception of primitivism is at work here it is in the figure of the 'Old Negro' which is in the process of being sloughed off by the new 'thinking Negro'. This figure, a 'historical fiction' or 'more of a formula than a human being – a something to be argued about, condemned or defended, to be "kept down", or "in his place", or "helped up", to be worried with or worried over, harassed or patronized; a social bogey or a social burden', has nevertheless shadowed the New, who has been obliged to invest in him through sentimental attachment and 'a sort of protective social mimicry forced upon him by the adverse circumstances of dependence' (Kolocotroni *et al.*, *Modernism*, p. 412). Locke therefore unashamedly sees Negro consciousness being gradually 'weaned' by public opinion, which must henceforth no longer 'paternalize', so that the Negro can increasingly take control of his own fate. One key factor in the process of 'shaking off the psychology of imitation and implied inferiority' is, Locke argues, the recognition of a modernist mission, 'acting as the advance-guard of the African peoples in their contact with Twentieth Century civilization' (p. 412, 416).

A more recent and major critical contribution to this debate has been Michael North's *The Dialect of Modernism: Race, Language and Twentieth-Century Literature* (1994). North's book highlights the significance of black American dialect in the formation of Anglo-American 'high' modernism, in the work of such writers as Gertrude Stein, William Faulkner, Ezra Pound and T.S. Eliot. What the idioms of negro speech and writing share with experimental modernism, North argues, is a fundamentally oppositional stance towards various culturally conservative lobbies, on both sides of the Atlantic, for the standardization and purification of language.

Hence, high modernists drew on such idioms as a resource, with varying degrees and kinds of acknowledgement, on the basis of an acquaintance with negro culture drawn, for example, from the vaudeville tradition, jazz and ragtime music, and images of the 'blackface' in cinema. More importantly, however, considering again Achebe's argument that African and by extension 'primitive' culture is seems only to be seen as an available backdrop or material for European or American issues, North demonstrates in detail how much negro writing, contained for example in Locke's anthology and principally in the work of writers such as Claude McKay, Jean Toomer and Zora Neale Hurston, is *itself* an experimental and distinctive mode of the avant-garde. More complicatedly still, such writers had to strive to extricate their own work from the models of mimicry of negro dialect or 'racial masquerades' perpetuated by modernists such as Eliot, Stein and Pound. An analogy of such ventriloquism could be found in the widespread practice in performance of 'blackface', the 'blacking-up' of the white artist, as exemplified by Al Jolson in the 1927 talkie film *The Jazz Singer*. North's study shows how these complex tensions within Harlem modernism can be revealed by comparing the famous and voluminous anthology *Negro*, compiled and edited by the rich heiress Nancy Cunard in 1934, with anthologies more internal to Harlem culture such as *The New Negro* or Zora Neale Hurston's sketchy and provisional 'The Eatonville Anthology' (1926) (see also Laura A. Winkiel, 'Nancy Cunard's *Negro* and the Transnational Politics of Race', *Modernism/modernity* 13:3, September 2006). With an extraordinarily diverse range of writing on, by or about the negro condition, from French surrealism to future Kenyan politician Jomo Kenyatta, Cunard's anthology, writes North, 'might have served as solid evidence of the rapprochement between African-American writing and Anglo-American modernism if the contributions from the modernists had not been either diffident or condescending' (*The Dialect of Modernism*, p. 190).

The human subject

'Enlightenment is founded and flounders upon the concept of self-knowledge.' Thus the critic Patricia Waugh highlights a key paradox that arises in the encounter between Enlightenment and modernism (*Practising Postmodernism/Reading Modernism*, London, Arnold, 1992, p. 91). Waugh refers to the sovereignty accorded to the individual human self by the secular optimism of the Enlightenment, as evinced by the founding philosophical *cogito* of René Descartes ('I think, therefore I am'), and illustrated by the dictum of Alexander Pope's 'Essay on Criticism', 'The proper study of mankind is man'. The broad Enlightenment proposition is that the boundless possibilities for human knowledge must embrace a growing understanding of human subjectivity itself, or even that such self-understanding is a precondition of the development of Enlightenment. Contradiction arises, however, when what it is we come to know is that we *cannot* know ourselves.

As we have seen in the section on language, above, Saussure's linguistics imply a displacement of human subjectivity, by reducing the sense of human agency in language: language is a pre-existent network of signs into which we are helplessly drawn, and through which subjectivity is constructed. A similar displacement or 'dethroning' of the subject takes place in the work of Karl Marx, via the forces of economics, and in that of Sigmund Freud, through the concept of the unconscious. These also suggest that we do not easily coincide with ourselves; that the human subject is always, in a sense, elsewhere.

We have already noted the importance of Karl Marx (1818–83) as a theorist of the perpetually revolutionizing tendencies of bourgeois modernity. Underpinning Marx's endorsement of communism was an extensive philosophical critique of capitalism. Marx identified a determining power in the relationship between economic base and superstructure, whereby the dominant economic mode of a society forms the substantial base or 'real foundation' that gives shape to the dominant ideas, institutions, and even cultural practices of that society. Marx strove to avoid any reductive sense of determinism or 'economism', and debates within Marxism have continually revolved around the nature of base–superstructure and on the degree of autonomy or independence possessed by elements of the superstructure. Nevertheless, Marxist thinkers insist on the extent to which our subjectivities might be shaped by the dominant economic systems of production and exchange – in the case of modernity, for example, by the mechanisms of capitalism. In the later Marxist work of Georg Simmel, a sociological thinker of some importance to modernism, this led to a landmark work on the philosophy of money, and to the theory that what characterizes the modern metropolitan consciousness is a tendency to calculation deriving from the capitalist money system.

Marx therefore also represents a *materialist* mode of thought, differing perhaps from Saussurean linguistic materialism and Darwinist evolutionary materialism, yet sharing with each the refusal of any metaphysics which might by definition draw on explanations that lay beyond the social and physical world. In this sense Marx's work developed in a complex critical dialogue with the tradition of German idealist philosophy, for example in the thinking of Hegel, who saw world history as the inevitable dialectical unfolding of a principle of Spirit. Marx is, then, responsible for a memorable statement of modernist paradox or inversion. In the Preface to *A Contribution to the Critique of Political Economy* (1859), he writes: 'It is not the consciousness of men that determines their being, but on the contrary, their social being that determines their consciousness'. Again, in the unravelling of Marx's writing, the word 'determines' proves to be far from simple. Human agency is as much a part of materialist causality as any other social or physical factor; hence, Marx's famous counterbalancing of revolutionary optimism with intellectual pessimism in his definition of history: 'Men make their own history, but they do not make it just as they please; they do not make it under circumstances chosen by themselves, but under circumstances directly encountered, given and transmitted from the past'. Thus, in the very moment and possibility of revolutionary change, 'the tradition of all the dead generations weighs like a nightmare on the brain of the living' (*The Eighteenth Brumaire of Louis Bonaparte*, 1852).

The rhetoric of modernist culture can sometimes sound like a repudiation of this complexity: 'make it new', effect a complete rupture with the past, build a truly modern world. But modernism is equally freighted by a sense that the conditions of individual freedom and self-possession necessary for this break are not what they seem. We carry within us, or are shaped and perhaps detained by, the not-self, that which shrinks from consciousness. Where in

Saussure and Marx this not-self takes the emphatically social forms of language and economics, in the work of Sigmund Freud (1856–1939) the social assumes the subtler and intimate form of the *unconscious*. For Freud, the unconscious is the means by which the human body accommodates itself to society and culture. As Schorske argues, Freud was a product of that Viennese *fin-de-siècle* liberalism which had suffered political displacement and a subsequent undermining of its claim to rational and artistic hegemony (Carl E. Schorske, *Fin-de-siècle Vienna: Politics and Culture*, Cambridge, Cambridge University Press, 1981, chs I and IV, for example). Like artists such as Gustav Klimt and Oskar Kokoshka, Freud's work was beginning to admit the underestimated significance of feeling and instinct in the structure of bourgeois lives. Having started out in the early 1880s as a doctor of medicine specializing in anatomy and physiology, Freud's developing interest in nervous diseases led him away from seeking purely physical explanations for conditions such as hysteria, and towards a model of the self in which traumas and experiences, often associated with childhood sexuality, are diverted and 'repressed' or 'sublimated', in other words converted into substitute forms, by the conscious mind.

When, Freud writes, a man becomes aware of the psychological truth that there are secrets which must be kept from himself, 'it looks as if his own self were no longer the unity which he had always considered it to be' (*Two Short Accounts of Psycho-Analysis*, Harmondsworth, Penguin, 1983, p. 97). The revolutionary model of human selfhood developed in Freud's later work was of a field of unstable and conflicting drives rather than of a single, unified entity. A new vocabulary embodies this complexity: 'ego' and 'id' only very roughly correspond to the consciousness and to the unconscious, while 'super-ego' approximates to the conscience. But perhaps the most revelatory aspect of this Freudian model is the large role given, in a range of key earlier works, *The Interpretation of Dreams* (1901), *Psychopathology of Everyday Life* (1904) and *Jokes and their Relation to the Unconscious* (1905), to those psychic mechanisms which resist, repress and transform our experiences, particularly those relating to the previously tabooed field of childhood sexuality. We do not, consciously, know the effects of these unconscious processes, but have indirect or symbolic apprehension of them in the involuntary production of, most famously, dreams, and of slips of the tongue (parapraxis).

Freud once famously claimed that the artists had been there before him – that is, that art and literature already made manifest those unconscious forces which in his work were taking the form of scientific theory for the first time. The subjective turn of modernism, and the coincidence of Freud's work with it, double and intensify this connection between psychoanalytic and artistic approaches to the unconscious. In visual art, as we have seen, surrealism seems to emerge in direct response to the Freudian model, concerned as it is with the dreamlike irruption of troubling or unfamiliar elements into the surface of the painting. Cubist or Expressionist human portraiture equally registers a sense that we know far less about ourselves than we (literally) think, and that painterly vocabularies, like psychological ones, needed to be stripped down and reconstructed in order to address the challenges posed by new models of the self. In literature, a central concept such as *stream of consciousness* can appear intimately linked to the random associations of the Freudian 'talking cure'; in chapter 7, we will look closely at the complex variants of this fictional technique. More broadly, Symbolist and Imagist principles in poetry, which we will examine in chapter 6, along with collage in Cubist art and montage in film, combine to form a modernist aesthetic in which the direct representation of unconscious material, unmediated by more traditional modes of narrative and explanation, comes to the fore. It is therefore unsurprising that film, coinciding with artistic modernism, very quickly emerges as the uniquely appropriate medium for an exploration of human subjectivity which went hand in hand with psychoanalysis.

In this light a fascinating cross-over text is H.D.'s *Tribute to Freud* (Oxford, Carcanet, 1971), written in 1944, because as well as being an Imagist poet and novelist, H.D. was also one of the founding editors of the influential film journal *Close Up* (1927–33) and, herself, an actor in avant-garde film. *Tribute to Freud* is a compelling account of the writer's own psychoanalysis with Freud in Vienna between 1933 and 1934, composed in both Freudian and modernistic terms. The account is as if poised between the wars, positing psychoanalysis as a means both of healing the personal damage to H.D. around the years of the First World War, and of anticipating the growing threat of the Second. H.D.'s own memories shuttle back and forth across the narrative in the manner of a talking cure, the centrepiece being her interpretation of the hallucinations projected onto the wall of her room while convalescing in Corfu after the war. H.D.'s profound affection for Freud shows through in her estimation of his 'very love of humanity' as expressed in his conviction of the universal, archetypal nature of unconscious structures, and in his desire to save humankind through self-knowledge. At times, the Freudian project emerges in heroic terms: 'I struck oil', she recalls Freud saying, 'It was I who struck oil. But the contents of the oil wells have only just been sampled. There is oil enough, material enough for research and exploitation, to last 50 years, to last 100 years – or longer' (p. 25). At other times, it is the uncoercive and subject-centred nature of psychoanalysis that is stressed: in Freud's method, 'the question must be propounded by the protagonist himself, he must dig it out from behind its buried hiding place, he himself must find the question before it could be answered' (p. 89).

In this context we return to the beginning of the current section and to Waugh's proposition concerning Enlightenment and the possibility of self-knowledge. As H.D. characterizes it, Freud's method abandons the principle of objectivity in knowledge: questions cannot be supplied by the analyst, nor even can the subject/analysand apply to her/himself questions supplied from outside. Yet, as is often noted, Freud is an impeccable product of a European tradition of Enlightenment rationality, applying systematic reason to the last bastion of human subjectivity, and in the process highlighting the limits of that very tradition. Similarly, while it is something of a commonplace to claim that modernist art turns inwards, or towards the recording of individual psychological experience, this process invariably produces a heightened sense of the slipperiness of that experience, and a displacement of ontology – the sense of being, subjective or otherwise – with epistemology: how do we or can we *know* being?

Selected reading

Bell, Michael, *Literature, Modernism and Myth: Belief and Responsibility in the Twentieth Century* (Cambridge, Cambridge University Press, 1997)

Important study charting the transition from major instances of modernist literary mythopoeia to later developments in the fiction of Marquez, Pynchon and Carter.

Bradshaw, David, 'Eugenics: "They Should Certainly Be Killed"', in ed. David Bradshaw, *A Concise Companion to Modernism* (Oxford, Blackwell, 2003), pp. 34–55.
Excellent brief survey of eugenics and modernist literature.

Childs, Donald J., *Modernism and Eugenics: Woolf, Eliot, Yeats and the Culture of Degeneration* (Cambridge: Cambridge University Press, 1997)
First sustained study of literary modernism and theories of eugenics.

Clifford, James, *The Predicament of Culture: Twentieth-Century Ethnography, Literature, and Art* (Cambridge, MA, Harvard University Press, 1988)
Starting from the modernist era, a stimulating set of essays on the ethnographic encounter, including sections on 'ethnographic surrealism', art collecting and museum cultures, and Edward Said's *Orientalism*.

Greene, Brian, *The Elegant Universe: Superstrings, Hidden Dimensions, and the Quest for the Ultimate Theory* (London, Vintage, 2000)
Chs 1–5 give a vivid, illustrated account of the problems addressed by Einstein in the special and general theories of relativity, and show how these point the way towards contemporary superstring theory.

Greenslade, William, *Degeneration, Culture and the Novel 1880–1940* (Cambridge, Cambridge University Press, 1994)
Very valuable study of the concept of degeneration and the influence of eugenics; see in particular chapter on Forster, Woolf, crisis of masculinity and shell-shock.

Harvey, David, *The Condition of Postmodernity*, especially Part Three, 'The Experience of Time and Space' and ch. 16, 'Time–Space Compression and the Rise of Modernism as a Cultural Force'.

Hutchinson, George, *The Harlem Renaissance in Black and White* (Cambridge, MA, Belknap Press, 1995)
An important study.

Kern, Stephen, *The Culture of Time and Space 1880–1918* (Cambridge MA, Harvard University Press, 1983)
Groundbreaking but accessible discussion.

Lefebvre, Henri, *The Production of Space*, trans. Donald Nicholson-Smith (1974; Oxford, Blackwell, 1991)
A key work on the philosophy of space in modernity.

Marcus, Laura (ed.), *Sigmund Freud's The Interpretation of Dreams: New Interdisciplinary Essays* (Manchester, Manchester University Press, 1999)
Essays which give a varied sense of Freud's text as a piece of modern

writing, including Robert Young's proposal that *Interpretation* 'was a
Gothic novel'.

Said, Edward W., *Culture and Imperialism* (London, Vintage, 1994)

Fascinating essays on Western cultural hegemony, including 'Two
Visions in *Heart of Darkness*' and 'Yeats and Decolonization'.

Stonebridge, Lyndsey, *The Destructive Element: British Psychoanalysis and
Modernism* (Basingstoke: Macmillan, 1998)

Good contextualizing of the complex and sometimes fraught encounter
between psychoanalysis and modernism in Britain.

Thacker, Andrew, *Moving Through Modernity: Space and Geography in
Modernism* (Manchester, Manchester University Press, 2003)

Very helpful survey of the spatial imperative in literary modernism.

Torgovnick, Marianna, *Gone Primitive: Savage Intellects, Modern Lives*
(Chicago and London, University of Chicago Press, 1990)

Lively essays on various modes of primitivism.

Whitworth, Michael H., *Einstein's Wake: Relativity, Metaphor, and
Modernist Literature* (Oxford, Oxford University Press, 2001)

Very interesting study of the understanding and appropriation of the
new physics in the work of writers such as Conrad, Eliot, Lawrence and
Woolf.

5
Modernist spaces

As we have seen in the section 'Time and space' in the previous chapter, modernism involves a bold rethinking of the common-sense conception of space as a neutral, empty vessel. Instead, space is assigned qualities which make it an active or positive entity. Correspondences can thus be traced between, for example, Einstein's theory of the material warping of space, and Picasso's refusal to identify space merely as background or context, in paintings such as *Les Demoiselles d'Avignon* (Figure 1 p. 5), or in the 1912 collage *Guitar*, where space seems to come into its own as a material rather than as an absence into which objects are placed. In a key theoretical work such as Henri Lefebvre's *The Production of Space* (1974), this new conceptualization of space is given a social and political dimension: spaces are *produced*, historically and ideologically, by different societies at different times.

This chapter examines the spaces of modernism from three perspectives: cities and their design; architecture; and sculpture. By exploring links between these perspectives, we will ask to what extent any distinguishing features of modernist 'spatial practice' can be identified. You might begin to think about the taken-for-granted status of the spaces you live and work in, and to consider how far these might be read through the lenses of modernism and modernity. How has modernism affected our experience of space, of built environments and of the cultural artefacts we shape and place within them?

Metropolis

> I love walking in London . . . Really, it's better than walking in the
> country.
>
> (Virginia Woolf, Mrs Dalloway (1925))

In examining the spaces of modernism, the city is an almost obligatory starting point. Along with many other commentators, Raymond Williams sees a 'decisive link' between the rise of historical avant-gardes and the production of a new social space in the form of the late nineteenth and early twentieth-century major cities or metropolises. In European capitals such as London, Paris and Berlin, quantitative change – rapid increases in population, which reached over 5, 3 and 2 million respectively by 1910 – becomes qualitative change, the production of new kinds of urban environment. The emergence of an international network of capitalism, driven by industrial and technological development, is crucial to this change, and highlights two typically modernist kinds of paradox:

- *Expansion/compression.* The city expands physically, yet becomes 'smaller' (David Harvey's 'time-space compression') as it partakes in a network of other centres between which new travel and communication technologies ease the flow of capital, ideas and people.
- *Planning/unplanned development.* Major late nineteenth-century transformations in cities such as Paris and Vienna were planned developments, applying principles of reason and geometry to the task of modernization. But the dynamism of expansion and the multifarious energies of different cultural identities inevitably gave an edge of unpredictability and irrationalism to the patterns by which the metropolis grew.

In propelling her protagonist Clarissa Dalloway into the streets of London to buy flowers for her party that evening, Woolf celebrates a counter-pastoral experience of metropolitan modernism that most of us now simply take for granted. Yet walking in the city is a relatively recent historical phenomenon, in its early days represented overwhelmingly in terms of the strange and 'unnatural'. This narrative can be traced back at least to the Romanticism of William Wordsworth's early draft of *The Prelude*, in which the

Wordsworthian persona, walking in London, finds a 'second-sight procession' of strangers passing before his eyes: every face is a mystery to him,

> And all the ballast of familiar life,
> The present, and the past; hope, fear; all stays,
> All laws of acting, thinking, speaking man
> Went from me, neither knowing me, nor known.

(Book VII, 1805)

Charles Baudelaire was to elaborate on this in terms of the symbolical proximity of the terms 'multitude' and 'solitude': we are far more intensely alone in the modern urban crowd, where we know no one, than we would be in a village, where people are far fewer but more likely to be intimately known. Thomas Hardy's *Tess of the D'Urbervilles* (1891) likens the statistical tendency of rural populations to drift towards the cities in the second half of the nineteenth century to 'the tendency of water to flow uphill when forced by machinery', an image taken up in the 'Unreal city' section of T.S. Eliot's *The Waste Land*, in which an automatized crowd of commuters 'Flowed up the hill and down King William Street,/ To where St Mary Woolnoth kept the hours/With a dead sound on the final stroke of nine'. This section of Eliot's poem declares an explicit linguistic debt to the work of Baudelaire, whose poetry and critical writing in the 1850s, perhaps more than any other literary source, helps to establish and explore the metropolitan character of modernism.

Invoking Baudelaire in this context, however, highlights another need to unsettle the taken-for-grantedness of walking in the city. In his widely influential essay 'The Painter of Modern Life' (1863), Baudelaire laid down a definition of the *flâneur*, a new sociological type of urban 'stroller' whose *modus vivendi* was to inhabit the city streets 'botanizing upon the asphalt'. In the essay Baudelaire bases this definition on two figures: 'M.C.G.' (the painter Constantin Guys), the lover of life who loves crowds more than anything else, moving into them '*as though into an enormous reservoir of electricity*', yet at the same time acting as a '*kaleidoscope*', mirroring the crowd's bewildering complexity, 'an ego athirst for the non-ego'; and the more general figure of the dandy or dandyism, an '*institution outside the law*', a man of leisure who possesses the time and money to inhabit and explore all aspects of the city, cultivating an egoistic and quasi-aristocratic originality to the extent of constituting, if somewhat ironically, '*the last flicker of heroism in decadent ages*' (see Koloctroni *et al.*, *Modernism*, pp. 102–8). The *flâneur* quickly becomes a symbol of untrammelled modernity, a freedom closely associated with the complex space of the city itself. Yet modernity and its freedom are, in that sense, emphatically gendered: the *flâneur* is masculine, for 'there could', as Rita Felski explains, 'be no female equivalent of the *flâneur*, given that any woman who loitered in the streets of the nineteenth-century city was likely to be taken for a prostitute' ('The Gender of Modernity', in eds S. Ledger, J.McDonagh and J. Spencer, *Political Gender*, London, Routledge, 1994, p. 145). What is walking the streets for the *flâneur* becomes street-walking for the woman. Woolf's writing, in *Mrs Dalloway* and in the closely related essay 'Street Haunting: A London Adventure' (1930), explores the more revolutionary possibility, though one made more viable, at least for the bourgeois woman, by changes in Britain after the First World War, of women's occupation of urban public space. In recent modernist studies, an important debate has emerged around the possibility or visibility of the feminine *flâneuse*, and along with Felski's essay you might consult here Elizabeth Wilson, 'The Invisible Flâneur', *New Left Review* 191 (Jan./Feb. 1992) and Janet Wolff, 'The Invisible Flâneuse: Women and the Literature of Modernity', *Theory, Culture and Society* 2:3 (1985).

What Malcolm Bradbury characterizes as the 'push and pull, attraction and repulsion' of the city in modernism is more critically articulated by Raymond Williams. A dominant 'ideology' of the modern city insists, Williams notes, upon the dehumanizing effects of enforced alienation and anonymity, the individual lost in the crowd. Behind this ideology we can trace the emergence of theories, combining psychological and sociological perspectives, which emphasize the distinctive and unprecedented mental characteristics of the people of the modern metropolis – for example, Gustav Le Bon's *Psychology of Crowds* (1895), and Georg Simmel's influential essay 'The Metropolis and Mental Life' (1903). Among the main effects of the 'rapidly shifting stimulations of the nerves' experienced in the city, Simmel numbers the *blasé* outlook, an attitude of reserve, and above all an 'essentially intellectualistic character' intimately related to the money economy and expressed in calculation, reducing the acts of daily life to a weighing and measuring of people and things in a manner of 'unrelenting hardness' (Kolocotroni *et al.*, *Modernism*, pp. 52–6).

Simmel's vision of metropolitan space is not however simply that of atomized individuals circulating in a void. He also identifies a 'totality of effects' within which the individual is not confined to the limits of their own physical body but 'embraces, rather, the totality of meaningful effects which emanates from him temporally and spatially' (Kolocotroni *et al.*, *Modernism*, p. 57). This sense of the city as a new *kind* of space, characterized by totalities and collectivities, is what informs Raymond Williams' much more positive alternative to the ideology of the modern city. For Williams, metropolises such as Paris, Vienna, Berlin, London and New York, offering themselves as 'transnational capitals of an art without frontiers', were characterized by 'a complexity and a sophistication of social relations, supplemented in the most important cases – Paris, above all – by exceptional liberties of expression' (*The Politics of Modernism: Against the New Conformists*, ed. T. Pinkney, London, Verso, 1989, pp. 34, 44). Thus, he argues, while the cities are centres of orthodoxy, both 'capitalist and imperialist' and the location of official artistic culture as enshrined in museums and academies, their growing 'miscellaneity' (fuelled primarily by immigration and networks of transport and communication) constitutes an opening-out of the space, enabling the formation of small groups and pockets of resistance and dissent. Famously, in the Swiss city of Zurich in 1916, the street Spiegelgasse housed Vladimir Lenin at number 6 and the Dadaist Cabaret Voltaire at number 1 ('Is Dadaism something of a mark and gesture of a counterplay to Bolshevism?', asked Hugo Ball) (Williams, *The Politics of Modernism*, p. 81).

The modern city is, then, an unprecedented space, both in its confrontation of the individual with their aloneness and singularity, and in its facilitation of new forms of culture and politics through openness, encounter and combination. It is not simply a *repository* of a universal human experience, but gives rise, it seems, to particular

human types and modes of behaviour – the bourgeois woman shopping in the department store; the *flâneur*; the clerk – which in turn
act on and shape metropolitan space.

Behind this image of an exhilarating if enervating openness,
however, it is important to note a history of the conscious design,
and hence control, or *development*, of metropolitan space, which is
equally a part of the narrative of modernity. Key instances are the
cities of Paris, Vienna and New York, around which there is a rich
critical literature concerning the implications of modern spatial
practice.

- *Paris and 'Haussmannization'*. The modern romantic image of
  elegant Parisian boulevards is indebted to a process of transformation in the 1860s. After the revolutions of 1848, Napoleon
  III sought to consolidate the bourgeois ascendancy in Second
  Empire France by reconfiguring the capital city. The Prefect
  of Paris, Baron Haussmann, masterminded this over seventeen
  years through the demolition of vast tracts of medieval Paris and
  the displacement of its inhabitants to new working-class enclaves,
  such as Belleville, on the outskirts of the city. Replacing the
  narrow lanes and close-knit, irregular buildings of the medieval
  period, Haussmann's modernized space included: wide, straight
  and spacious 'boulevards', surfaced with macadam rather than
  stone, allowing for the first time swift road passage across the
  city, ease of access and the possibility of effective surveillance
  (in other words, nowhere to hide); effective systems of sewerage
  and water supply; open spaces in the form of parks and public
  squares; the creation of a new commercial sector and new patterns of consumption, based around the shops and cafés that
  took advantage of the spaciousness of buildings and pavements.
  T.J. Clark writes that, on Haussmann's own estimation, 'the new
  boulevards and open spaces displaced 350,000 people; 12,000 of
  them were uprooted by the building of the Rue de Rivoli and Les
  Halles alone'; by 1870, 'one-fifth of the streets in central Paris
  were his creation; he had spent 80 million francs on sewers, and
  2.5 billion francs on the city as a whole; at the height of the fever
  for reconstruction, one in five Parisian workers was employed in
  the building trade' (*The Painting of Modern Life: Paris in the Art*

of Manet and His Followers, London, Thames & Hudson, 1985, p. 37). This history allows us to rethink Paris, still regarded by many people as the 'cultural capital' of the world, in the terms of Marx's concept of modernity as 'creative destruction'. For Clark, Haussmann's boulevards 'laid waste the city', while for David Harvey they embody 'the tyranny of the straight line' or, in the words of Henri Lefebvre, 'an authoritarian and brutal spatial practice'.

- *Vienna and the 'Ringstrasse'*. At the same time as the Haussmannization of Paris, a very similar development was taking place in Vienna. Following the revolution of 1848, liberals won concessions from the Imperial centre and came into ascendancy in the city. Viennese population and commercial growth doubled between 1840 and 1870. From around 1860, the transformation began of a circular space separating the old city from the growing outer suburbs, which had previously served the functions of fortification and defence. The *Ringstrasse* became a municipal space of public administrative buildings, galleries and dwellings which, according to Carl Schorske, 'surpassed in visual impact any urban reconstruction of the nineteenth century – even that of Paris' (*Fin-de-siècle Vienna: Politics and Culture*, Cambridge, Cambridge University Press, 1981, p. 26). As in Paris, a progressive modernity was expressed both in democratic emancipation and in the containment of resistance – the installation of an unprecedented public utility system, and the construction of wide thoroughfares to 'maximise mobility for troops and to minimise barricading opportunities for potential rebels' (Schorske, *Fin-de-siècle* pp. 30–1). The precise spatial character of the *Ringstrasse* also appears, in Schorske's fascinating reading, as a means of embodying a collective public spirit while preserving the essential individualism of liberal politics. The thoroughfares constitute a 'vast, continuous circular space', almost self-sufficient in the sense that linking streets to the inner city and outer suburbs are almost negligible; buildings are placed in clusters or in isolation rather than in organic relationship; lines of trees serve to divert the eye from the height of the buildings and to emphasise horizontality instead. Schorske writes: 'The several functions represented in the buildings – political, educational, and cultural – are expressed in spatial organisation as equivalents. Alternate centres of visual interest, they are related to each other not in any direct way but only in their lonely confrontation of the great circular artery, which carries the citizen from one building to another, as from one aspect of life to another. The public buildings float unrecognised in a spatial medium whose only stabilising element is an artery of men in motion' (*Fin-de-siècle*, p. 36).

- New York and Robert Moses: It seems a dramatic shift from the incipient nineteenth-century modernisms of Vienna and Paris (Benjamin's 'capital of the nineteenth century') to the exemplary modernism of New York in the twentieth century. Yet comparisons have been drawn between Haussmannization and the work of Robert Moses in New York from the late 1920s through to the 1960s. In a personal, heartfelt chapter, Marshall Berman recounts his horror at the devastation wreaked in his native Bronx by Moses' automotive expressway of the 1960s, imposing a brutally aggressive extension of modernity over a built environment which was already felt to be elegantly 'modern' by inhabitants such as Berman. This is seen by Berman as a warped mutation of an originally benign utopian project on Moses' part, typified by his work in the late 1920s and 1930s on New York parks. The first of these, Jones Beach State Park, opened in Long Island in 1929, and was, Berman contends, 'a public space radically different from anything that had existed anywhere before', its abstract clarity of horizontal space and form reminiscent of 'the diagrammatic paintings of Mondrian', and broken only by two Art Deco bathhouses and a water tower, the latter thematizing the effect of a modern skyscraper (Berman, *All That Is Solid Melts into Air*, pp. 296–7). By 1934, many other sites of pastoralized renewal existed across New York thanks to Moses and to the Roosevelt New Deal emphasis on public finance. By the 1950s, however, Moses had developed an ingenuity for manipulating the public authority system so that municipal funding could coincide with the aspirations of private developers. As the 'power broker' (Harvey, *The Condition of Postmodernity*, p. 69, following R. Caro) of this process, Moses oversaw a system of highways and bridges which cut through the lived environment of New York, ruthlessly dismantling communities and effectively subordinating the space of the city to the transport network that now traversed it. We see, in other words, how the 'development of modernity has made the modern city itself old-fashioned, obsolete' (Berman, *All That Is Solid Melts into Air*, pp. 306–7).

(A coda, however, to Berman's account of New York modernity. In selecting his own community and the impact of Moses' work within a general transformation on the lines of the International Style of Architecture, Berman's account does not contain any references to the emergence of two key communities of avant-garde modernism in specific areas of New York: Harlem and Greenwich Village. Alain Locke in the key anthology *The New Negro* (1925) explains that Harlem emerged from the post-Civil War migrations that took black Americans 'not only . . . toward the North and the Central Midwest, but city-ward and to the great centers of industry', but that its metropolitan character radically diversified the notion of a homogeneous negro identity: 'It has attracted the African, the West Indian, the Negro American; has brought together the Negro of the North and the Negro of the South; the man from the city and the man from the town or village; the peasant, the student, the business man, the professional man, artist, poet, musician, adventurer and worker, preacher and criminal, exploiter and social outcast. Each group has come with its own separate motives and its own special ends, but their greatest experience has been in the finding of one another.' The result is a creative metropolitan environment comparable to those inhabited by James Joyce or Franz Kafka: 'Harlem has the same role to play for the New Negro as Dublin has had for the New Ireland or Prague for the New Czechoslovakia' (*The New Negro*, in Kolocotroni *et al.*, *Modernism*, pp. 413–14). Look back in this book to chapter 4, the section on primitivism, and ahead to chapter 8, the section on music, for a sense of the importance of literature and jazz in the Harlem Renaissance.)

An important paradox re-emerges. If the metropolis fosters the explosion of heterodox artistic forms and ideas we call modernism, it can appear to do so in the face of the modernization of urban space since the mid-nineteenth century. The rational planning and regulation of Haussmann's Paris or the Viennese *Ringstrasse*, which we associate with *modernity*, acts as a kind of bourgeois incitement to *modernism*, as if the latter arose to contest the heavily controlling and anti-revolutionary rationality of modernity. This is evident in the contrasting visions of Viennese urban designers Camillo Sitte and Otto Wagner, whose reactions to *Ringstrasse* Vienna were, in the first case, to endorse free-form irregularity and a return to spaces with a human, communal and organic connection and, in the second case, to outdo the quickly superseded elegance of the *Ringstrasse* in the pursuit of a stripped-down, purely functional, utilitarian and technologically contemporary aesthetic (see Schorske's account in the chapter 'The *Ringstrasse*, its Critics, and the Birth of Urban Modernism', in *Fin-de-siècle*).

Yet, at the same time, many aspects of spatial modernism of the twentieth century, from Bauhaus design to Moses' New York, can be read as continuations of the rational impulses of 1860s city design. These are not simply intractable contradictions, but signs again of the fact that modernism can be 'modern' (rational, developmental, progressive, planned) or 'anti-modern' (irrational, unpredictable) depending on the instance. Let us take this up in our discussion of architecture and the comparison, which follows, of two specific modernist buildings.

Architecture

'Building is the ultimate goal of all artistic work.' This statement, from Walter Gropius' Bauhaus manifesto of 1919, shows how the concept of 'building' attained an expanded significance in artistic modernism, encapsulating a constructivist spirit and a belief that modernist art should be practical in orientation and capable of intervening in modern life for the better. Much of this aspiration became focused on domestic space, and the figure of the home. In the same year as Gropius' manifesto, Sigmund Freud's short essay on the uncanny (*Unheimlich*) subtly located the primal dread associated with this concept in the proximity of the 'homely' and 'unhomely', while the French thinker Gaston Bachelard was later to theorize the powerful role of the house in imagination, dream and the workings of the unconscious (*The Poetics of Space*, 1957). Le Corbusier wrote in 1923 that the 'problem' of the house had 'not yet been stated', and that as a result 'we are to be pitied for living in unworthy houses, since they ruin our health and our *morale*' (*Towards a New Architecture*, p. 10, 18).

Let us stage a comparative reading of two early modernist houses, the Casa Batllo (built 1904–6, Figure 13) in Barcelona by the architect Antoni Gaudi (1852–1926), and the Steiner House (1910, Figure 14) in Vienna by Adolf Loos (1870–1933). Like many of Gaudi's projects, Casa Batllo was the renovation of an already-existing building and façade. But Gaudi's transformation distinguished the house utterly from its surroundings. You may note the following features:

- asymmetry, particularly in the hat-shaped roof and in the disposition of the balconies;
- irregularity: windows of different shapes and sizes;
- balconies like theatrical masks or birds' nests;
- bulging pillars as if in a state of plasticity;
- other unpredictable forms of ornamentation, such as the upper-left tower;
- stone carved and polished until it looks like soft moulded clay; and
- few straight lines and no sharp edges or corners, leaving a soft and flowing feel.

The façade is decorated with coloured plates and tiles that glitter in the sun. In the interior, wavy, undulating lines and polished surfaces of various materials create a cave-like and hallucinatory effect. The impression is of the transformation of a building into a living, if somewhat fantastic, organism.

Compare Loos' Steiner house:

- strict regularity of form;
- symmetry of windows;
- concrete without decoration; and
- angularity.

Figure 13 Antoni Gaudi, Casa Batllo (1904–6)

Figure 14 Adolf Loos, Steiner House (1910)

STOP and THINK

- Which design do you prefer, and why? What are the criteria for your decision? Is it possible or desirable to make a distinction between aesthetic and functional criteria, and to venture two judgements based on these different criteria?
- Which of these architectural styles has had most impact on the built environments we inhabit today? Can you think of any buildings that are comparable in either case?
- Think now in terms of economic rather than artistic criteria. How would these houses compare in terms of cost of production, and what might the implications be for their relative social and economic potential as architectural models that might be reproduced?

This comparison may well seem to you a rather biased exercise from the start, if as I suspect – though I stand to be corrected here – you 'prefer' Gaudi's Casa Batllo, because of its sensuous, vivacious beauty. Because of the variety and unexpectedness of the design, it is certainly easier to the untrained eye to identify distinctive features in the Gaudi house. Yet the style – or anti-style? – of Loos' house is more familiar to us; and, indeed, is a prototype of a form which became, if anything did, the 'official' architectural language of modernism, as well as a powerful influence on the built environment of the twentieth century.

The Steiner house was a forerunner of a broader architectural movement which, through various influences, linked modernist building to the concept of 'functionalism' – that is, to the idea that the form of a building should not be imposed through some prior conception of a decorative style, but rather should follow simply from the functions the buildings perform for the humans living in them. The relevant influences would include:

- The Dutch journal *De Stijl*, articulating a particularly purist vision of the potential of abstract design for transforming human life, dominated by architectural theory in Theo van Doesburg, but also involving the painter Piet Mondrian.

- Russian Constructivism, for example the work of Tatlin (see chapter 3), with its strong connection between architectural function and revolutionary social regeneration
- The most prominent individual figure, the French painter and architect known as Le Corbusier (Charles-Edouard Jeanneret-Gris), who began architectural practice in Paris in 1922 but who was already known for his collaborations with the painter Amedée Ozenfant (1886–1966) on the manifesto *After Cubism* (1918) and the journal *L'Esprit nouveau* (The New Spirit) (1920–5), the latter title explained as 'a spirit of construction and synthesis, shaped by a lucid idea'. Slightly later works such as *Towards an Architecture* (1923) and *Urbanisme* (1925, translated into English as *The City of Tomorrow*) established Le Corbusier as the key theorist and polemicist of modernist architecture. His buildings, which can seem relatively few in comparison to his theoretical influence, include houses such as Maison la Roche, Paris (1922–4), the Villa Savoye, Poissy (1929–31), religious establishments such as the Dominican Convent 'La Tourette' at Eveux-sur-L'Arbesle and the Ronchamp chapel of Notre Dame du Haut (1950–5), and the municipal mass housing commission outside Marseilles, the Unité d'Habitation (1945–52).
- The direction taken by the Bauhaus under the influence of Walter Gropius, and encapsulated in the construction of the flagship Dessau building, to which the Bauhaus relocated in 1926.
- The later influence of the Bauhaus under the leadership of Ludwig Mies van der Rohe, who after the demise of the Bauhaus became the leading exponent of the modern skyscraper, exploiting the combined constructive possibilities of reinforced concrete, steel and sheet glass.
- *Neue Sachlichkeit* in Germany, signalling a reclamation of mimesis and objectivity in art.
- The formation in Switzerland in 1928 of the International Congress of Modern Architecture (CIAM), with Le Corbusier as a prime mover.
- In 1932, the exhibition 'The International Style', curated by Henry-Russell Hitchcock and Philip Johnson at the Museum of Modern Art, designed to introduce European architectural modernism to American audiences. This in conjunction with

bodies such as CIAM consolidated the association of modernist architecture with 'international style', in other words with a universalism which transcended national boundaries and flattened out local particularities.

The pre-eminence of functionalism and the International Style raises a number of critical questions concerning the spatial practices of modernism. From the outset, for example, it is clear that modernism here connotes a lack of adornment, a bareness or sparseness linked to *emancipation*. Adolf Loos again led the way, in a famous article (1908) in which he stigmatized ornament as 'excrement', not simply criminal in nature but a kind of 'degeneracy' equivalent to scrawling obscenities on toilet walls (see Kolocotroni *et al.*, *Modernism*, pp. 77–81). Cultural evolution was held to be directly dependent upon the repudiation of ornament, breaking the necessity for humanity to be 'kept down in the slavery of decoration.' The moral piety of this position is expressed in the frequency of the term 'purity' in such contexts; 'Purism' was for example the term used by Le Corbusier and Ozenfant to designate and endorse a form of painting that would restore a machine-like purity of representation to natural objects after the supposed distortions and abstractions of Cubism.

It is therefore implied that people would be emancipated by functionalist modernism, as if through the application of a universal system of democracy. In the words of the *De Stijl* manifesto of 1918, 'The old is connected with the individual. The new is connected with the universal' (Harrison and Wood, *Art in Theory*, p. 278). Reinforced concrete becomes, on this perspective, the modernist material par excellence, with a rich metaphorical significance: like macadam, the road surfacing material central to Haussmann's Paris, it is cheaply and easily made and, like a levelling agent, applicable to all building in all social and cultural contexts. Architectural historians have not been slow to link these high modernist ideals to models of classicism. 'Le Corbusier fell in love with reinforced concrete', writes Stephen Gardiner, 'because its structural frame freed space in the way that the Greek column and beam had previously done' (*Introduction to Architecture*, Oxford, Leisure Books, 1983, p. 117). This is a comparison with an original locus of democracy as well as with an ancient ideal of beauty. However, as Bruno Zevi points out, what Le Corbusier discovered on a Greek expedition as a young man was a 'heretical' *anti*-classicism differing markedly from the images and ideas of Greece perpetuated by the 'Hellenism' of the European *beaux-arts* tradition (not one Greek temple, Zevi maintains, has 'the proportions institutionalized in the abstract idea of the "Greek temple"'). Instead, along with urban grids similar to those of the modern metropolis, Le Corbusier found subtly ornate mouldings informed by 'a vibrant Greek arithmetic' and 'isolated volumes, autonomous prisms in the light, freely situated over an irregular landscape and cast in elementary geometrical schemes' (Bruno Zevi, *The Modern Language of Architecture*, New York, Da Capo Press, 1994, pp. 29, 98, 102).

This free and irregular siting of 'isolated volumes' suggests something of the emancipation implicit in the interior as well as the exterior of modernist buildings. The aim here was to challenge static hierarchies in the domestic interior – drawing room, dining room, kitchen, for example – and to dismantle the position of mastery implicit in a three-dimensional perspective (parallel to the unpicking of single-point perspective in painting). The aim as articulated in *De Stijl* theory, writes Zevi, and as exemplified in Gropius' Bauhaus building at Dessau, was to free space by 'decomposing' it, breaking up the 'box' into panels, and separating the joinings between planes – ceiling, walls, floor – so that light could penetrate the interior. 'Once the box has been dismembered', writes Zevi, 'the planes no longer form closed volumes, containers of finite spaces. Instead the rooms become fluid and join up and flow in a moving continuum', and 'there is no vantage point from which you can grasp the whole' (p. 31).

Notice here how the advantages of the regulated functionalist space seem to turn into their opposites – fluidity, movement – comparable perhaps with Le Corbusier's gratification at the unpredictabilities within classical Greek architecture. At the heart of continuing debates around modernist architecture is the question of how far the democratic emancipation of functionalism is an *idealized* concept which contrasts with the actual experience of living in those spaces. In a very practical sense, functionalism realized its utopian potential by fulfilling the widespread need in post-First and Second World War European societies for low-cost, mass-produced housing on a large scale. John Willett shows how this applied in particular to central Europe, first in Vienna from 1923, where socialist architects pioneered a scheme of mass social rehousing, and then from 1925 on a larger scale across Weimar Germany, and in particular in the cities of Frankfurt, Berlin and Stuttgart. While the ideas of Le Corbusier, Gropius and Mies van der Rohe lay behind many of the buildings and estates that appeared with great rapidity in this period, functionalism came to dominate because, as Willett puts it, of 'the more humdrum activities of countless lesser architects and, above all, its harnessing to a major social aim' (*The New Sobriety*, p. 124). As part of the regeneration of German society, the architecture of vast estates such as Ernst May's Romerstadt, north of Frankfurt, was accompanied by a movement of subjective health, fitness and efficiency, as if the function of the new domestic space was to reacquaint people with the outdoors, sunlight and open space. Wandering round the estate, the French sculptor Maillol commented that 'until now, everything I have seen of modern architecture has been cold; but this is not cold – on the contrary.' His companion Count Kessler confirmed that 'this architecture only expressed the same new sense of life that was turning the young to sport and nakedness' (quoted in Willett, *The New Sobriety*, p. 132).

On the other hand, it has become common to associate functionalist spaces with a joyless uniformity and brutalism from which ordinary people required liberation, demonstrating thereby the uneasy proximity between utopia and dystopia. Commentators often cite the view of Charles Jencks, a key theorist of the postmodern in architecture, that the dynamiting of the Pruitt-Igoe housing estate in St Louis, Missouri, on 15 July 1972, was an iconic moment of modernist failure, though Harvey has argued that social conditions were at least as responsible for this failure as the architecture itself. Critiques can be found in Prince Charles' consistent campaign for a return to brick-based vernacular building, starting from his notorious characterization of the new extension to London's National Gallery as a 'monstrous carbuncle'; or in Jane Jacobs' classic account, *The Death and Life of Great American Cities* (1961), where the corporate strangulation of the diverse life of cities such as Baltimore is aesthetically labelled as a 'Great Blight of Dullness.'

Functionalism can thus be seen to inform both the wrongheaded rational egalitarianism of the modern housing estate, creating ugliness and uniformity, and, in Mies van der Rohe's breathtaking skyscrapers of Chicago and New York for example, sublime vertical monuments to the power and competitive inequalities of corporate capitalism. Henri Lefebvre traces this phenomenon directly back to the Bauhaus around 1920, and the discovery of 'a new conception, a global concept, of space', showing crucial practical connections 'between industrialization and urbanization, between workplaces and dwelling places.' As it was in the nature of such a conception of space to be adopted in a programmatic way, Lefebvre provocatively concludes that the Bauhaus was therefore responsible for 'the worldwide, homogeneous and monotonous architecture of the state, whether capitalist or socialist', and 'an authoritarian and brutal spatial practice', involving 'the effective application of the analytic spirit in and through dispersion, division and segregation' (Lefebvre, *The Production of Space*, pp. 124–6, 308). This is echoed in Willett's argument that the increasing cultural and political 'sobriety' of the Weimar period provided amenable conditions for Hitler's National Socialists from 1933 onwards.

For this reason, it is important to remember that modernism includes Gaudi as well as Bauhaus, and that the 'official' association of modernist architecture with a universal 'tyranny of the straight line' might need to be modified. Recent work such as Elizabeth Darling's *Re-forming Britain: Narratives of Modernity before Reconstruction* (London, Routledge, 2006) and Romy Golan's *Modernity and Nostalgia: Art and Politics in France between the wars* (New Haven and London, Yale University Press, 1995) demonstrate that national and regional specificities were crucial to the reconstructive value of architecture and design in the inter-war years, including in the case of Golan's argument a movement in French art and design away from the machine aesthetic and towards a putatively more conservative and 'rusticizing' organicism without ever necessarily ceasing to be modernist. Gaudi's Catalan influence still reverberates, inspiring spatial practices which align more clearly with the dynamic and rebellious principles of aesthetic modernism – disorder, excess and spontaneity, for example. Nikolaus Pevsner initially excluded Gaudi, as a 'freak', from his very rationalistic account of the modern movement, *Pioneers of Modern Design* (1936), only to feel obliged to include him in a second edition. Recalling here the dictum that there are no straight lines in nature, it is interesting to consider the role of the nature–artifice dialectic in modernist architecture, and in particular the tendency for the organic to act as a shifting centre of value. Gaudi's work is variously described as Expressionist or Mannerist, the latter implying an undoing of classical styles through an exaggerated use of them. From Loos through the Bauhaus to the International Style, it could be claimed that the removal of artifice and ornamentation constituted a return to the simplicity of natural form. However, against the accusations of gratuitous artifice to which Gaudi was prone, it might equally be claimed that the florid, even monstrous excrescences of his buildings follow a principle of *natural* growth. Conversely, the radical pursuit of functionalist purity can itself be seen as the pursuit of a *style* (of anti-style). This explains the division in the movement after 1928 between functionalists and 'formalists', as discussed in Tim Benton's excellent survey essay 'Building Utopia' (2006). In a further turn, Gaudi can then appear to illustrate the propensity of nature for instability and unpredictability, his distorted extensions of turn-of-the-century Art Nouveau distasteful to official modernism, yet embraced by the Surrealists, who found in the workings of the unconscious a truer version of natural productivity than anything to be found in Enlightenment reason.

Perhaps fittingly, Gaudi's crowning achievement, the extraordinary Sagrada Familia Roman Catholic cathedral in Barcelona, begun in 1903, is still growing, and may always remain unfinished, a testament to an imagination that could produce, in the words of Robert Hughes, 'a large building that denied its own rigidity'. In Hughes' colourful account, the Sagrada is 'Desire made concrete', a Dalí-esque 'soft architecture, juicy architecture, the architecture of ecstasy' (*The Shock of the New*, p. 237). Henri Lefebvre similarly stresses that Gaudi 'did for architecture what Lautréamont did for poetry: he put it through the bath of madness'; but in a more complex and equivocal reading, Lefebvre notes that a 'naturalness boldly identified with divine transcendence' can also turn into a 'mockery' of that which it seeks to revere: the Sagrada is a 'risible consecration' in that it 'causes modern space and the archaic space of nature to corrupt one another' (Lefebvre, *The Production of Space*, p. 232).

Alongside Gaudi in this emphasis on modernist space and the 'natural', though with more apparent proximity to the official modernist tradition, we might place the American architect Frank Lloyd Wright (1867–1959). Wright had already completed a substantial body of work, including the Unity Church at Oak Park, 1906 (which influenced De Stijl) and the Robie House, Chicago (1908–9), by 1910, when his selected writings were published in Europe and began to be widely influential. 'Organic architecture', for Wright, signified a design style of intimate relationship between inhabitants, buildings and environment, rather than an adherence to 'nature' as such. However, a recurrent feature of his buildings was their permeability to natural surroundings, achieved through the use of traditional materials – wood, brick, stone – and an aesthetic of the liberation of interior space, using cantileverage to free up corners so that light could enter, and reducing walls to surfaces, wherever they were not load-bearing, in order to minimize the distinctions between inside and outside. The essential change, he wrote, was 'from box to free plan and the new reality that is *space* instead of matter . . . Space may now go out or come in where life is being lived, space as a component of it' (quoted in Zevi, *Modern Language of Architecture*, p. 40). Wright's buildings tend to have a strong horizontality, and their solid angularity can superficially recall the International Style. Wright was far more influenced, however, by traditional Japanese domestic architecture than by the imperatives of technological modernity, and such solidity could be illusory: a dematerializing impulse in Wright, the displacement of matter by space, had an ironic correlative in the notorious physical fragility of some of his designs. Among the stories surrounding the magnificent Fallingwater house at Bear Run, Pennsylvania (1939), perched on a rock ledge above a waterfall, it is said that Wright finally dismantled the scaffolding himself, because the builders did not share his confidence about the house's stability, and indeed that certain supports were added to the building by the engineer and without Wright's knowledge!

'Organic architecture', wrote Wright, 'is the architecture of democratic freedom'. Despite its associations with, or appropriation by, oppressive state technocracy, modernist architecture is consistently informed by this utopian view that the renewed disposition of space can enable healthier and better lives. Despite the prevalence of 'functionalism' as a descriptive category, principles of natural harmony and aesthetic beauty remained central, unexpungeable principles for individual architects, albeit often appearing unfamiliar guises. Le Corbusier's chapel of Notre Dame du Haut, Ronchamp, France (1950–5), with its curving, boat-like roof seemingly lifted clear of the supporting walls, encapsulates these principles, as if they had always informed his work. Yet we should perhaps be wary of the tendency to think loosely, as it is easy to do, of the revolutionizing effect of modernist spatial practice on everyday life. The final words of Le Corbusier's manifesto *Towards a New Architecture*, published some six years after the Bolshevik Revolution, are: 'Architecture or Revolution. Revolution can be avoided.'

Sculpture

The turn taken by sculpture in modernism can be directly linked to the kind of narrative around modernist visual art presented in chapter 2. That is to say, there are key modes of sculpture – Cubist, Futurist, Constructivist, for example – which break the contract with classical representation and verisimilitude, within the same complex range of ideas and contexts that we explored in that chapter. Instead of reiterating that narrative here, however, I want to begin with what is particular to sculpture itself, which is that it involves the aesthetic manipulation of 'plastic' materials, as well as the disposition of the subsequent bodies in space. I also want to continue the emphasis on how we *read* modernism, by basing this section almost entirely around a very close analysis of certain sculptural objects by the American critic Rosalind Krauss, in her book *Passages in Modern Sculpture* (1977), a key source text to which I have already referred in this book. Krauss, who is Professor of Modern Art and Theory at Columbia University in New York, was, with Michael Fried, a very important, though not uncritical, interpreter of Clement Greenberg's work, and did much to introduce Greenberg's influential formalist theory of modernism as self-critique to a wider audience.

One of the first and perhaps curious points made by Krauss in *Passages in Modern Sculpture* is that sculpture is in fact about time as well as space. Time and space cannot be separated in the analysis of sculpture, she argues, because 'into any spatial organisation there will be folded an implicit statement about the nature of temporal experience' (p. 4). To understand this it might help to refer back to modernist architecture, and to the way in which the freeing of space in buildings affects the nature of human movement in them, movement being something that happens in time as well as in space. Bruno Zevi for example draws attention to Le Corbusier's concept of '*promenade architecturale*', architecture to walk through, as embodied in the famous Villa Savoye at Poissy, where a fully visible ramp cuts through the house from ground floor to roof garden. In this, and for example in this idea that every room in a house should have a different floor material, Zevi sees the potential of architecture to raise consciousness about the dynamic nature of modernity, and to empower inhabitants by alerting them to the possibility of shaping their own movement through time. Invoking Einstein's relativity, whereby any event is necessarily localized in time and in space, Zevi thus endorses 'open design that is constantly in process, invested with time consciousness, and unfinished' (*Modern Language of Architecture*, p. 53).

In a similar if more nuanced idea, Krauss sees modernist sculpture as informed by an awareness that it is located 'at the juncture between stillness and motion, time arrested and time passing' (p. 5). However, her account of the origins of modernist sculpture place a different emphasis on the value of movement in time. It begins with a comparison of two examples of *relief*, the mode of sculpture in which figures are seen to emerge from a flat or curved surface. These are the *Gates of Hell* (1880–1917) by Auguste Rodin (1840–1917), Krauss' initial reference point for modernism, and *La Marseillaise* (1833–6) by Francois Rudé, which is installed on the Arc de Triomph in Paris. The latter depicts the progressive, Enlightenment force of the French Revolution with a combination of mortal and mythical figures, a winged 'victory' flying over a lower frieze of soldiers; the former depicts scenes from Dante's *Divine Comedy*. Because both then claim to tell part of a story, this narrative impulse necessarily implies a sense of time.

Krauss shows how Rudé's combination of vertical and horizontal axes gives a very strong sense of movement, as if the lower figures emerge from the plane of the relief on the right hand side, curve outwards, and then recede back into the plane on the left. The viewer, facing the sculpture head-on, is thus persuaded that they have sufficient knowledge to make two kinds of deduction: one concerning the further unseen dimension of depth from which the figures have emerged, and another concerning the totality of the historical narrative of the Revolution, from the past into the future.

Rodin's *Gates*, by contrast (Figure 15), seem to obstruct wilfully the possibility of this knowledge, and instead to 'dam up the flow of sequential time'. Krauss observes that, while in their original conception the *Gates* were to consist of eight separate panels arranged in a narrative sequence, by the time of the third version the divisions between these panels had been almost completely erased, and a crucifix-like abstract figure, a 'large static icon', has been 'implanted in the midst of the dramatic space.' A number of other features work firmly against the possibility of deducing from the fragments of figures a deeper knowledge of some whole from which they have emerged. Only two of the many sets of figures relate to the *Divine Comedy* itself; Rodin uses exact repetitions of figures, as if to deny logical narrative sequence; the effect of shadow reveals the 'isolation and detachment' of the figures from the ground, so that the ground feels solid and opaque, rather than something we can see through; and to further emphasize the latter, the disposition of the figures appears warped, as if they do not obey the scientific logic of bodily structure. Summing up this comparison in terms of the overall appearance of the sculptures, we might say that where Rudé's composition has a tightly composed coherence and sense of direction and purpose, Rodin's appears random, fluid, asymmetrical and unfinished.

Krauss concludes that what is newly modernist about this strategy in Rodin's *Gates of Hell* is the way in which it contests a heroic but discredited model of Enlightenment rationality – a model she also finds signified, in Sergei Eisenstein's film of the Russian Revolution *October* (1927–8), in the figure of a mechanical peacock. Rodin's art is 'intensely hostile' to the rationalism that claims powers of prediction, and therefore mastery, based on knowledge

Figure 15 Auguste Rodin, *Gates of Hell* (1880–1917)

gained in the past. Thus, his work disrupts the linear coherence
of narrative time. Krauss aligns this with the phenomenological
theories of Edmund Husserl (1859–1938), for whom meaning is
'synchronous with experience, rather than necessarily prior to it'
(*Passages in Modern Sculpture*, p. 28), which in turn resonates with
the modernist thinking of Henri Bergson's 'creative evolution' or
Gertrude Stein's narrative techniques, where growth and production, whether of the personality, or of a work of art, or of wider
processes in nature, are strictly unforeseeable and unpredictable,
and can only be understood rationally and scientifically once they
have come into being.

Starting with her close reading of Rodin and Rudé's sculptures,
therefore, Krauss sets up favoured and unfavoured versions of
modernism which she then applies schematically to successive
instances of sculpture. Krauss evaluates in the sculptural representation of human or other material objects the same narrative
principle she found in relief sculpture. Henri Matisse, for example,
was strongly influenced by works of Rodin's such as *Flying Figure*
(1890–1) and *The Walking Man* (1900). These are fragmented figures, torsos without heads or entire limbs, and they plainly show
various marks – cuts, gouges, pinches and indentations – which
reveal the processes of clay modelling, without trying to efface these
by achieving a smoothed final product. The versions in bronze also
retained many of the accidents of the foundry-casting process, air
holes and bubbles for example. In Matisse's *The Serf* (1900–3),
the *Jeanette* series (1910–13), and in a series of reliefs of the naked
female *Back* (1909–31), a similarly rough-hewn, unfinished quality works towards a sense of the *unreadability* of the human frame.
Despite being reliefs, the *Backs* do not allow the viewer the mastery
of being able to deduce the front of the figure; walking around *The
Serpentine* (1909), a leaning woman whose limbs are plainly still
coils of clay, the viewer is constantly surprised by perspectives
which do not seem to obey anatomical rules, providing, as Krauss
notes of some of Rodin's work, 'no angle of view that would be "correct" – no vantage point that would give coherence to the figures'
(*Passages in Modern Sculpture*, p. 25). This is encapsulated in the
Austrian modernist poet Rilke's comment on Rodin's monument
to Balzac (1897), the head of which was as if '"living at the summit

of the figure like those balls that dance on jets of water"' (Krauss, *Passages in Modern Sculpture*, p. 31). The design style in question, which Krauss relates to the Art Nouveau heritage of Antonio Gaudi and Henry Van de Velde, is one that simply 'does not concern itself with the internal structure of an object' (Krauss, *Passages in Modern Sculpture*, p. 33).

We do not have to agree with Krauss' broad interpretation of a division between 'a sculpture of reason and a sculpture of situation' in order to appreciate the value of her close reading of individual works. Krauss' schema draws our attention again to a fundamental division in the way modernism might be theorized. On one side of the divide, modernism is seen to extend and refine the rationalist project of the Enlightenment, stressing intellectualism, analysis and the power of prediction. On the other side, it reveals the illusions and limitations of mastery though accumulated knowledge, and instead stresses the value of experience and intuition. Included in the latter alongside the work of the 'private' Rodin and Matisse, as Krauss' argument unfolds, is the sculpture of Pablo Picasso, Vladimir Tatlin, Constantin Brancusi (1876–1957), Marcel Duchamp and Alberto Giacometti. Included in the former are Umberto Boccioni (1882–1916), Naum Gabo (1890–1977), El Lizzitsky and László Moholy-Nagy.

To some extent Krauss' schema is about the orientation of identifiable movements. Despite being at opposite ends of the political spectrum, for example, Krauss sets Futurism and Constructivism together in their preoccupations with technology and industrial culture. This led to a shared view of sculpture, Krauss argues, as 'an investigatory tool in the service of knowledge', and to a disposition towards 'the intellectual domination of things' (*Passages in Modern Sculpture*, p. 45, 67). She is thus able to connect the Futurist Boccioni's *Development of a Bottle in Space* (1913, Figure 16) with the work of the Russian sculptor Naum Gabo, who taught at the Bauhaus between 1922 and 1932. Boccioni's *Development* is an abstract still life with, at its centre, a nested series of bottle-like shapes cut away at the front to reveal parts of the shells of the bottles slightly rotated in relation to each other. This, Krauss argues, gives the sculpture a strong core of absolute stillness around which various relative motions occur. The viewer is 'immobilized' in front of

Figure 16 Umberto Boccioni (1882-1916): *Development of a Bottle in Space* (1913)

the sculpture, yet at the same time freed into its 'conceptual space', which transcends the limitations of experienced space and allows the viewer the effect of being able to see all sides of the object at once, as if in the form of an ideal, 'disembodied' intelligence. Krauss writes:

> It attempts to outrun the partial information that any single view would allow a perceiver to have of that object. It seems to proceed from a notion of the poverty of brute perception since, in any one moment of seeing, much of the actual surface of the bottle will be obscured from view. By overcoming that poverty, the bottle can be known in terms of a full conceptual grasp of the thing. (*Passages in Modern Sculpture*, pp. 43–4)

Krauss then attributes the same 'conceptual penetration of form' to a series of heads sculpted initially out of cardboard and plywood by Gabo between 1915 and 1917, and to *Column* (1923), in which began to develop his signature material of transparent and coloured plastics. Gabo's technique of 'stereometry' cuts away the surface of the heads and faces to reveal a set of intersecting planes, giving a sense of the previously hidden volume of the heads, and their principle of structure, as geometric objects. In a similar way, the transparent planes of *Column* give access to the axial core of the object; the clear plastics are, Krauss asserts, the perfect material for Gabo's idealist or 'intellectualist' position.

At the same time, Krauss' counter-narrative of sculptors who contest this modernist will-to-power involves identifying luminous exceptions *within* movements. Futurism and Constructivism, she argues, build on the essentially Cubist impulse of art as 'research', a tool of knowledge. However, Picasso's Cubist reliefs of 1914, such as *Violin* and *Guitar* – crucial compositions in the emancipation from two-dimensional illusionism and the integration of a sculptural, mixed-material element into painting – depart tellingly from this principle. For Krauss, Picasso's reliefs do not announce the transcendence of limited perception by the absolute knowledge of conceptual space, but instead manage to display these various sculptural perspectives or languages side by side, so that their mutual relativity is dramatized. Similarly, within Russian Constructivism, Vladimir Tatlin's abstract *Corner Relief* of 1915 implicitly refutes Gabo's and Boccioni's idealism by denying the idea of a central axis and instead posing to the viewer a series of questions about balance: the composition is delicately suspended across the corner of a room, with a mixture of solid planes and supporting cables of extension. No comprehensive perspective, real or ideal, is allowed, and the actual siting of the work confirms an interest in the dynamics of actual rather than conceptual space. Translated into the heroic projection of Tatlin's *Monument to the Third International* (see the discussion in chapter 3), Krauss finds these principles in evidence in a transparent displacement of structure from interior to exterior, and in the differential rotations of the tower, providing the experience of movement in real time rather than (in the case of Gabo's *Column*) having past and future collapsed into a static summation of time as a totality. 'For Tatlin', Krauss concludes, 'technology is placed visibly at the service of a revolutionary ideology through which history might be shaped; for Gabo, it is a model of absolute knowledge through which the future is given rather than found' (*Passages in Modern Sculpture*, p. 62).

This emphasis on individual exceptions then leads to what

looks like a highly unlikely parallel between two sculptors, Marcel Duchamp (1887–1968) and the Romanian Constantin Brancusi (1876–1957). Krauss admits that their practices could not seem farther apart. We associate Duchamp with the presentation as art of 'readymades', found objects 'slipped into the stream of aesthetic discourse', and therefore with little or no 'sculpture' in the sense of a handling and shaping of material. By contrast, almost half of Brancusi's work involved the extremely labour-intensive carving of wood or stone, just as the typically smooth and highly polished surfaces were the results of many hours of painstaking work. Brancusi's most well-known work includes the early, ovoid head-shapes with varying degrees of feature, such as the *Head of a Sleeping Child* (1908), *Sleeping Muse* (1910), *Newborn* (1915) and *The Beginning of the World* (1924), and the various *Birds in Space* of the mid-1920s, smoothly abstract, single feather-like projections tapering down to a very slender point just above the base.

Krauss insists, however, that the sculptures of Duchamp and Brancusi are alike hostile to logical connection and cause-and-effect explanations. Duchamp overtly severs the causal chain between author and text, maker and product, and breaks with the idea of representation, his 'sculptures' thereby working to stimulate a curiosity about how meaning in art is constructed. But Krauss also detects a determination in Brancusi to 'deflect' an ideal geometry and to be obstructive towards that kind of analysis, implicit in Boccioni or Gabo for example, which seeks to get to the heart of the internal structure of a form. When we look closely at Brancusi's ovoid forms, we find subtle 'deformations', and in the case of *The Beginning of the World*, for example, a seemingly perfectly ovoid bronze on its side, it is the placement of the object on a circular metal base that further contributes to that effect. Krauss writes that the effect 'is to insure a difference in kind between the reflections that will register on the lower portion of the form and those that will fall upon its upper half'; the play of light on the upper half, contrasting with the 'velvety darkness' of the reflected shadow on the lower half, destabilizes our sense of the object and emphasizes that it is the situation of the object, and thus the placing of it as a work of art, that prevails over perfection of form. In a similar way, the *Birds in Space* seem not quite to make sense in that space, their slender low point seeming to defy the logic of a centre of gravity (a metal rod had to be inserted into the marble versions before they could be carved). The work of Duchamp and Brancusi, Krauss concludes, 'questioned the very role of narrative structure', and the role that scientific explanation might play in it, 'by gravitating toward that which is unitary and unanalyzable' (*Passages in Modern Sculpture*, p. 103).

I have concentrated your attention in this section solely on Krauss' analysis because it acts as a model of the way we might attempt to 'read' a non-linguistic modernist artefact, transferring to that artefact qualities of 'time' and 'narrative structure' that we would be more likely to find, for example, in a work of fiction. In the next two chapters we turn to the analysis of literary texts.

Selected reading

Benton, Tim, 'Building Utopia', in *Modernism 1914–1939: Designing a New World*, ed. Christopher Wilk (2006) pp. 149–224.

Brooker, Peter, and Andrew Thacker (eds), *Geographies of Modernism* (London, Routledge, 2005)

Eclectic volume of interdisciplinary essays typifying the growing investigation of space and geography in the new modernist studies.

D'Souza, Aruna and Tom McDonough (eds), *The Invisible Flâneuse? Gender, Public Space and Visual Culture in Nineteenth-Century Paris* (Manchester, Manchester University Press, 2006)

A stimulating volume updating debates in these interlocking areas.

Frampton, Kenneth, *Modern Architecture: A Critical History* (London, Thames & Hudson, 1980)

A wide-ranging and copiously illustrated survey.

Jencks, Charles, *Modern Movements in Architecture* (Harmondsworth, Penguin, 1977)

Interesting comparison with Pevsner, with whom Jencks takes issue for his 'unified' conception. This book takes a fascinating 'pluralistic' approach by comparison.

Krauss, Rosalind E., *Passages in Modern Sculpture* (Cambridge, MA and London, MIT Press, 1977)

Indispensable for an understanding of modernist sculpture, characterized by detailed and highly theorized formal analysis.

Parsons, Deborah L., *Streetwalking the Metropolis: Women, the City and Modernity* (Oxford, Oxford University Press, 2000)

Detailed discussion building valuably in the flâneur/flâneuse debates.

Pevsner, Nicholas, *Pioneers of Modern Design: from William Morris to Walter Gropius* (Harmondsworth, Penguin, 1977)

One of the first to define a 'Modern Movement' with the first edition of this book in 1936, Pevsner takes an evolutionary/gradualist approach to architecture and design from the mid-nineteenth century to 1914 (see Jencks, above).

Schorske, Carl E., *Fin-de-Siècle Vienna: Politics and Culture* (Cambridge, Cambridge University Press, 1979)

Erudite and compelling, deeply historicist analysis of the crisis of Austrian liberalism in turn-of-the-century Vienna, with especially valuable material on the *Ringstrasse*, Freud's *Interpretation of Dreams*, Klimt and Schoenberg.

Zevi, Bruno, *The Modern Language of Architecture* (New York, Da Capo, 1994)

Thought-provoking and unusual in its parallels.

6

Modernist poetry

Reading the modernist poem

We have seen, in chapter 4, the general importance of the 'linguistic turn' in modernist thought. Of all the written forms of modernism, poetry, with its characteristic intensity of language, might be expected to exemplify this state of affairs. As we begin to explore modernist poetry in this chapter, however, I will draw attention to a paradox that soon becomes evident: as poetry becomes more interested in the enigmas of expression and communication, it simultaneously aspires to *transcend* the condition of language, or to turn poetic language into other things: music, sound, performance, image, alternative languages. How do we account for this? And how might it relate to our ongoing discussion of issues such as modernist autonomy and the history and politics of modernist forms?

Let us begin with a close reading of a modernist poem, 'Anecdote of the Jar' by the American poet Wallace Stevens (1879–1955). 'Anecdote' could be said to show the linguistic turn at work, and exemplifies a peculiarly modernist combination of difficulty and simplicity, prompting the critic Glen Macleod to see it as an essentially Dadaist poem which 'could describe the creation of a ready-made' and reflects 'the combination of intellectual seriousness and deadpan humour that characterizes New York Dada' (Macleod, in Levenson, *Cambridge Companion to Modernism*, p. 210).

Anecdote of the Jar
I placed a jar in Tennessee,
And round it was, upon a hill,

It made the slovenly wilderness
Surround that hill.

The wilderness rose up to it,
And sprawled around, no longer wild,
The jar was round upon the ground
And tall and of a port in air.

It took dominion everywhere.
The jar was gray and bare.
It did not give of bird or bush,
Like nothing else in Tennessee.

STOP and THINK

- The poem begins with disproportion, or a disorientation of
  perspective: the small jar is 'placed', not in a cupboard, but
  in the US state of Tennessee. Similar jarrings of perspective
  (pun intended!) are created by apparent contradictions: line
  6, 'sprawled around' hardly suggests control, yet the wilderness is 'no longer wild'; lines 7 and 8, the jar is 'round upon
  the ground', yet at the same time 'tall and of a port in air'.
  What happens if you try to visualize what is going on in this
  'anecdote'?
- Examine the use of rhyme and rhythm in the poem. Look at
  rhyming words and where they occur; count syllables in lines,
  noting stressed (heavy) and unstressed (light) syllables. Are
  the patterns regular, irregular or a mixture of the two? Think
  about how these things impact upon your ability to read the
  poem aloud.
- The vocabulary of the poem seems simple; it does not send
  you scurrying to the dictionary. Yet there are oddities of
  expression. Look for example at the phrase 'of a port' in line
  8, or at the final two lines of the poem: the phrase 'give of',
  and the confusing double negative, 'It did not . . . /Like nothing else . . .'. What are the effects of these ambiguities as you
  read the poem?
- Now stand back and assess the import of the poem as a
  whole. Perhaps the jar has a symbolic value, making of the
  anecdote a kind of allegory. Let us assume that the jar can

represent artefacts in general, and the ability of humans to make art, while the positioning of the jar represents the effects of introducing human-made things into the world. What kinds of reading are then made possible?

My suggestions are these. 'Anecdote of the Jar' has a deceptive simplicity: it is easy to read, but difficult to fathom. It calls to mind the playful observations of Samuel Beckett's character Celia, regarding the tragi-comic, anti-heroic figure of the novel *Murphy*, whose words:

> went dead as soon as they sounded; each word obliterated, before it had time to make sense, by the word that came next; so that in the end she did not know what had been said. It was like difficult music heard for the first time. (*Murphy*, 1938; London, John Calder, 1977, p. 27)

Beckett echoes here the 'deadpan humour' that McLeod finds in Stevens' 'Anecdote', and reminds us of the poem's playfulness. The oddities and ambiguities of the poem belie the apparently childlike simplicity of its statements, often frustrating our quest for clarity. Such frustration seems to be embodied in the curious giving and withholding of pattern in the structure of the poem. The regular octosyllabic lines are unpredictably interrupted: at line 4, 'Surround that hill', where the number of syllables is abruptly halved, and at line 10, where there are six. Rhyme seems perversely irregular. The flat repetition of 'hill' in the first stanza feels like a travesty of rhyme; in the second stanza there is a clustering of internal rhymes ('around', 'round', 'ground') but none at the end of the lines; yet the end of line 8, 'air', initiates a run of three straight rhymes ('everywhere' and then 'bare'), crossing the stanzas in a way that denies any sense of rhyming pattern and makes the lines feel like three isolated statements. It is as if the poem does not know how to arrive at a rhyme scheme.

A symbolical or allegorical reading of the poem might proceed as follows. The jar is a work of 'art' in the broadest sense, and art is one of the many ways in which humans make their mark on, or intervene in, the natural world. When we make art, we change the way the world looks: when we make a focal point in nature, for example with a piece of sculpture, or even a 'gray' and 'bare' jar, things by definition *appear* to arrange themselves around it, as our eye is drawn to it. This calls to mind the Dadaist strategy of reflection upon what is or is not art, and of asking if art might be the definition of an activity or context rather than an inherent property of something: think of Duchamp's deployment of the 'readymade' urinal, *Fountain*. Art can thus assume a quasi-magical or ritualistic power, creating order out of 'slovenly wilderness': the jar is 'placed' carefully, and certain quasi-archaic expressions suggest a sacredness, nobility or for-mality – the inversion 'round it was', instead of 'it was round'; the phrase 'of a port', suggesting a grace of de*port*ment.

Such power may not be necessarily benign, however. We can take 'dominion everywhere' with our interventions, not just cre-ating pattern and order but subduing nature to our own inter-ests, so that it is no longer itself but subordinate to the human. Does art bring us closer to the world, or does it separate us? My own reading of the difficult line 'It did not give of bird or bush' is that the jar, as an autonomous work of art, holds itself aloof, makes no compromises or accommodations with nature. What is at stake here is not so much the particular work of art, as the value that we attach to the general idea of art; while the jar itself might be simple, 'gray' and bare' it can be elevated by being used or thought of as art (Duchamp's *Fountain* again). This brings us back to the strange inconsistencies of the poem itself: the tokens of 'high' cultural capital ('round it was', 'of a port'), yet the bald simplicities of statement; the deployment of rhyme and rhythm, yet in apparently incoherent ways. At times, the poem can show a perfect adjustment of form to idea, for example in those two truncated lines, where the sharp shock of 'Surround that hill' expresses the immediate power of the jar to arrange and organize the wilderness, while the elongated vowels of 'jar', 'gray' and 'bare', as if stretching out to cover the spaces left by the two missing syllables, express the expan-sionism by which the jar can take 'dominion everywhere'. At other times, however, the poem seems determined to disrupt or break any sense of an organic fit between art and life.

Qualities of bareness and self-sufficiency are shared by jar and poem alike, and any specific references to historical or political context (apart from 'Tennessee') are strenuously avoided. But exactly this autonomy reminds us of questions of the social and political functions of art in the modern world, just as abstraction does in the realm of visual art. Repudiation of context can look like a form of emancipation, the work of art becoming a utopian space; the simplicity of the poem can imply transparency of access, and a kind of straightforward democracy reminiscent of De Stijl or Bauhaus design principles. On the other hand, the poem can appear overbearing in its obscurity, and suggest analogies between the production of art and the colonizing processes of Western imperialism.

From the 'difficult music' of Stevens' *Anecdote*, in which I have tried to show how openness and multivalency can be the direct product of difficulty (such multiplicity being a property of poetic expression per se, but heightened perhaps within the modernist poem), let us now examine in more detail the question of a connection between modernist poetry and musicality.

Symbolism and music

The movement known as Symbolism(e), revolving around Paris between the 1870s and 1890s, is generally acknowledged as the starting point of modernist poetry. While principally associated with the work of Stéphane Mallarmé (1842–98), Paul Verlaine (1844–96) and Arthur Rimbaud (1854–91), it is often seen to be inaugurated by the earlier poetry of Charles Baudelaire (1821–67). Less pivotal figures included Gerard de Nerval (1808–55) and Villiers de L'Isle-Adam' (1838–89), while a slightly later transmutation of Symbolism into the poetry of Decadence featured the work of Jules Laforgue (1860–87) and Tristan Corbières' (1845–75), which was particularly influential on the early poetry of T.S. Eliot.

In keeping with modernism's dual identity as a movement both of theory and of practice, prose texts such as Arthur Symons' *The Symbolist Movement in Literature* (1899) or W.B. Yeats' *The Symbolism of Poetry* (1900) have played a large part in consolidating the idea and influence of Symbolism. In another of these, *Axel's*

Castle: A Study in the Imaginative Literature of 1870–1930 (1931;
London, Fontana, 1969), one of the first critical studies of literary modernism, the American critic Edmund Wilson offered the
following as a 'doctrine' of Symbolist poetry:

> Every feeling or sensation we have, every moment of consciousness,
> is different from any other; and it is, in consequence, impossible to
> render our sensations as we actually experience them through the
> conventional and universal language of ordinary literature. Each poet
> has his own unique personality; each of his moments has its special
> tone, its special combination of elements. And it is the poet's task to
> find, to invent, the special language which will alone be capable of
> expressing his personality and feelings. Such a language must make
> use of symbols: what is so special, so fleeting and so vague cannot be
> conveyed by direct statement or description, but only by a succession
> of words, of images, which will serve to suggest it to the reader. (p. 24)

While Wilson's is a serviceable definition to start with, I'll go on
to suggest that it does not fully capture the complexities of the
Symbolist aesthetic, nor does it accurately pinpoint the nature
of Symbolist musicality. A familiar reference point for the latter
is Baudelaire's poem 'Correspondances' from *Les Fleurs du mal*
(1857), whose first two stanzas are as follows:

> La Nature est un temple où de vivants piliers
> Laissent parfois sortir de confuses paroles;
> L'homme y passe à travers des forêts de symboles
> Qui l'observent avec des regards familiers.

> Comme de longs échos qui de loin se confondent
> Dans une ténébreuse et profonde unité,
> Vaste comme la nuit et comme la clarté,
> Les parfums, les couleurs et les sons se répondent.

> [Nature is a temple whose living pillars
> Sometimes let out confused words;
> Man passes through forests of symbols
> That observe him with familiar expressions.

> Like prolonged echoes that merge far away
> In a deep and shadowy unity,
> Vast as the night and the moonlight,
> Perfumes, sounds and colours answer each to each]

The poem evokes *synaesthesia*, a principle of the interchangeability of sense effects. 'We now *hear* undeniable rays of light, like arrows gilding and piercing the meandering of song', wrote Stéphane Mallarmé of 'certain new states of our poetic mind' inspired by the synthesizing musical forms of the German composer Richard Wagner (1813–83) (Kolocotroni *et al.*, *Modernism*, p. 125). In part the suggestion is that this conflation of hearing and sight is a physical state, provoked by the sound of the poem in itself. Even if you don't know French, you might ignore my translation of the above, in order to try to 'hear' the musicality of the original, in line with T.S. Eliot's sometime observation that the ideal hearer of his poetry would have no knowledge of English. (One of the most memorable poetry readings I ever heard was in Russian, to a mesmerized British audience, by Joseph Brodsky.) So, for example, Baudelaire uses the word '*parfois*' (sometimes) to chime musically with 'parfums' (perfumes). But synaesthesia may also be communicated as a condition of semantic or semiotic uncertainty. Words as signs, but like perfumes, colours or sounds, set off a chain of effects which can neither be contained nor predicted.

In the work of the art critic and philosophical novelist Walter Pater (1839–94), the main disseminator of Symbolist principles in Britain, this linking of poetry to an expanded sense of the *aesthetic* also became associated with the tendency in modernity to 'regard all things and principles of things as inconstant modes or fashions' – in the terms of James Joyce's *Ulysses* (1922), an 'ineluctable modality'. Whether we consider the outer physical world, or the inner world of thought and feeling, we become aware merely of a continuous flux of elements and sensations: the stream of consciousness is compared with the flow of a river in summer heat, in that both are literally composed of the same physical elements. This blending of physical forces, outer and inner, impresses itself on the act of cognition itself. In his famous conclusion to *The Renaissance: Studies in Art and Poetry* (1873), which itself is often seen to be an early experiment in modernist poetical prose, Pater writes:

> At first sight experience seems to bury us under a flood of external objects, pressing upon us with a sharp and importunate reality, calling us out of ourselves in a thousand forms of action. But when reflection begins to act upon those objects they are dissipated under

its influence; the cohesive force seems suspended like a trick of magic; each object is loosed into a group of impressions – colour, odour, texture – in the mind of the observer. (*Selected Writings of Walter Pater*, ed. Harold Bloom, New York, Signet, 1974, p. 59)

On the explicit subject of poetry, Pater contrasts an initial and superficial function which is to address the 'mere intelligence', for example in the moral and political didacticism of Victor Hugo, with a more profound aspiration. In the 'ideal types of poetry', Pater argues, 'form' and 'matter' are indistinguishable; rather than being able to separate out some clear message or subject, the reader of poetry in its ideal condition encounters 'a certain suppression or vagueness of mere subject, so that the meaning reaches us through ways not distinctly traceable by the understanding' (p. 56). The ultimate art form in which these conditions of 'pure perception' are found, or created, is music, so that Pater's ideal goals for poetry are contained in the declaration that 'all great art aspires to the condition of music'.

We need to pause here to reflect on musicality as it is applied to poetry, and in doing so to distinguish this condition from the more traditional sense in which the histories of poetry and song, for example, have been closely interrelated. Rather, poetry might transmit something which is direct, experiential and unamenable to translation or paraphrase, and the sensual effect of music on us might be an appropriate *analogy* for that mode of communication. It is not that language can be used to approximate musical sounds (although this too is often part of the Symbolist effect), but that it possesses an immediacy by virtue of communicating something in an autonomous and symbolic sense rather than in a literal sense which could immediately be translated into meaning. Similarly, we can say that a piece of music can have a profound effect on us without ever considering what it 'means'.

This takes us directly back to the pivotal figure of Stéphane Mallarmé, whose weekly Paris salons were the organizing point for an array of proto-modernist writers and artists, the poet having established himself as the muse or priestly mediator of a new, rarified aesthetic, positing an idealized mode of poetic utterance which was inherently resistant to the practical realms of commerce, politics and technology. In 'Crisis in Poetry', drafted between 1886 and

1895, Mallarmé consistently resorts to musical analogies to describe the ways in which Symbolist poets were loosening and subverting the 'cut and dried rules' of 'official prosody' (prosody is the theory and practice of versification). 'Each soul is a melody', he writes, 'its strands must be bound up. Each poet has his flute or viol, with which to do so'; this is not, however, a purely unfettered individualism, because with the 'ever-ready keyboard' of 'orthodox verse', 'any poet with an individual technique and ear can build his own instrument', dedicated 'to Language'. And in an uncanny anticipation of the modernist music of Arnold Schoenberg, which we will discuss in chapter 8, Mallarmé observes that once the 'artificial metronomes' of traditional metrics have been abolished, 'there is joy for our ears alone in perceiving all possible combinations and interrelationships of twelve tones' (Kolocotroni *et al.*, *Modernism*, p. 124).

We find therefore in Mallarmé's early modernism a sense of tenacious discipline and theory which, along with the work of Rimbaud in particular, have proved resonant for much more recent, postmodernist thinking about language and subjectivity. In what Theodor Adorno described as Mallarmé's 'materialistic programme', works of literature are 'not inspired', wrote Mallarmé, 'but made out of words'. If the poem is to be 'pure', he insists, 'the poet's voice must be stilled and the initiative taken by the words themselves, which will be set in motion as they meet unequally in collision' (Kolocotroni *et al.*, *Modernism*, p. 126). This challenge to the intimate link between language and self is identified by later twentieth-century philosophers such as Derrida as an early rupture in a Western tradition of logocentrism, attacking Romantic–humanistic notions of genius and inspiration which insisted that speech was the authentic expression of the self, and that by this token writing was a kind of speech *manqué*, a fallen condition always aspiring towards speech (see, for example, Derrida's essay 'The Double Session', in *Dissemination*, trans. B. Johnson, London, Athlone Press, 1981). For Rimbaud, the strength and suffering of the individual poet lay in the recognition that '*I* is someone else' (Kolocotroni *et al.*, *Modernism*, p. 109); instead of the construction 'I think', Rimbaud suggested that thought is something that happens to us (as in 'I am thought'), and which in the process gives rise to the concept of the 'I'. Something very similar is implicit in the Bergsonian notion of lifeforce, or *élan vital*, expressed as a general condition of thought of which egos are only individual instances; the later twentieth-century 'new Bergsonism' of the French philosopher Gilles Deleuze was to take up this idea.

In this light we might begin to see the limitations of Edmund Wilson's emphasis on the uniqueness of individual 'personality' and the incommunicability of personal experience in Symbolism. While the work of Mallarmé and Rimbaud is more complex than the search for a personal poetic language, it is also bound up in history in a way that Wilson's emphasis on individualism cannot acknowledge. In a very astute reading, Peter Nicholls asserts that 'Rimbaud's poetics is, in fact, hardly intelligible without reference to the revolutionary Paris Commune of 1871 and its bloody suppression' (Nicholls, *Modernisms: A Literary Guide*, p. 31). Refusing individuality along with all kinds of conformity as aspects of a repressive Christian, capitalist and imperialist society, Rimbaud's impersonal forces are revolutionary as well as poetical impulses. His poems, all written between the ages of 15 and 21, are still shocking in their hallucinatory force, often confronting sexual and religious taboos with a breathtaking explicitness and sense of depravity: see for example 'Seven-Year-Old-Poets' and 'Drunken Boat' of 1871, and the long sequence *A Season in Hell* of 1873, in which Rimbaud is already leaving behind the apparent constraints of verse form for a looser, mixed prose-poetry.

Where Symbolist principles are carried over into T.S. Eliot's early anti-Romanticist theorizing, for example in the essay 'Tradition and the Individual Talent' (1919), they produce the formula, not only that the successful communication of unique feeling in poetry is directly proportionate to the *impersonality* of the language used, but that the poet does not in fact have a 'personality' to express, but only a medium, which effects an *escape* from personality. The mind of the poet is merely a catalyst for the achieving of certain poetic effects; though, Eliot adds, with a subtle twist which somehow reinstates the Romantic notion of genius he otherwise appears to dismantle, 'only those who have personality and emotions know what it means to want to escape from these things' (Eliot, in Kolocotroni *et al.*, *Modernism*, p. 371). In the essay 'Hamlet' (1919), the formula of the 'objective correlative' constitutes another version of this search for poetic impersonality.

Eliot's early thinking – the 'objective correlative', the poet's mind as a 'shred of platinum' – reinforces the 'materialism' of Mallarmé and Rimbaud. Yet there remains a sense, inherent in Edmund Wilson's emphasis on the 'vague', 'fleeting' and suggestive nature of Symbolist language, that Symbolism extended the project of Romanticism in its insistence that imagination could give access to truths which lay hidden beneath the veil of reason and normality. Crucial to the concept of the symbol in both movements was this resistance to definite meaning, embodying a revolt against the inexorable rise of an industrial, bureaucratic and administrative ethos variously labelled as 'instrumental reason' (Adorno and Horkheimer) or 'technologico-Benthamism' (F.R. Leavis). In the words of Arthur Symons, the aim of the symbol was to make visible 'the soul of things', and to do so meant repudiating 'exteriority . . . rhetoric . . . [and] a materialistic tradition'.

In two poets in particular, W.B. Yeats (1865–1939) and Rainer Maria Rilke (1875–1926), this dimension of Symbolism is uppermost. From early collections such as *Crossways* (1889) and *The Rose* (1893), shaped by his interests in mystic religion and the supernatural, Yeats built a corpus of yearning lament for a neo-Platonic 'faeryland' and associated concepts, before the reign of the 'merchant and the clerk'. Yet Yeats' lyric and conversational poetry was not simply the backward-looking pursuit of a 'Celtic Twilight': it also aimed to partake in the imaginative construction of a modern Ireland, and to redress the historical denigration of the Irish people. In its middle and later stages Yeats' work was coloured by an ongoing tension between aesthetic and political principles; as he became interested in Symons' work and in Symbolist poetics, so in the early 1900s he became increasingly disillusioned with the nationalist political culture (for example, in the philistine reaction to Synge's *Playboy of the Western World*, when it was performed in 1907 at the Abbey Theatre, Dublin, the site of the Irish national theatre established by Yeats and Lady Gregory in 1904). In postwar collections such as *The Wild Swans at Coole* (1919) and *Michael Robartes and the Dancer* (1921), Yeats' poetry combined a delicate beauty with a compressed density of meaning. While never the most obvious example of modernist rupture and defamiliarization, Yeats had arguably been travelling towards a Symbolist aesthetic since his declaration in 'Nationality and Literature' (1893) that in poetry 'the most obvious distinction between the old and the new is the growing complexity of language and thought'.

Like the poetry of Yeats, that of Rilke combines modernist innovation in form with a profound suspicion of modernity as such; for Peter Nicholls, Rilke typifies a German-language modernism which tended (for example, also in the prose fictions of Thomas Mann) 'to value a radical aesthetic for its capacity to bring release from a claustrophobic social environment' rather than from the principle of tradition per se (*Modernism: A Literary Guide*, p. 138). In his early career Rilke had written lyric poetry and reflective prose, most notably the *Notebooks of Malte Laurids Brigge* (1910). It is however on the later poetic sequences, the *Sonnets of Orpheus* and the *Duino Elegies* (1923), that Rilke's reputation as a great modernist, and his influence on later British modernist poets such as W.H. Auden, rests. The voice from the outset is anguished, confessional and intensely serious, seeming to possess none of the impersonal detachment of Mallarméan or Eliotic symbolism. The poems grapple openly with the mystery of life and the enigma of death or not-being, a struggle embodied in the recurrent figure of angels as subjects of address. In a way comparable with Walter Benjamin's thesis in his essay 'The Storyteller', with Cézanne's still-life paintings or with Bergson's concept of *durée*, Rilke's later work addresses the decline in the value and authenticity of experience within a heavily mediated modernity, continuing the emphasis in his earlier work on the renovation of our relationships with *things*. Impersonality or Symbolist suggestiveness is achieved, if at all, through the generalized treatment of the human condition in a travelling circus (the Fifth elegy), motherhood and fatherhood (the Third and Fourth elegies), or in the relationship with animals (the Eighth elegy). Part of the mythology of Rilke's consuming identification of art with life was that the completion of the elegies was closely followed by his own final illness.

Imagism

From the identification of modernist poetry with music, let us now examine its association with the visual image. At one point in T.S.

Eliot's 'Prufrock', the persona's narration breaks down under the pressure of trying to explain a lost opportunity; a hiatus occurs, taking the form of a juxtaposition of two lines:

> It is impossible to say just what I mean!
> But as if a magic lantern threw the nerves in patterns on a screen:

after which the poem resumes its diffident questioning of motives and outcomes.

In the face of the apparent inadequacy of language, Eliot's Prufrock here aspires towards a direct and unmediated projection of his condition: language is replaced by 'the nerves in patterns on a screen', drawing perhaps on the 1895 discovery of X-rays. This translation of word into image leads us to the formation and characteristics of Imagism, a central movement in Anglo–American modernist poetry.

Imagism emerged in London between the years 1908 to 1914, taking the form of various groupings (societies, clubs) which more or less modelled themselves on the formation of Symbolism in the cafés of Paris some thirty years earlier. A forerunner was T.E. Hulme's Poets' Club of 1908; following a satirical review by F.S. Flint in the *New Age* periodical, unfavourably comparing the Club to the intellectual dynamism of the Symbolists, Hulme and Flint collaborated in a new, unnamed group which met, initially in March 1909, in the 'Tour Eiffel' restaurant in Soho. This group was soon energized by the appearance of the American poet Ezra Pound, by Hilda Doolittle (H.D.) and Richard Aldington in 1911 and, when Pound left after the publication of the first Imagist anthology in 1914, by the rich American patron and poet Amy Lowell, who went on to orchestrate three further anthologies during the war years.

STOP and THINK

Imagism presents an intriguing study of the relationship in modernism between theory and practice. Put simply, while Imagism was announced in a welter of principles and manifestos, the poems supported by this superstructure were, of their nature, extremely slight and fragile. Look first at this juxtaposition of theory and practice.

According to Ezra Pound in his essay 'A Retrospect' (1918), the main principles of the Imagists were as follows:

1. Direct treatment of the 'thing' whether subjective or objective.
2. To use absolutely no word that does not contribute to the presentation.
3. As regarding rhythm: to compose in sequence of the musical phrase, not in sequence of a metronome.

Pound also included the following injunctions:

- 'An "Image" is that which presents an intellectual and emotional complex in an instant of time'.
- 'It is the presentation of such a "complex" instantaneously which gives that sudden sense of liberation; that sense of freedom from time and space limits . . .'
- 'Use no superfluous word, no adjective which does not reveal something'.
- 'Go in fear of abstractions'.
- 'Don't be descriptive; remember that a painter can describe a landscape much better than you can'.
- 'Harder and saner . . . "nearer the bone" . . . It will be as much like granite as it can be, its force will lie in its truth, its interpretative power . . . We will have fewer painted adjectives impeding the shock and stroke of it . . . austere, direct, free from emotional slither' (Quoted in Kolocotroni *et al.*, *Modernism*, pp. 374–6.)

Now read the following Imagist poems.

Autumn Haze
Is it a dragonfly or a maple leaf
That settles softly down upon the water?

(Amy Lowell)

You Are Like the Realistic Product of an Idealistic
  Search for Gold at the Foot of the Rainbow
   Hid by the august foliage and fruit
    of the grape vine,
     twine
      your anatomy
       round the pruned and polished stem,

chameleon.
 Fire laid upon
 an emerald as long as
 the dark King's massy
one,
could not snap up the spectrum for food
 as you have done.

(Marianne Moore)

In a Station of the Metro
The apparition of these faces in the crowd;
Petals on a wet, black bough.

(Ezra Pound)

- Think about precise ways in which individual poems do or do
  not match up to the criteria laid down by the Imagist poets.
- Are the Imagist criteria shown, by the poems, to be consistent, or are they contradictory?
- Would you suggest any alternative criteria that might help us
  to evaluate the success or failure of these poems?

My suggestions are these. In Lowell's 'Autumn Haze', might
the word 'softly' be superfluous? Given that the manipulation
of 's' and 'f' sounds elsewhere have already done the work
of establishing softness as a quality within the poem, does
'softly' make too explicit what is already implicit, and therefore resemble what Pound disparagingly calls 'description'?
Marianne Moore's poem, through its over-explicatory title,
surely announces itself as a clever antithesis to Imagist principles, even though the poem itself is Imagistic in its concrete
form and in the brilliant image of the chameleon snapping
up the spectrum for food, leading overall to a sense that the
poem has a satirical relation towards its own aesthetic. Pound's
poem, in its verblessness, gives a sense of suspension, 'an intellectual and emotional complex in an instant of time'; but the
poem also has a surprisingly narrative structure, which Imagism
does not seem to allow for, and which imports movement by
another means. As we move across the three lines (including
the title), we move upwards – underground, human faces,

the boughs of a tree – as if following the escalator I somehow (why?) assume to be there. Also, while the third line asks to be read as a metaphor of the human faces, the structure of the poem can also imply that it is poised, or poises itself, between machinery and nature – a fitting modernist scenario, perhaps.

It may seem unsurprising that the Imagists' minimalist strategies did not meet with universal approval, even from within modernism itself. Quarrelling with Richard Aldington, the Harlem poet Jean Toomer insisted that, 'Overnight, our voice and our hearing have not shrunk to an eye' (quoted in North, *The Dialect of Modernism*, pp. 171–2). Perhaps Toomer here underestimated the importance of context. The London Imagists vigorously repudiated what they saw as the tired and outdated culture of poetry in Britain at the beginning of the twentieth century. They saw this poetry as variously sentimental, post-romantic in its reverence for nature, bloated by the Victorian tendency for long-winded rhetoric and storytelling, narrowly didactic, nationalistic and imperialistic. In its place, therefore, they sought to develop a harder, more precise, purified and minimalist poetics, as if poetry were to be boiled down to its essence. We might identify other prominent features, as a kind of alternative to Pound's formalistic strictures, as follows:

- a noticeable masculinism, for example in Pound's insistence on hardness and precision, avoiding 'emotional slither';
- a renewed classicism, for example in H.D.'s mythic Greek scenarios, but also in T.E. Hulme's notorious condemnation of romanticism as 'spilt religion', set against a classicism defined in terms of finiteness, restraint and reserve; and
- an orientalism or, more precisely, a gravitation towards Far Eastern linguistic forms. The haiku, a three-line, seventeen-syllable lyric form emerging from Japanese Samurai culture of the sixteenth century, became the perfect model for the Imagist aspiration towards the compression of meaning into a single unit, 'an intellectual and emotional complex in an instant of time'.

It might also be noted that Pound's apparently macho posturing is directed towards the principle of an exacting rigour, and a concreteness, in the *choice* of words, rather than in the nature of the words themselves. If the concreteness of the image was in this sense a means of emancipation, beyond the terms of gender, Pound also found this in the *ideogram*, or Chinese written character, a knowledge of which he derived from the scholar Ernest Fenollosa, whose work *The Chinese Written Character as a Medium for Poetry* Pound was to edit in 1919. The ideogram is a pictorial mode of language, working through the juxtaposition of two representations to form a third thing, a statement in effect, contrasting with the more linear and extended Western model in which meaning is created by the combination of words strung out across the line (or, in Woolf's terms, the 'railway line') of the sentence. So, instead of writing 'the cup is bright', the Chinese ideogram represents 'cup sun-moon'. This directness of meaning avoids what Pound called the 'soul-obsession' of Western languages; the point resembles Nietzsche's critique of the infirmity of a language which, for example, through the role of the subject in the phrase 'the lightning flashed', divides a single event into two, stating it once as cause ('lightning') and again as effect ('flashed'). We can see the significance, in Pound's writing, of Oriental languages and their implications for cultural difference, as an anticipation of the work of anthropologists Whorf and Sapir in the domain of linguistic relativity (see chapter 4).

Mina Loy and H.D.

As we see in the examples above, Imagist images were often of almost unthinkably fragile and provisional things and situations. Helen Carr has argued that, while there was undoubtedly misogyny in the attitudes of Hulme and Pound as well as other male modernists, they 'did much more to assist women writers than their predecessors' by contributing to an aesthetic of impersonality which condemned any association of poetry with a vague and effusive effeminacy ('Imagism and Empire', in eds Howard J. Booth and Nigel Rigby, *Modernism and Empire*, Manchester, Manchester University Press, 2000, p. 84). Virginia Woolf similarly argued that women's writing in the twentieth century, even of romance narratives, should not become the 'dumping ground' of the emotions. The critical tradition on modernist poetry continued to tell a predominantly masculine story (my own account has done so too, thus far), focusing for example on the 'men of 1914', until texts like Gillian Hanscombe and Virginia L. Smyers' *Writing for Their Lives: The Modernist Women 1910–40* (London, Women's Press, 1987) began the process of biographical reclamation, stressing also the crucial importance of transnational networks in literary modernism per se. Critics such as Claire Buck and Diana Collecott initiated a serious critical appraisal of the work of H.D. (Hilda Doolittle, 1886–1961), and this has now been extensively developed, with recent critics for example reading H.D. from the perspectives of cinema (Susan McCabe) and democracy (Rachel Potter). Scholarly work has taken a little longer to catch up with Mina Loy (1882–1966), but recent critics such as Potter, Cristane Miller and Alex Goody are now making up this ground.

I focus on Loy and H.D. here, however, in order to stress that no unitary story can be told about modernist women's poetry, and that no single conception of an emancipated woman poet can apply to such different writers as these. Both were extremely well connected with an international avant-garde, with Loy's early attachments being to Marinetti and Italian Futurism, while H.D. was an editor of Dora Marsden's *Freewoman* and became part of the Imagist group. As Rachel Potter has argued, neither's modernism allowed for an easy accommodation to the principles of liberal democracy, and by extension this places both in an ambivalent relationship with political feminism. Loy's work, admired by fellow artists in its time and place, fell into complete discredit after the modernist period. It is characterized from the outset by a use of jazzy, syncopated rhythms, a stridency and assertiveness of voice, and a willingness to take on taboo subjects. *Parturition* deals with the intense pain of giving birth; in 'a congested cosmos of agony', Loy's persona is able to overhear an encounter between lovers and to reflect on 'The irresponsibility of the male'. Alongside this polemicism, however, the poem reflects in a complex way on the decentring and confusing sense of self that agony creates:

> Locate an irritation   without
> It is   within
>   Within

It is without
The sensitized area
Is identical   with the extensity
Of intension

I am the false quantity
In the harmony of physiological potentiality
To which
Gaining self-control
I should be consonant
In time

A Futuristic, geometric–scientific vocabulary is at work here which, along with the spatial/textual freedom assumed, enables Loy to give a distanced treatment to the disorientation. As the extract shows, Loy tends to deal in the unit of the single line, often short, with less attention paid to metre. Instead, the poetry is driven by an insistent metaphorizing and elaboration of images whose risky excess at times might explain the critical disfavour her work found. *The Widow's Jazz* reflects on her missing (presumed dead) husband Arthur Cravan from the context of a jazz club in which her 'white flesh quakes to the negro soul': 'Cravan/colossal absentee/the substitute dark/rolls to the incandescent memory/of love's survivor/ on this rich suttee/seared by the flames of sound/the widowed urn/holds impotently/your murdered laughter'.

A comparison of Loy's improvisational modernist gestures with H.D.'s poetry might be made through the theme of H.D.'s well-known Hellenism. Loy's poem *Marble* begins:

Greece has thrown   white shadows
sown
their eyeballs with oblivion

A flock of stone
Gods
perched upon pedestals

A populace
of athlete lilies
of the galleries

Loy's irreverence, especially in the second stanza, is that of the outsider or tourist in the gallery; there is a sense of Futuristic impatience with a world that has consigned itself to oblivion. Ancient Greece is however the arena of H.D.'s Hellenic poems, the symbolic site of their Imagistic modernity, even if mixed with certain conscious archaisms, as in the following opening sequences:

Priapus
Keeper-of-Orchards
(D.I.)

I saw the first pear
As it fell.
The honey-seeking, golden-banded,
The yellow swarm
Was not more fleet than I,
(Spare us from loveliness!)
And I fell prostrate,
Crying.
Thou hast flayed us with thy blossoms;
Spare us the beauty
Of fruit-trees!

Hermes of the Ways
(D.I.)

The hard sand breaks,
And the grains of it
Are clear as wine.

Far off over the leagues of it,
The wind,
Playing on the wide shore,
Piles little ridges,
And the great waves
Break over it.

Tonally, H.D.'s work clearly conveys greater restraint, partly through a distinctly plainer vocabulary, and partly through attention to line length and rhythm (note the incantatory repetition of 'spare us' in the first poem and 'it' in the second). Imagism is at work; both poems were in the anthologies spread across 1915 to 1917. The delicacy of H.D.'s poems, however, as Rachel Potter has argued, lies also in their exploration of a borderline between 'psychological states and the world of objects'; this vulnerability of self, briefly glimpsed also in Loy's *Parturition*, pervades H.D.'s work, and helps to contextualize both her bisexuality and her life-long engagement with psychoanalysis (the film *Borderline*, 1930, directed by Kenneth McPherson, and in which H.D. acted, can also contribute to a psychoanalytic reading of her work). Even in H.D.'s most worldly and extended poem, *Trilogy* (1944–6), which bears comparison with Eliot's *Four Quartets* (see below) and opens with images of railings being torn down to make armaments, the over-riding Hellenism is the context in which the continuing relevance of the poet and the Word is endorsed in the midst of cultural ruin. Widely contrasting though they are as poets, the embrace of mod-ernism enabled both Loy and H.D. to circumvent the contestable category of 'feminine' writing.

Rereading Pound and Eliot

We have seen how modernist poetry tends to aspire, in various ways, towards transcending the condition of language itself, or at least Western language: through musicality; through the visual image; or through the deployment of other languages. These three central features can be seen to combine in the work of the two most prominent, although perhaps over-mythologized, poets of Anglo-American 'high' modernism: Ezra Pound and T.S. Eliot. In early collections such as *Personae* (1908–10) and *Ripostes* (1912), Pound's poetry focused on European medieval and Renaissance contexts, mixing myth and history, and renovating the poetic diction of these periods through the use of modern idiom and rhythm. The collec-tion *Cathay* (1915) demonstrated Pound's fascination with Chinese culture and the work of Fenollosa, and roughly coincided with his disengagement from Imagism and attachment to the English Vorticists, who had taken up the influence of Italian Futurism. *Hugh Selwyn Mauberley* (1920) saw Pound in more satirical and diagnostic mode, an analysis of a 'botched civilization' analogous to the poetry of Yeats' middle and Eliot's early periods.

Pound's most distinctive modernist achievement was the long sequence of the *Pisan Cantos* (1925–62), combining imagistic mini-malism with epic proportions. Pound's aspirations in the *Cantos* were both encyclopaedic and universalistic, drawing on Homer and Dante but also on the example of Robert Browning's long narrative

poem *Sordello* to create a critical account of the emergence of
modernity through vast swathes of Italian and ancient Chinese history. 'Narrative' is nevertheless not what the *Cantos* present, despite
their overriding concern with the preservation and understanding
of history; their form is unpredictable, swinging from lyric expression and ideogrammatic language (often literally) to fragments
of historical texts. The poem is frequently preoccupied with the
economics of earlier periods, and slips into transcribing chronicled
accounts of highly specific economic processes and transactions, in
a way that has often led to the questioning of its value *as* poetry. A
recurrent emphasis is on the condemnation of usury. An unsympathetic reading would identify this with anti-Semitism, and with
Pound's notorious commitment to Mussolini and Italian fascism; a
more sympathetic reading might see a critique of the influence of
capitalism on modern subjectivities, aligning Pound for example
with the sociologies of Marx, Weber and Simmel.

While T.S. Eliot's central position in the development of modernist poetry remains unquestioned, recent accounts have sought to
modify the nature of this position from the perspective of ideological critique. For example, Anthony Julius' *T.S. Eliot, Anti-Semitism,
and Literary Form* (Cambridge, Cambridge University Press, 1995)
indicted Eliot's poetry for its perpetuation of anti-Jewish images
and ideas, while more recently contributors to the volume edited by
Cassandra Laity and Nancy K. Gish, *Gender, Desire and Sexuality
in T.S. Eliot* (Cambridge, Cambridge University Press, 2007) have
drawn attention to its gendered dimensions and biases. Like Pound
an American émigré who established his literary reputation in
London, the trajectory of Eliot's career is also, somewhat notoriously, a movement towards the political right, albeit, in a rather
more safely traditional sense than Pound, through the embrace of
Anglo-Saxon institutions as encapsulated in his triple declaration
of being classicist in literature, royalist in politics and Anglo-
Catholic in religion. In the poetry of the 1910s, Eliot quickly established himself as the main Anglo-American inheritor of French
Symbolism and Decadence, even while maintaining an explicit distance both from these and from the immediate context of Imagism.
In the collections *Prufrock and Other Observations* (1917) and *Poems*
(1920), Eliot fashioned the distinctive poetic voice of ironic, urban

angst and sexual neurosis, in poems which became an indispensable feature of the modernist reading list: 'Preludes', 'Portrait of a Lady', 'The Love Song of J. Alfred Prufrock', 'Rhapsody on a Windy Night', 'Gerontion'.

The ideological movement of Eliot's work might best be assessed, however, through a comparison of his two longer, landmark works, *The Waste Land* (1922) and *Four Quartets* (1936–44). *The Waste Land* was a collection of poetic fragments until coaxed into the form of a single coherent work by the editorial interventions of Ezra Pound. The relationship between the coherent and the fragmentary remains, however, one of the key critical questions through which to address the poem. Structured loosely around the Grail legend and anthropological perspectives on cultural rituals marking life and death, the subject of the poem is the decline of the cohesive powers of myth in modernity, along the lines of Nietzsche's theory of the preponderance of Apollonian over Dionysian principles (see *The Birth of Tragedy*, 1872). The elusive, protean form of the poem across its five parts embodies this ambivalence, a constantly shifting combination of verse forms, quotations, voices and registers held together by logics drawn both from music (the recycling of theme and motif) and collage (the juxtaposition of diverse elements, as in the synthetic Cubism of Picasso and Braque, the posters of Heartfield or the films of Eisenstein).

Critical history has been divided over the seemingly self-appointed diagnostic claims made by the poem, as an account of the ills of civilization and of the role of high culture in constructing a bulwark against popularization and democratization. For F.R. Leavis, in *New Bearings in English Poetry* (1932), Eliot's linguistic mastery – 'exquisitely sure', 'subtle variations', 'perfect control' – was achieved in the face of the 'peculiar difficulties' facing a poet in the twentieth century: the dumbing-down of culture, the fact that the poem could be comprehended by only an increasingly 'tiny' minority. In contrast to this critical vocabulary, David Craig's Marxist account of the 'defeatism' of *The Waste Land* reflected witheringly on Eliot's 'sour and *un*lovely' Cockney pub women, the vulgar snobbery of the construction of the 'small house agent's clerk', and the poem's 'groundless idealizing' of the past, fuelled by a 'warped revulsion from the modern'. Surely, Craig insisted,

it is time to see the poem for what it really is: 'not as a centrally
wise diagnosis of "mass civilization" and its ills but as the acme of
conservatism made into art' (*The Real Foundations: Literature and
Social Change*, London, Chatto & Windus, 1973, p. 212).

More recent critical readings have sought to combine a celebration of *The Waste Land*'s experimentalism with a more relaxed
sense of its ironic, even comedic relationship with other popular
discourses – the latter underlined by the tendency to note that
Eliot's original working title for the poem was 'He Do the Police in
Different Voices', a comment on impersonation taken from Charles
Dickens' novel *Our Mutual Friend*. Robert Crawford argues that
voice, or more precisely the eruption into the poem of many different and often scarcely articulate cries and voices, is what helps
the poem, itself, to function 'as a primitive ritual' (*The Savage and
the City*, Oxford, Clarendon Press, 1990, p. 141). Cairns Craig
maintains that, on the basis of this polyphonic quality, the poem
has a rich undecidability, its real existence 'not on the page, but
in our completions of it' (*Yeats, Eliot, Pound and the Politics of
Poetry*, London, Croom Helm, 1982, p. 231). Both readings are a
counterweight to the established reputation of the poem as a kind
of intimidating scholarly exercise or crossword puzzle – a reputation secured by Eliot's addition of a footnote apparatus. The latter,
Peter Ackroyd notes, was subsequently acknowledged by Eliot to
be an act of 'bogus scholarship'; Ackroyd's lively cultural history
of *The Waste Land*'s reception again attempts to dislodge the image
of high seriousness by pointing to its 'jazzy', populist or celebrity
cult status, typified by Evelyn Waugh's *Brideshead Revisited* scene
in which the gay aesthete Anthony Blanche recites extracts through
a megaphone from his Oxford rooms, and by suggesting that the
notes might be strategically linked to Eliot's awareness of the
growth of literary studies as a university discipline. *The Waste Land*
does not, then, simply stake out a claim to a position within 'high'
or minority culture, but dramatizes the tensions between high and
low, minority and mass, which permeate modernism in its relationship to modernity.

Overtly less open to these polyphonic readings, however, is *Four
Quartets*. Largely written among the ruins of a blitzed London
during the Second World War, the poem grapples with the paradox

of attempting to delineate a condition of faith which, by definition, lies beyond the reach of words. This is the Eliot who had converted to Anglicanism in 1927, and who seemed committed to pursuing a high-Church theology. *Four Quartets* could therefore be said to have a more didactic motivation than *The Waste Land*. However, there is also stylistic flexibility across the *Quartets*, principally in the form of an oscillation between an intense lyric voice, in which the earlier Symbolist Eliot can be recognized, and a newer discursive voice of a highly personal and confessional nature. So, for example, following a sequence that begins with the invocation of apocalyptic scenarios, 'Whirled in a vortex that shall bring/The world to that destructive fire/Which burns before the ice-cap reigns', we find:

> That was a way of putting it – not very satisfactory:
> A periphrastic study in a worn-out poetical fashion,
> Leaving one still with the intolerable wrestle
> With words and meanings. The poetry does not matter.

On one level, these two modes represent the elements of Christian worship that Eliot sought to combine in his high Anglicanism: in lyric, an approximation to the distanced and ritualistic expression of Catholicism; in discourse, a reflection of the Protestant belief in salvation through the individual's personal relationship with God. This is not, however, simply a distinction between the poetic and the prosaic; Eliot's reflective passages manage to take on a powerful poetic intensity even when their ostensible function is to frame and question the possibilities of poetry itself. Such ironic framing or metapoetic devices suggest that the poem has more in common with a latent, sceptical postmodernism than a modernistic search for elusive absolutes.

Yet *Four Quartets* remains a profound meditation on modern experience as this is shaped and constrained by concepts of time and space; the poem twists these concepts into unrecognizable and paradoxical forms, hinting consistently at the possibilities of Christian redemption through epiphanic moments of escape or transcendence, 'The point of intersection of the timeless/With time' ('The Dry Salvages'). In a vivid passage from the final quartet, 'Little Gidding', an encounter is staged in a bombed-out city between a poetic persona and a figure whose Christ-like characteristics are blurred by the cultural 'forgetting' of faith – a 'familiar compound ghost/Both intimate and unidentifiable'. The figure issues a bleak valediction for humanity, whose 'exasperated spirit' will proceed from 'wrong to wrong' unless restored, in an image of Symbolist synaesthesia, 'by that refining fire/Where you must move in measure, like a dancer'. As in *The Waste Land*, Eliot is drawn to states of suspension or in-betweenness, and to the simultaneous conferring and withholding of conditions of renewal. The pursuit of the timeless moment is 'an occupation for the saint', the rest of us needing to be content, in the terms of Eliot's high-Church ritual, with 'prayer, observance, discipline, thought and action'; even the authenticity of the act of prayer itself may be hollowed out, as in the injunction 'You are here to kneel/Where prayer has been valid'. Yet the act of reading the poem is subtly offered as an alternative to this void, a form of exploration whose end is 'to arrive where we started/And know the place for the first time'.

Beyond universalism and Eurocentrism

It should not overly surprise us that Americans such as Pound, Amy Lowell and Eliot were the driving forces behind modernist poetry in Britain. Modernism, as we have seen, is characterized by a transnational exchange of ideas and by the experiences of the *émigré* artist. But in America itself, Pound and Eliot in particular did not receive universal acclaim. In his 1951 autobiography, the poet William Carlos Williams (1883–1963) argued that each had succumbed too easily to a Europeanism which made their work derivative, pessimistic and ultimately conformist. *The Waste Land* became a focus of this critique: like an atom bomb, Williams asserted, the poem had laid waste to a whole cultural world, his own immediate response being to rebuild a more optimistic expression in the mixed prose-and-poetry form of *Spring and All* (1923). Hart Crane's (1899–1932) exuberant *The Bridge* (1930) mimics the high classicism of 'The Waste Land' in its structure and cadences, but in its own reassembly of fragments the reference points are modern American authors – Melville, Whitman and Emily Dickinson – as much as the classical writers.

We are accustomed then to find a universalism in modernist

poetry, an aspiration towards the transcendence of particularities of time and place: Hulme's appeal to classical values of restraint or, in the words of *Four Quartets*, 'A condition of complete simplicity'; the epic scale of the work of Pound and Eliot in particular; the search for a 'purified' poetic language, for example in Imagism and the concept of the ideogram; the splicing of languages and cultural references from the perspective of an unfixed cosmopolitanism. Recent critical work has, however, begun to identify a regional or provincial impulse in modernist poetry, starting ironically with the Americans themselves. In *Devolving English Literature*, for example, Robert Crawford argues that the very strategies used by Eliot and Pound to construct a sophisticated sense of historical tradition and, particularly in the case of Eliot, to invent an authentic 'Englishness', simultaneously define those writers as insider–outsider Americans. Eliot's invention of European and English traditions was, Crawford argues, 'one of the most "making new" of American productions'; we are also reminded of Pound's contention of 1912 that, 'when you pin an American down on any issue of fundamental importance, "you get – at his last gasp – a quotation" (*The Savage and the City*, p. 231). In an earlier work, Crawford had highlighted the intimate links between concepts of the savage and of the city in Eliot; in the later book, he suggests that primitivism was cultivated by provincial modernists as the necessary Other or 'dark' side of a civilized cosmopolitanism. In this paradoxical condition, the 'impurities' of demotic language, for example in *The Waste Land*, are not simply resolved into the higher purified form of the classical artefact, but retain some of the oppositional energy of the marginalized cultures from which they are drawn. Michael North's important work, which I have referred to at various points elsewhere in this book (see the section on Primitivism in chapter 4), intersects with Crawford's argument, in stressing how important, if ambivalent, Negro dialect was to the substance of Eliot and Pound's actual avant-garde resistance to linguistic standardization and purification movements on either side of the Atlantic. On this reading, modernism strives to *become* a dialect, rather than to transcend particularity and enter the universal.

What, then, characterizes a modernist poetry founded ostensibly on a native Americanism? In William Carlos Williams and Wallace Stevens, for example, connection may be traced as a certain emphasis on a poetry of 'things', linking Williams' anti-Platonic dictum 'no ideas but in things' with Stevens' assertion that 'poetry means not the language of poetry but the thing itself, wherever it may be found' (quoted in Frank Kermode, *Wallace Stevens*, 2nd edn, London, Faber, 1989, p. 2). This refusal of the ethereal may also, speculatively, be linked to professional identity: Williams remained a practising pediatrician, while Stevens trained as a lawyer and became Vice-President of the Hartford Accident and Indemnity Company, in a career lasting nearly forty years. Resisting the European romanticist image of poetry as a Mallarméan priestly calling, there is a brisk worldliness in the work of Williams, and a concrete philosophical speculativeness in Stevens, and in each a fresh and constantly surprising mode of perception and choice of phrase for which Whitman is a more obvious reference point. Yet paradoxically, 'abstraction' is a key term in Stevens' poetry, and the strange aphoristic challenge of his work (which we have already seen in *Anecdote of the Jar*) connects inevitably with the intellectual traditions of Dada and Surrealism.

Perhaps the key to each poet's Americanness lies in a quotation from John Dewey used by Williams in the prefatory notes to his long (five-books) poem *Paterson*: 'The local is the only universal, upon that all art builds'. This certainly helps to grasp the form of *Paterson* (1946–58), which blends into a single image a river, a man and a city ('a man is indeed a city'), but grounds this elaborate trope in an exuberant montaging of found linguistic materials, poetry and prose, drawn from the spectrum of everyday American life (for an account of what the 'Russian montage' of early Soviet films meant to Williams, see David Kadlec, 'Early Soviet Cinema and American Poetry', *Modernism/modernity* 11:2, April 2004). Stevens' key works, less muscular and even playfully dandyish in tone at times, come in the form of collections of shorter poems, such as his first collection *Harmonium* (1923), *Ideas of Order* (1936) and *Transport to Summer* (1947), the latter of which culminates in the extended work *Notes Towards a Supreme Fiction*, comparable perhaps to Eliot's *Four Quartets* in its sense of making an ultimate and reflexive statement, and rooted in Stevens' belief in the human propensity to move from practice to theory or in the view that life is the sum of our propositions about it.

Another 'devolved' poetic modernism, and one which could be said to be surviving or even prospering, is located by Crawford in British cultural traditions. He notes the importance but neglect of the Scottish communist poet Hugh McDiarmid, whose epic work *A Drunk Man Looks at a Thistle* (1926) responds overtly to *The Waste Land*. McDiarmid's poem offers a vibrant alternative, in Scots dialect, to Eliot's safely canonized text. Further evidence of *The Waste Land*'s provocative intertextual effect can be found in the Welsh poet David Jones' meditation on the First World War, *In Parenthesis* (1937), and in *Briggflatts* (1966), the highly acclaimed work by the equally neglected Northumbrian poet Basil Bunting. The richly textured musical nature of this poem, along with the use of dialect combined, as in McDiarmid, with a broader geography of cultural reference, are a riposte to the more narrowly ideological Englishness of the 'Movement' poetry which came to dominate in the 1950s. As Keith Tuma and Nate Dorward, as well as Tim Armstrong, have recently suggested, Bunting's poem sparked a revival of modernist poetry in 1960s Britain, for example in the work of Lee Harwood, J.H. Prynne and the Cornish poet W.S. Graham, driven by regionalism and sustained by a fragile network of small presses (Tuma and Dorward, 'Modernism and anti-Modernism in British Poetry', and Armstrong, 'The Seventies and the Cult of Culture', in eds Laura Marcus and Peter Nicholls, *The Cambridge History of Twentieth-Century Literature*, Cambridge, Cambridge University Press, 2004). In the same volume, Peter Middleton traces the uncertain fortunes of an embattled British modernist poetry beyond the 1970s, a corpus whose powers of persistence are perhaps encouragingly confirmed by the appearance of Rod Mengham and John Kinsella's anthology, *Vanishing Points: New Modernist Poems* (Cambridge, Salt Publishing, 2004).

To raise the question of the persistence of modernist poetry in the here and now is again to challenge the confining of modernism to its early twentieth-century moment. It is also to reopen the question of the determining characteristics of modernism if these are not solely to be provided by chronology. By what means are we to distinguish contemporary modernist poetry within a context to which terms like postmodern and post-colonial are most readily applicable? How might modernist regionalism or provincialism differ from the postmodern exploration and celebration of multicultural hybridity? Peter Middleton's recent essay, 'Poetry after 1970', provocatively stages this debate, satirizing the playfulness, 'itch to experiment' and prevalence of the personal voice in postmodernism. Against these tendencies, then, Middleton's offers a vigorous intellectualism that we might profitably read back into, as it were, the modernist poetry of the modernist period: the belief that the poem is 'capable of challenging the public sphere, investigating history and science, making discoveries', that it anticipates the later insights of literary theorists, and that it can dramatize language as the (unconscious) site of subjectivity and desire rather than as the transparent display of personal confession (Middleton, in Marcus and Nicholls, *Cambridge History of Twentieth-Century Literature*, pp. 770–1).

Selected reading

Beasley, Rebecca, *Theorists of Modern Poetry: T.S. Eliot, T.E. Hulme, Ezra Pound* (London, Routledge, 2007)
   Demonstrates the important links between poetic theory and the drive towards social reform in modernism, with particular emphasis on the critique of democracy.
Crawford, Robert, *Devolving English Literature* (Oxford, Clarendon Press, 1992)
   See ch. 5, 'Modernism as Provincialism', for an alternative view of 'high' modernist poetry, equating the work of McDiarmid with that of Pound and Eliot.
Dowson, Jane, *Women, Modernism and British Poetry 1910–1939: Resisting Femininity* (London, Ashgate, 2002)
   An important survey assessing the neglected work of British poets such as Anna Wickham, Edith Sitwell, Charlotte Mew and May Sinclair, but set also in the context of international networks and the influence of American poets such as H.D., Amy Lowell and Marianne Moore.
Kristeva, Julia, *Revolution in Poetic Language* (1974), trans. Léon S. Roudiez (New York, Columbia University Press, 1984)
   Pioneering theoretical study.
Mengham, Rod, and John Kinsella (eds), *Vanishing Points: New Modernist Poems* (Cambridge, Salt, 2004)
   A valuable starting point for assessing how and why modernist poetry might persist.

Nicholls, Peter, *Modernisms: A Literary Guide* (Basingstoke, Macmillan, 1995)

Contains a strong emphasis on Symbolism in the opening chapters of the book: ch. 1 on Baudelaire, 2 on Mallarmé and Rimbaud, 3 on Verlaine and 4 on Laforgue, Corbière, Pater and Whitman.

Smith, Stan, *The Origins of Modernism: Eliot, Pound, Yeats, and the Rhetorics of Renewal* (New York, Harvester Wheatsheaf, 1994)

Excellent on social and political contexts.

Stead, C.K., *The New Poetic: Yeats to Eliot* (London, Hutchinson, 1977)

First published in 1964, but an excellent introduction to Eliot, Yeats and Pound, which has stood the test of time well.

7

Modernist fiction

The art of modernist fiction

The modernist novel emerged out of a simultaneous upheaval in theory and in practice. Factors in this upheaval range from the emergence of a critical discourse on the novel as a form of 'art', from Flaubert onwards and notably in the writing of Henry James, to material changes in the printing and publication of fiction and in reading habits – in Britain, for example, after 1894, through the decline in influence of the circulating libraries, and of the 'triple-decker' model of the novel, leading to a freeing of the constraints on both the writing and the reading of fiction (see my 'Modernists on the Art of Fiction', in ed. Shiach, *The Cambridge Companion to the Modernist Novel*, Cambridge, Cambridge University Press, 2007, pp. 15–31).

To the extent that fictional prose and the novel are already distinctively 'modern' forms, emerging as the vehicles of increasingly secular and commercial societies in the eighteenth century, the issues driving modernist fiction are comparable to those facing modernist painting, as these were explored in chapter 2. How adequate is the 'realism' of the novel to the transformations of early twentieth-century modernity? Conversely, if the modernist novel develops greater autonomy, how does this affect its continuing commitment to the recording and interpretation of the modern world?

Let us begin to pursue these questions by examining the fictional prose of the English modernist Virginia Woolf, whose desire to break with established fictional practice was boldly articulated in essays and reviews. The exercise takes the form of a comparison between two passages in which a central female character is intro- duced: the first is from Arnold Bennett's novel *Anna of the Five Towns* (1902), and the second from Woolf's novel *Mrs Dalloway* (1925).

[1.] Anna Tellwright stood motionless for a second in the shadow of the doorway. She was tall, but not unusually so, and sturdily built up. Her figure, though the bust was a little flat, had the lenient curves of absolute maturity. Anna had been a woman since seventeen, and she was now on the eve of her twenty-first birthday. She wore a plain, home-made light frock checked with brown and edged with brown velvet, thin cotton gloves of cream colour, and a broad straw hat like her sister's. Her grave face, owing to the prominence of the cheekbones and the width of the jaw, had a slight angularity; the lips were thin, the brown eyes rather large, the eyebrows level, the nose fine and delicate; the ears could scarcely be seen for the dark brown hair which was brushed diagonally across the temples, leaving of the forehead only a pale triangle. It seemed a face for the cloister, austere in contour, fervent in expression, the severity of it mollified by that resigned and spiritual melancholy peculiar to women who through the error of destiny have been born into the wrong environment. (Arnold Bennett, *Anna of the Five Towns*, 1902; Harmondsworth, Penguin, 1984, p. 19).

[2.] Mrs Dalloway said she would buy the flowers herself.

For Lucy had her work cut out for her. The doors would be taken off their hinges; Rumpelmayer's men were coming. And then, thought Clarissa Dalloway, what a morning – fresh as if issued to children on a beach.

What a lark! What a plunge! For so it had always seemed to her when, with a little squeak of the hinges, which she could hear now, she had burst open the French windows and plunged at Bourton into the open air. How fresh, how calm, stiller than this of course, the air was in the early morning; like the flap of a wave; the kiss of a wave; chill and sharp and yet (for a girl of eighteen as she then was) solemn, feeling as she did, standing there at the open window, that something awful was about to happen; looking at the flowers, at the trees with the smoke winding off them and the rooks rising, falling; standing and looking until Peter Walsh said, 'Musing among the vegetables?' – was that it? – 'I prefer men to cauliflowers' – was that it? He must have said it at breakfast one morning when she had gone out on to the terrace – Peter Walsh. He would be back from India one of these days, June or July, she forgot which, for his letters were awfully dull; it was his sayings one remembered; his eyes, his pocket-knife, his smile, his grumpiness and, when millions of things had utterly vanished – how strange it was! – a few sayings like this about cabbages. (p. 5)

What are the key areas of contrast between these two pieces of fiction?

- *Outer–inner*. Anna Tellwright is introduced via her outward appearance – precise details of her physique, clothes and face. There is no access to her thoughts or consciousness. In contrast, the introduction to Clarissa Dalloway contains no physical description. We have, however, an intimate glimpse of her consciousness, plunging immediately into a vivid memory from Clarissa's life over thirty years ago.

- *Stasis–movement*. Anna does not move: she is made temporarily 'motionless', framed, like a painting, in the doorway. Clarissa is in motion: she launches out to buy the flowers herself, while her mind is also mobile, taking us back to the scene at Bourton.

- *Certainty–uncertainty*. We know exactly where Anna is and what she looks like. There are other expressions of certainty: she became a 'woman' at seventeen; the narrator also generalizes about certain kinds of women who develop a 'resigned and spiritual melancholy' through being born into 'the wrong environment'. By contrast, the introduction to Clarissa throws the reader into uncertainty. Where is Clarissa? Why is she buying flowers? Why do the doors need to be taken off their hinges? What and where was Bourton? Who is Peter Walsh?

- *Prose–poetry*. The description of Anna contains no similes or metaphors – nothing figurative at all, until the tentatively symbolic 'it seemed a face for the cloister' It proceeds through straightforward declarative statements – short balanced sentences, or longer sentences clearly divided up by commas and semi-colons. Scientific objectivity is suggested by geometrical vocabulary – 'angularity', 'level', 'diagonally', 'triangle' – and the impersonality of this description is reinforced by the repeated use of 'the' rather than 'her' to describe Anna's face. The description of Clarissa, however, contains simile and metaphor – 'as if issued to children on a beach', 'the kiss of a wave' – and is characterized by a vocabulary of figurative expressivity: 'lark', 'plunge' (twice), 'squeak', 'burst', 'flap', 'kiss', 'winding', 'rising', 'falling' (notice how many of these are verbs of movement). Sentences are long and unbalanced, complicated by a variety of devices – exclamations and question marks, parentheses, dashes, quotations – which seem to represent the spontaneous prompt-ings of Clarissa's mind rather than any rules of order or stylistic elegance. To appreciate this unpredictability, try reading aloud the sentence which begins 'How fresh' and ends 'was that it?'.

STOP and THINK

- We are by now familiar with the way in which the modernist text makes its reader work hard. Is the description of Clarissa more challenging than that of Anna? If so, how and why? What might the reader gain from such difficulty?
- Bennett's novel can be firmly located within that late Victorian/Edwardian genre known as 'social realism'. But, as we have seen in the work of Cézanne and Cubism, modern-ists often challenged ostensibly realist forms in the name of a more tenacious realism. Is there a realism in Woolf's descrip-tion of Clarissa that challenges Bennett's version of realism?
- Consider the view that Woolf's challenge is not simply to Bennett's mode of realism, but to a certain set of assump-tions about *women*, which his realism reinforces. Look again at the highlighted distinctions between the passages: outer–inner, active–passive, certainty–uncertainty, prose–poetry. How might Woolf's artistic representation of Clarissa be linked to the struggle for women's emancipation in the early twentieth century? Conversely, can Bennett's depiction of Anna be in any way connected with the kind of patriarchal structures and ideas that feminists were challenging? What and how does each passage *know* about the woman it repre-sents? For example, according to whose or what criteria was 'the bust . . . a little flat'? What does it mean to say that Anna had been a woman 'since seventeen'? (menstruation? sexual

experience? or assuming some kind of responsibility?); the
statement is perhaps not so factual as it first seems, showing behind the 'objectivity' of masculine knowledge a high
degree of value judgement.

In her critical writing, Woolf stated quite explicitly that her fiction was partly driven by the need to offer a distinct alternative
to Bennett's technique. In two famous essays, 'Modern Fiction'
(1919) and 'Mr. Bennett and Mrs. Brown' (1924), Woolf cat-
egorized Bennett's fiction, alongside that of H.G. Wells and John
Galsworthy, as 'materialist', a term which in this context has
negative connotations. The work of these three highly popular
and respected British novelists of the Edwardian and Georgian
periods was, she argued, locked into the past, in two senses: first,
it had not noticed the extent to which 'life or spirit, truth or reality' had changed; second, it was still using the traditional forms of
nineteenth-century realist fiction. To acknowledge the one meant
to transform the other. Despite having been freed, in the later
1890s, from the 'triple-decker' structure, novelists, Woolf argued,
still conscientiously constructed their 'two and thirty chapters',
with the obligatory inclusion of plot, comedy, tragedy, love and
an air of probability, according to a design 'which more and more
ceases to resemble the vision in our minds' ('Modern Fiction', in
ed. Peter Faulkner, *A Modernist Reader: Modernism in England
1910–1930*, London, Batsford, 1986, p. 108). Moreover, as 'materi-
alists', Bennett, Wells and Galsworthy expended immense industry
on the quasi-scientific analysis of human and social phenomena, and
in so doing lost sight of the very thing they sought to capture. How,
Woolf asked, would Bennett respond to the challenge of describing
'Mrs. Brown', the archetypal, anonymous woman sitting opposite
him in the railway carriage? 'Begin by saying that her father kept
a shop in Harrogate. Ascertain the rent. Ascertain the wages of
shop assistants in the year 1878. Discover what her mother died of.
Describe cancer. Describe calico. Describe –'. But Woolf interrupts
the imaginary narrative, throwing the clumsy 'tool' of Edwardian
materialist analysis out of the window, because, she writes, it has
given us a house, 'in the hope that it will enable us to deduce the

human beings who live there', and because it is entirely inappropriate for the twentieth-century woman novelist ('Mr. Bennett and Mrs. Brown', in Faulkner, *A Modernist Reader*, pp. 123–4).

Woolf's alternative aesthetic is articulated in a now-famous passage from 'Modern Fiction'. Any 'ordinary mind' on an 'ordinary day' is bombarded with innumerable impressions, 'an incessant shower of innumerable atoms', and were it not for the tyranny of novelistic convention, the writer would be free to try to capture this complexity:

> Life is not a series of gig lamps symmetrically arranged; life is a luminous halo, a semi-transparent envelope surrounding us from the beginning of consciousness to the end. Is it not the task of the novelist to convey this varying, this unknown and uncircumscribed spirit, whatever aberration or complexity it may display, with as little mixture of the alien and external as possible? (Faulkner, *A Modernist Reader*, p. 108)

It is impossible to avoid comparing this Woolfian fictional manifesto, in its desire to capture impressions and multiple perspectives, with modernism in the visual arts. The enigmatic phrases 'luminous halo' and 'semi-transparent envelope' seem to introduce a note of mysticism; yet at the same time, in their suggestion of an interaction between subject and object, they are consonant with that change of scientific paradigm which, for A.N. Whitehead, constituted a challenge to the 'materialism' of the seventeenth century, and which saw modern(ist?) science 'taking on a new aspect which is neither purely physical, nor purely biological' (*Science and the Modern World*, Cambridge, Cambridge University Press, 1927, p. 129).

Woolf's determination to convey 'life' as scrupulously and faithfully as possible is also, of course, to a large extent consistent with the history of the novel. Her aesthetic alerts us to the dangers of constructing a convenient foil or straw man, 'the traditional nineteenth-century realist novel', from which modernism could be said to make its revolutionary break. You might notice that that the bewilderingly unpredictable prose of the *Mrs Dalloway* passage is actually still under the control of that staple of traditional fiction, the omniscient (or 'third-person') narrative voice, drifting in and out of a familiar device, *free indirect narration* (the narrative echoes or mimics the speech or thought patterns of a character, without identifying them as such with quotation marks – so, for 'Mrs Dalloway said she would buy the flowers herself', we read '"I will buy the flowers myself", said Mrs Dalloway'). Was not a version of this ironic device perfected by Jane Austen, in fact?

The *complexity* of Woolf's stance on realism is highlighted by the following qualifications. First, despite the wit and persuasiveness of her essays, one doesn't of course have to agree with Woolf's critique of Bennett (as I indicated at the end of chapter 3, John Carey's work is certainly proof of this). The use of social realism for the purposes of analysing social conditions and their injustices is, in the period in question, an acknowledged feature of a progressive, left-leaning politics of reform and emancipation. For a sustained critique of how modernism, in its inward or psychological turn, could be seen to renege on the possibility of understanding society as a whole, see again the work of the influential Hungarian Marxist critic, Georg Lukács (1885–1971). Woolf, Lukács claimed, was an extreme example of the modernist tendency to 'identif(y) what is necessarily a subjective experience with reality as such, thus giving a distorted picture of reality as a whole' ('Franz Kafka or Thomas Mann?', in *The Meaning of Contemporary Realism*, London, Merlin, 1963, p. 51). Rather more pointedly, Terry Eagleton saw this subjectivity as inevitably shaped by a relatively privileged class background: 'from what kind of social standpoint', he argues, 'does lived experience appear utterly shapeless and chaotic? Virginia Woolf may well have experienced her life in this way, but her servants are less likely to have regarded their days as deliciously fluid and indeterminate' (*Ideology: An Introduction*, London, Verso, 1991, pp. 48–9).

Second, Woolf brings a distinctive element to the critique of realism, and one which became crucial in the development of later twentieth-century feminist criticism. This was the insight that the realist gaze might be an implicitly male gaze, turning women into objects, denying them full subjectivity. In an influential essay, the film theorist Laura Mulvey was to see this gaze as the default mode of Hollywood mainstream cinema, embodying the split between active/male and passive/female ('Visual Pleasure and Narrative Cinema', in *Visual and Other Pleasures*, London, Macmillan, 1989). Realism, Woolf suggests, is a gendered category, making her own modernist reclamation and reinvention of it all the more significant. While the full force of experimentalism in this respect emerged in novels from the mid-1920s onwards – *Mrs Dalloway*, followed by *To the Lighthouse* (1927) and *The Waves* (1931) – Woolf had been preceded by two British contemporaries, whose contribution to a fictional modernism voicing women's experience lay in the development of the technique known broadly as 'stream of consciousness'. Dorothy Richardson's multi-volume work *Pilgrimage* (1915–67) is highlighted below (p. 230–3). May Sinclair's (1863–1946) novels *Mary Olivier: A Life* (1919) and *The Life and Death of Harriet Frean* (1922) were extremely important elements in an emergent feminist aesthetic, building on the use of psychoanalytic materials to explore female desire and its encounter with social repression in novels such as her own *The Three Sisters* (1914) and Rebecca West's *The Return of the Soldier* (1918).

The emergence of modernist fiction

Three main elements might be identified in a nineteenth-century prehistory drawn mainly from French, Russian and American fiction:

- *Symbolism*. A primary influence on Baudelaire's poetry had been the early, unsettling short fictions of Edgar Allan Poe. Poe's tales, typified by 'The Fall of the House of Usher' (1839), trace the shadow of a degeneration or decay at the heart of modernity (Baudelaire's 'fleurs du mal'), combining the principles of analysis and detection with an allusive Gothic symbolism in a way that made them prime material for a psychoanalytic approach to literary criticism. In the inwardness of their 'morbid' self-analysis and often highly mannered prose, Poe's tales are a key reference point for the emergence of so-called 'Decadent' and *fin-de-siècle* writing, whose fictional apogee could be said to be represented in France by J.-K. Huysmans' enigmatic *Against Nature* (1884). In this novel Des Esseintes, the aristocratic anti-hero, retreats from the squalor encountered as a *flâneur* on the streets of Paris, virtually sealing himself into his house in Fontaney, an exile only interrupted by the delivery of the rare and unusual artefacts with which he surrounds himself, and by the doctor who comes to treat his growing yet indefinably modern malady. *Against Nature* is an extraordinary antithesis both to realism and to romanticism; Des Esseintes' preference for cultural ingenuity over mere nature is mirrored in a prose that is almost overladen with references, as if bearing the weight of an overdeveloped culture is a condition of modernity itself. The model of Huysmann's decadence reappears throughout later modernism, principally in the work Marcel Proust and James Joyce, and re-merges distinctly in Djuna Barnes' narrative of 1920s European salon culture, *Nightwood* (1936).

- *Naturalism*. It would be a simplification to say that the 'natural' associations of Naturalism are antithetical to the 'degenerative' associations of Symbolism; both are important in the emergence of modernist fiction, and sometimes overlap. Gustave Flaubert (1821–80), a key figure for Huysmans, exemplifies this ambivalence. The modernism of *Madame Bovary* (1857) was seen to lie in the pitiless, sardonic realism with which Emma Bovary's betrayal of her dull, petit-bourgeois husband was represented. Yet in his letters, Flaubert is a Mallarméan Symbolist, aspiring to write a novel about 'nothing', spending an entire day refining the style of a single sentence, and insisting that *Madame Bovary* is neither based on any 'actual occurrence' nor contains any of the author's own feelings or autobiography. In other words, Flaubert represents the novelist in terms of an Eliotic aesthetic of impersonality: 'An artist must be in his work like God in creation, invisible and all-powerful; he should be everywhere felt, but nowhere seen' (Kolocotroni *et al.*, *Modernism*, p. 97). This combination of aesthetic autonomy and Naturalist investigation is precisely that discerned by Rosen and Zerner in the paintings of Flaubert's contemporary, Gustave Courbet, as we discussed on p. 36.

A more unambiguous source of the movement known as Naturalism are the novels of Emile Zola (1840–1902), though even here Zola insisted on connecting their artistic organization with the music of Wagner. What came to distinguish this category from Realism was Zola's determination to create an analogy between scientific experimentation and the writing of fiction. In his Rougon–Macquart series of novels of the 1870s and 1880s,

Zola claimed to apply the determining principles of heredity and environment to the history of a family in Second Empire France. This scientific ultra-realism also meant dispensing with any moral taboos concerning subject matter; hence, through for example the treatment of sexual depravity within industrial labouring communities in *Germinal* (1885), or prostitution in *Nana* (1880), Naturalism in Zola's hands came to signify, to the European bourgeoisie, scandal and dubious sexual morality as much as rigorous scientific analysis. In writing in English, the Irish novelist George Moore (1852–1933) became the clearest exponent of a Zolaesque Naturalism, claiming to have written in *Esther Waters* (1894) a more direct and honest account of the young, fallen woman than was to be found in Thomas Hardy's *Tess of the D'Urbervilles* (1891), despite the latter's self-conscious treatment of the 'ache of modernism'.

Rather than the conscious rupturing of language or the sense of difficulty that we see as a Symbolist legacy to literary modernism, Naturalism brought to modernist fiction a heightening and intensifying of the realist impulse, and the widening of fiction's remit out into previously tabooed areas. Where the Naturalist pursuit of physical fact and the Symbolist search for a unique language of subjectivity might be said to coincide was in the distinctly psychological turn taken by fiction of the later nineteenth century.

• *The psychological turn*. The early novel had already been distinguished by the strength of its individual psychologies (Robinson Crusoe and Moll Flanders; Emma Woodhouse and Jane Eyre), and fictions of the later nineteenth century show a more marked turn towards the individual case study, as in the tortured Raskolnikov of Fyodor Dostoevsky's *Crime and Punishment* (1866). Modernist fiction, however, tends towards the elusiveness and intractability, as well as the complexity, of subjectivity – qualities in the face of which the standard devices of the realist novel, such as linearity, omniscience and closure, might prove inadequate.

An analysis of the typical modernist figure of the clerk is a good starting point. In 'Bartleby the Scrivener' (1853) by Herman

Melville, Bartleby begins to greet every request made by his manager with variants on the formula, 'I would prefer not to'. Bartleby's
recalcitrance remains inscrutable throughout the story; the formula,
as Gilles Deleuze puts it, is 'ravaging, devastating, and leaves nothing standing in its wake', including the character or consciousness
of Bartleby himself, to which we have no access (*Essays Critical and
Clinical*, trans. Daniel W. Smith and Michael A. Greco, London,
Verso, 1998, p. 70). By contrast, another account of the modern
clerk, Fyodor Dostoevsky's *Notes from Underground* (1864), takes
the form of a diary or confession, following the narrator's tortu-
ous attempts at explaining his own 'paradoxical' consciousness.
Underground man reproduces the dilemma of a key modernist reference point, Shakespeare's Hamlet; 'to think too much is a disease,
a real, actual disease', so that he remains caught between reflection
and the actions he needs to take to rectify his sense of powerlessness.

Virginia Woolf's *Mrs Dalloway* contains another enigmatic clerk-
psyche. Septimus Smith represents one of the first fictional representations of the condition of post-war psychological damage known
as 'shell-shock'. Septimus is treated by an ordinary doctor and by a
world-famous Harley Street specialist; the one maintains that there
is 'nothing whatever the matter' with Septimus, prescribing sport
and an extra bowl of porridge every morning; the other insists that
Septimus is a case of 'complete physical and nervous breakdown',
prescribing isolation, rest and a cessation of all stimulation. We
sense, however, that the truth about Septimus lies somewhere
between these two unequivocal diagnoses, in a liminal region where
it is far more difficult to distinguish, as Sir William habitually does,
between 'madness' and 'sanity'. Septimus is therefore a border
figure, 'neither one thing nor the other', and in a variety of ways: in
the enigmatic social and economic modernity of his status as a clerk;
in his sexuality, where masculinity and marriage are complicated
by his unresolved feelings for the dead officer Evans; in his symbolic status as the 'other' or alter-ego of Clarissa Dalloway, herself
ambiguously poised in terms of sexuality; and in his shell-shock.

Psychoanalysis itself could be said to have occupied just such
a liminal space. As William Greenslade shows in *Degeneration,
Culture and the Novel* (Cambridge, Cambridge University Press,
1994), Freudian theory was initially opposed and derided by the

British medical establishment. How could one treat, scientifically, something as intangible as the unconscious, by definition impossible to apprehend directly? Was not the concept of the unconscious itself unscientific? W.H.R. Rivers' pioneering treatment of the condition of shell-shock had begun to demonstrate that it was possible to achieve practical success through psychoanalytic methods. An analogous fictional technique, directly approaching what can only, as it were, be indirectly represented, was that of the narrative refracted through an unstable or unreliable 'centre of consciousness'. Key examples of this extremely subtle fictional modernism are *What Maisie Knew* (1897) by Henry James and *The Good Soldier* (1915) by Ford Madox Ford. James' novel uses a form of omniscient narration filtered through the consciousness of the child, Maisie, as she observes the questionable actions of the adults around her; Ford's American narrator John Dowell naively relates the tale of his wife's infidelity at the hands of the enigmatic Englishman, Edward Ashburnham. What situates these profound and complex stories on what Randall Stevenson calls a '"fault-line" between Victorian and modernist fiction' (*Modernist Fiction*, p. 28) is their shift towards the nature and psychology of the perceiver and away from any stable sense of the perceived world. However, the modernist novel also began to adopt a more explicit technique which Stevenson identifies in Ford's later, epic four-volume work of wartime experience, *Parade's End* (1924–8), and whose broad principle – the liberation of a 'stream of consciousness' – suggested a parallel with the Freudian method of the 'talking cure'. As 'stream of consciousness' is a somewhat overused phrase in the study of fictional modernism, the next section examines some practical examples.

Stream of consciousness

'Consciousness does not appear to itself chopped up into bits, it is nothing jointed, it flows'. In a founding work of modern psychology, *Principles of Psychology* (1890), William James originated the famous definition of a 'stream of consciousness' – 'Immortal phrase of the immortal James!', intones D.H. Lawrence in full satirical mode, 'Oh stream of hell which undermined my adolescence! I felt it streaming through my brain, in at one ear and out at the other'

(*Fantasia of the Unconscious and Psychoanalysis of the Unconscious*, Harmondsworth, Penguin, 1977, pp. 102–3). Lawrence touches on the profound influence of the definition. Freud's work, he felt, aimed at finding the source of the stream. The sense of a complex and uncategorizable fluidity made James' definition resonate more widely in modernist thinking, however – through, for example, Pater's aesthetics of sense experience, or Bergson's conception of a continually, unpredictably unfolding *élan vital*. How did modernist fiction respond to the challenge of 'stream of consciousness'? Here are three examples:

1. '"Yes I certainly do see that very clear Dr. Campbell", said Melanctha, "I see that's certainly what it is always made me not know right about you and that's certainly what it is that makes you really mean what you was always saying. You certainly are just too scared Dr. Campbell to really feel things way down in you. All you are always wanting Dr. Campbell, is just to talk about being good, and to play with people just to have a good time, and yet always to certainly keep yourself out of trouble"' (Gertrude Stein, 'Melanctha', *Three Lives*, 1909; Harmondsworth, Penguin, 1990, p. 86).

2. 'Tranquil moonlight lay across the room. It surprised her like a sudden hand stroking her brow. It seemed to feel for her heart. If she gave way to it her thoughts would go. Perhaps she ought to watch it and let her thoughts go. It passed over her trouble like her mother did when she said, "Don't go so deeply into everything, chickie. You must learn to take life as it comes. Ah-eh, if I were strong I could show you how to enjoy life". Delicate little mother, running quickly downstairs clearing her throat to sing. But mother did not know. She had no reasoning power. She could not help because she did not know. The moonlight was sad and hesitating. Miriam closed her eyes again. Luther . . . pinning up that notice on a church door . . . (Why is Luther like a dyspeptic blackbird? Because the Diet of Worms did not agree with him.) . . . and then leaving that notice on the church door and going home to tea . . . coffee . . . some evening meal . . . Käthe . . . Käthe . . . happy Käthe' (Dorothy Richardson, *Pilgrimage*, vol. I, London, Dent, 1967, p. 169).

3. '[. . .] and Gibraltar as a girl where I was a Flower of the mountain yes when I put the rose in my hair like the Andalusian girls
used or shall I wear a red yes and how he kissed me under the
Moorish wall and I thought well as well him as another and then
I asked him with my eyes to ask again yes and then he asked me
would I yes to say yes my mountain flower and first I put my
arms around him yes and drew him down to me so he could feel
my breasts all perfume yes and his heart was going like mad and
yes I said yes I will Yes' (James Joyce, *Ulysses,* Oxford, Oxford
University Press (World's Classics series), p. 732).

Example 1: Gertrude Stein studied for a brief period under William
James at Harvard. This extract from the story 'Melanctha' (1909) is
not so much a stream of *consciousness* as of *speech*, as the quotation
marks clearly indicate. Melanctha Herbert, a vibrant young woman
with a troubled and dramatic life, explains her feelings to Dr. Jeff
Campbell, who has become her lover. Several features suggest the
rhythms and spontaneity of ordinary speech: repetition, in particular of the terms 'certainly' and 'always'; clumsy syntax ('made me
not know right about you', 'always to certainly'); the ungrammatical
colloquialisms ('was' for 'are' or 'were' in the first sentence) and the
distinct lack of abstract or differentiated vocabulary. In an often-
acknowledged irony, the black American novelist Richard Wright
viewed this technique, as practised by the white German-American
Jewish intellectual Stein, as a pioneering fictional rendering of black
American vernacular. However, there is also a quality of excess that
makes it difficult simply to 'hear' Melanctha's words as speech.
'Certainly' occurs just a little too often to be feasible, along with
the repeated formal address 'Dr. Campbell'. The obscurities of
Melanctha's language can seem exaggerated: the shift within a sentence, for example, from her failure to understand Jeff ('made me
not know right') to the sense that he always really means what he
says. The extract seems to hover, then, between colloquial speech
and a more stylized mode of expression; partly, we 'hear' it, but
partly too this is a very 'written' language which, perhaps, represents what Melanctha *is* rather than simply recording what she says.
If this stream-like language can be said to embody Melanctha, it
does so principally through a *struggle* for expression, denoting the

unclassifiability and marginality of a person whose voice had barely been heard in the fictional tradition. Stein's very stylized stream of consciousness is highly distinctive, its closest parallel perhaps to be found in the narration of the quirky publisher's secretary, Pompey Casmilus, in the unjustly neglected English writer Stevie Smith's *Novel on Yellow Paper* (1936).

Example 2: *Pointed Roofs* (1915), the first volume of Dorothy Richardson's multi-volume novel *Pilgrimage*, is often seen as a start-ing point for fictional stream of consciousness, thanks largely to an early review of the work by the novelist May Sinclair which referred to a sense of the protagonist Miriam Henderson's 'stream of con-sciousness going on and on' (Sinclair, 1918, quoted in Kolocotrini *et al.*, *Modernism*, p. 353). This extract shows how the technique might present modernism, not as an abrupt break, but as a seam-less evolution in fictional form. Miriam lies in bed, reflecting upon the challenges of her life as a young and inexperienced governess in Germany. The mode of narration subtly mutates, from omnis-cient narration ('Tranquil moonlight'), to free indirect speech ('If she gave way to it', 'Perhaps she ought'), to the reported speech of her mother and finally, when Miriam re-closes her eyes, to her own stream of consciousness. Various devices prefigure the sense that this is a release of unconscious forces: the moonlight itself as a stimulus (as in T.S. Eliot's poem 'Rhapsody on a Windy Night', where the 'lunar' effect is to 'Dissolve the floors of memory/And all its clear relations'); the idea of letting thoughts 'go'; the memory of her mother's words; and the idea of her mother having 'no reason-ing power'. The stream itself is then simply a stream of associations, linked by ellipsis, a device that suggests both the continuous and the unfinished. Miriam reverts to a train of thought about Germany and Martin Luther; this provokes a memory of a joke revolving around the Diet of Worms, in a way reminiscent of Freud's theory of jokes and their intimate relation to the unconscious; the stream then con-nects two prominent feelings in Miriam's own unconscious, the act of profound revolt (Luther's challenge to the established Church), and the cosy domesticity and companionship she had left at home in England – tea, coffee, evening meal, 'happy Käthe'.

Example 3: In this famous conclusion to James Joyce's epic novel *Ulysses* (1922), Molly Bloom lies in bed, reflecting back on her long-suspended sexual life with her husband Leopold, and on coupling in the same bed with her lover Blazes Boylan earlier that day. She concludes by reminiscing about the first time she gave herself to Leopold. The opening ellipsis is mine, because the absence of punctuation makes intervention literally like the act of jumping into the running stream of Molly's consciousness. In Joyce's model of stream of consciousness here (although there are several other models at work in various chapters of *Ulysses*), the conventions of grammar, syntax, punctuation, even down to the ellipses deployed by Richardson, are simply irrelevant to the principle of free linguistic flow. There is no omniscient narrative voice to help us place and interpret the flow; Joyce dispenses with this 'metalanguage', as the critic Colin McCabe put it in a pioneering study (*James Joyce and the Revolution of the Word*, London, Macmillan, 1979). Nothing is stable or predictable: the simple past tense is interrupted by a future, 'shall I wear a red', which seems equally to be part of Molly's recollection; syntax begins to break under the strain of memory and passion: 'would I yes to say yes my mountain flower'. 'Yes' is an ambiguous punctuation of the stream, signifying Molly's assent to Leopold but also, in its gathering repetition, the intensity of Molly's approach to penetration or orgasm – 'Yes'. Yet, while suggesting the sheer spontaneity of the moment, the upper-case 'Y' takes the reader back to the opening 'Yes' of the whole 'Penelope' section of the novel, suggesting an organic cyclicality which is also representative of the myth of womanhood that Molly embodies.

The marked differences between these three passages show that there is no simple label to be attached to stream of consciousness in the modernist novel; see Anne Fernihough's essay, 'Consciousness as a Stream', in Shiach, *Cambridge Companion to the Modernist Novel*, to pursue this issue with more reference to Henri Bergson's thought. Two key examples of American modernism further emphasize the point. William Faulkner's (1897–1962) major novels are *The Sound and the Fury* (1929), *As I Lay Dying* (1930), *Light in August* (1932) and *Absalom! Absalom!* (1936). In the first, Faulkner began a sustained experiment in using stream of consciousness and multiple perspective as a means of exploring 'the construction of identity across racial and sexual difference' (Trotter, 'The Modernist Novel', in Levenson, *Cambridge*

Companion to Modernism, p. 89) in his native American South. *The Sound and the Fury* has the feel of a tour de force; among its four narrators is Benjy Compson, whose arrested development renders him unable to grasp the relations of the objective world, while producing a narrative of rich subjective intensity. The radical socialist writer John Dos Passos (1896–1970) similarly began his modernist experiment in the 1920s with *Manhattan Transfer* (1925) and extended it in the 1930s through the epic trilogy *U.S.A.* (1930–6). Where Faulkner's technique stressed alternating consciousnesses, Dos Passos' fourfold narration in *U.S.A.* stressed technologies of communication and perception in its account of the approach to the Wall Street Crash and the Depression: omniscient narration mingled with the fragmentary vision of the 'Camera Eye', newsreel or newspaper collage, and journalistic biography (though, for a suggestion of how Faulkner's fictions are also informed by the emergence of new recording technologies, see Armstrong, *Modernism: A Cultural History*, pp. 112–14). These works reveal the limitations of the concept of the modernist psychological turn, if and when this is conceived purely in terms of the workings of individual minds. Rather, the subjective becomes a means of reapproaching fiction's obligation to explore and analyse collective and historical phenomena, as the next sections indicate.

Narrative time and space

Stream of consciousness, with its impressions of immediacy and unpredictability, no doubt contributed to a sense of the formlessness of modernist fiction. May Sinclair claimed to have heard other novelists complaining about a lack of art in Dorothy Richardson's fictions – that 'they have no beginning and no middle and no end, and that to have form a novel must have an end and a beginning and a middle'. While there may, Sinclair admits, be something in this requirement, it 'depends on what constitutes a beginning and a middle and an end' (Kolocotroni *et al.*, *Modernism*, p. 353). The formal structure of modernist fictions needs, however, to be understood in conjunction with rapidly changing conceptions of time and space, such as those implicit in Bergson's philosophy or in relativity physics (see chapter 4).

In terms of economies of scale, this does not produce any single norm for modernist fiction: epic novels thrive, such as Proust's *In Search of Lost Time* or Joyce's *Ulysses*, while the short story, for example in the hands of Katherine Mansfield or D.H. Lawrence, undergoes a resurgence, as if fictional narrative borrowed productively from Imagist poetics. The novella, hovering ambiguously between the proportions of novel and short story, becomes equally emblematic of great modernist fiction, for example in Joseph Conrad's *Heart of Darkness* (1902), Henry James' *The Turn of the Screw*, Katherine Mansfield's *In a German Pension* (1911) or D.H. Lawrence's *The Fox* (1923).

An awareness of 'time–space compression' has inevitable impacts on fictional form. Broadly speaking we could characterize the fiction of the nineteenth century as endorsing a model of time as linear and homogeneous, typified by the *Bildungsroman*, the narrative of individual growth and identity. Plots, sequences of events which initially obscure and then gradually reveal their relations of causality, can also be built into the structure of beginning–middle–end. Fictional modernism, however, combines a number of the following structural characteristics:

- beginnings *in media res*, involving uncertainty of orientation;
- 'open', ambiguous endings;
- the weakening or disappearance of plot;
- chapters structured according to a loosely 'symbolic' logic, or written in different styles;
- the presence of apparently inconsequential or 'non'-events;
- simultaneity of events within short time-spans;
- inconsistencies in the notation of time: the extended treatment of moments, the fleeting description of longer periods, for example; and
- multiple and shifting narrative viewpoints and, often as a consequence, the disruption of sequential time, for example through digression or memory flashbacks.

The time span of James Joyce's *Ulysses*, and of Virginia Woolf's *Mrs Dalloway*, is a single day. In *The Rainbow*, D.H. Lawrence spends several pages on the intense, moonlit sheaf-gathering scene between Will and Anna, yet elsewhere summarizes years of Anna's life in a matter of paragraphs. For the reader of Stein's *Melanctha*, progression through the narrative is also a circling back, so that s/he encounters the beginning a second time, in the form of an identical sentence, close to the end of the narrative. The reader of modernist fiction soon comes to realize that there is no consistent correlation between time and space; discussion of the relationship between them in modernist fiction has tended to revolve around the concept of 'spatial form', coined by the American critic Joseph Frank (see *The Widening Gyre*, 1963). In spatial form, as in a painting of analytic Cubism, different moments in time are said to occupy the same *space*, simultaneously, rather than to succeed each other as points on a line. The concept captures well the anti-linear complexities of modernist narrative; in *Mrs Dalloway*, for example, two 'moments' separated by over thirty years are experienced simultaneously, so that the 'now' of the novel's opening sequence is divided, and Clarissa is at once a teenager and a menopausal woman.

However, it is well to remember that for Bergson, it was precisely the tendency to spatialize time that reduced and impoverished our capacity to *experience* it as *durée*. Perhaps the most uncompromising attempt to embody a Bergsonian 'continuous present' in fictional form is in Gertrude Stein's *Melanctha*, where the consistent reiteration of 'Melanctha Herbert' and her situations and qualities seems to imply that nothing about Melanctha can be taken for granted or fixed at a point in space, and that what she is must continually be rebuilt and experienced anew, from sentence to sentence.

The archetype of a modernist reworking of time and space is Marcel Proust's eight-part *In Search of Lost Time* (1913–27). In its elements of social satire on the France of the Second Empire, readers new to Proust may be surprised to find some of the familiar lineaments of nineteenth-century realist fiction. The novel's treatment of its themes, however, is a complex dismantling of linear temporality, in which the recollections of the Jamesian centre of consciousness, the narrator Marcel, are assembled according to his own inner logic, resulting in what Randall Stevenson, summarizing Gérard Genette's reliance on Proust for his narratological study *Narrative Discourse* (1972), describes as 'a kind of inventory of narrative techniques and strategies'. Proust's novel addresses the philosophical problem of recovering the past by famously enacting a distinction between two kinds of memory, voluntary and involuntary. While much of the novel consists in Marcel's painstaking efforts to reconstruct consciously his own personal development and that of late nineteenth-century France, it is punctuated by rare moments of involuntary memory. At these moments, a physical stimulus – the taste of a Madeleine pastry dipped in tea, a piano sonata by the musician Vinteuil, tripping on an uneven paving stone – produces a memory so vivid that it is less a mental image or concept than an entire physical condition of embodiment. These, the novel implies, are the only moments at which time can be truly regained or redeemed; voluntary memory, for all its importance in the essentially human work of historical imagination and explanation, is strictly secondary, being prone to partiality and distortion.

Proust's work in this sense has close affinities with the concept of *mémoire involuntaire* as elaborated in Henri Bergson's *Matter and Memory* (1911). Bergson questions the tendency to conceive of the function of memory in spatial terms, for example as slides stored in a mental cabinet and then projected onto a screen in the 'theatre' of the mind. Instead, Bergson claims, memory is an actualized physical state: we do not *have* memories, but *are* them for the time of their duration. We are reminded of the concept of *durée* and the sense of time as experience rather than as objectively measurable quantity. T.S. Eliot's *Four Quartets* attempt to encapsulate this as a mystic condition in the formula, 'To be conscious is not to be in time' or in the image of music heard so 'deeply' that 'it is not heard at all, but you are the music/While the music lasts' (*Burnt Norton*, II, line 84; *The Dry Salvages*, V, lines 210–12). For Walter Benjamin, whose superb essay 'On Some Motifs in Baudelaire' weaves Proust into a reading of Baudelaire's lyric poetry and their joint relation to the crowd and the city in modernity, it is necessary to invoke Freud's theory of memory traces (and their implicit connection with trauma), which are 'often most powerful and enduring when the incident which left them behind was one that never entered consciousness' (Benjamin, *Illuminations*, p. 162).

The results of this emphasis in Proust is a novel in which time possesses extraordinary qualities of warping and expansion. For Samuel Beckett, in his acute and creative long essay on Proust, the novel allows its people to occupy in time 'a much greater place than that so sparingly conceded to them in space', while 'the whole of Proust's world comes out of a teacup' (*Proust and Three Dialogues with Georges Duthuit*, London, John Calder, 1965, p. 12, 34). Out of the initial Overture, detailing memories from the narrator's childhood family holidays in Combray, the model of the two paths labelled Swann's Way and the Guermantes' Way becomes the basis of an exploration of ambivalences of class, power and sexuality in the upper bourgeois and aristocratic circles that Marcel and the central enigmatic figure of Swann move in.

Another famous vehicle of this warping of time is the Proustian sentence. Finely crystallizing the challenges of reading literary modernism, Samuel Beckett writes of the 'chain-figure of the metaphor', which often extends to breaking point the dimensions of Proust's sentences:

> It is a tiring style, but it does not tire the mind. The clarity of the phrase is cumulative and explosive. One's fatigue is a fatigue of the heart, a blood fatigue. One is exhausted and angry after an hour, submerged, dominated by the crest and break of metaphor after metaphor: but never stupefied. The complaint that it is an involved style, full of periphrasis, obscure and impossible to follow, has no foundation whatsoever. (*Proust and Three Dialogues*, p. 88)

Proust's experiment with time and space inevitably invites comparison with that of James Joyce. There is a close similarity between the Proustian *mémoire involuntaire* and the Joycean 'epiphany', intense experiential moments of consciousness whose transfigurative potential connects to the orthodox religious context from which the term is drawn. The epiphany is a central device in Joyce's fiction from the early *Dubliners* stories, through *Portrait of the Artist as a Young Man*, to *Ulysses*. Joyce's later modernism, however, belonging more securely to the practices of the European avant-garde, calls for a new and contrasting conception of time and space that highlights the limits of Proust's transgression of realism.

The stories of *Dubliners*, critically excoriated by contemporary Dublin folk for the bleak and unforgiving 'realism' of Joyce's depiction of the city, are organized through a chain of artistic motifs that are passed on and discarded as we move through the volume. In *Portrait*, the linear and physical growth of Stephen Dedalus from toddler to young artist is recorded across six chapters, the stages however depicted not in terms of a familiar realistic causality but in terms of a style of writing which modulates according to the stage in Stephen's development. The early chapters of *Ulysses* promise to consolidate the reader's knowledge of Stephen by switching the focus to a day in his life, the famous 'Bloomsday', 16 June 1904, although this indicates that the day also belongs to Leopold Bloom, the cuckolded Jewish advertising salesman and 'Everyman' figure, whose status as a prosaic father-figure for Stephen is confirmed in their meeting at the end of the day. But the 'Aeolus' chapter institutes an unprecedented break in this pattern; while the subject is a meeting of journalists in the offices of a newspaper, the style is a series of fragments prefaced by satirical journalistic headlines. The pattern resumes in the next two chapters, but the breach in the realist fabric has been made: from 'Wandering Rocks' onwards, the chapters are written in a medley of styles, as if to catalogue and in the process, as Joyce himself put it, to exhaust and have done with the various available modes of writing. Here style, it appears, has prevailed over realist content, and the time and space of the novel are the time and space of *writing* or *textuality*.

The radical nature of Joyce's transformation of fiction is intimately tied to the notions of flight and exile informing his relationship, and that of the character Stephen, with his Irish cultural and religious background. As Stephen puts it to his friend Cranly:

> I will not serve that in which I no longer believe, whether it call itself my home, my fatherland or my church: and I will try to express myself in some mode of life or art as freely as I can and as wholly as I can, using for my defence the only arms I allow myself to use – silence, exile, and cunning. (*Portrait of the Artist as a Young Man*, 1916: Harmondsworth, Penguin, 1976, p. 247)

Trying to awake himself, in the words of Stephen and in an echo of Marx, from the 'nightmare' of history, Joyce's deployment of 'arms' meant an assault on the bourgeois novel and its realist contract. His exuberant reinvention of the language of fiction, where language becomes (in *Finnegan's Wake*) the novel's world, constitutes at the same time an imaginative escape from, and a transfiguration of, his home culture. T.S. Eliot's assessment of the 'mythic method' in *Ulysses*, the use of the Homeric parallel, as a way of conferring order upon the 'futility and anarchy of contemporary history', probably tells us more about Eliot than it does about Joyce, though both are *émigré* artists. Eliot's flight was towards the sense of order in English literary culture and identity, from which position his hybrid cosmopolitan writing could emerge; Joyce, although the figure of the rootless intellectual gravitating between Paris, Rome, Trieste and Zurich, could be said never to have left Dublin in imagination, while transforming that city – not, then, one of the centres of metropolitan modernity – through a radical fictional aesthetic which seems to refuse all traditional order and cohesion.

Joyce's modernizing spirit, through which time and space become *metafictional*, or self-conscious aspects of the novel itself, comes to define an Irish narrative modernism characterized by linguistic play, irreverence and reflexivity, as for example in Samuel Beckett's *Murphy* (1938) or the fictions of Flann O'Brien, such as *At Swim Two Birds* (1939) or *The Third Policeman* (1940). Beckett's first novel *Murphy* is a darkly comedic exercise, a kind of philosophical cartoon, whose subject is partly the explosion of novelistic discourse, just as the eponymous anti-hero of the novel is exploded (twice!) towards its climax. The novel plays incessantly with fictional discourse, pausing at one point to satirize the realist imperative (a list of Murphy's lover Celia's vital statistics, which for example declares her wrist to be 6 inches and her calf 13 inches, but her age and instep 'unimportant'), and at another to satirize the psychological turn of the modernist novel (the narrative is interrupted in chapter 6 in order to consider how Murphy pictures his own mind). Yet *Murphy* is far from reducible to reflexive linguistic or narrative play. As a helper in a mental asylum, Murphy's scandalous success with the patients, and his relationship of intimate non-communication with the schizophrenic Mr Endon, constitute both a powerful critique of institutionalized psychiatric 'care' and a moving model of peaceful co-existence at a time when Europe was once again on the verge of war. Declan Kiberd has also argued that the comic, anti-heroic but fiercely intellectual Murphy acts as a subtle deconstruction of embedded English stereotypes of the 'Irishman' (*Inventing Ireland: The Literature of the Modern Nation*, Harvard University Press, 1996). In the end, faced with a fundamental decision in his relationships with the patients, Murphy votes unhesitatingly for their 'little' world over the 'big' world, as much a political as a philosophical or aesthetic preference.

The modernist novel of irony

Another important strand in the modernist novel looks initially rather unlike the kinds of experimentalism evident in the fictions of stream of consciousness or time–space compression, and much more like a continuation of previous tradition. This strand can also be located geographically: it is central European, focused for example around Vienna, the polyglot capital of the Austro-Hungarian empire, Prague, or Trieste, the Italian border city to which James Joyce also gravitated. I call this 'the modernist novel of irony'. A continuity is again established with the highly developed use of irony implicit in the earlier novel; in modernist prose, however, the ironic mode is developed to an extreme, all-encompassing pitch, as if it is the necessary analytic tool of a modernity founded on paradox, unable to fully declare itself because perpetually 'pregnant with its contrary' (Marx and Engels).

A leading source of this voice of irony in modernist fiction is the German novelist Thomas Mann (1875–1955), with works stretching from the early novella *Death in Venice* (1912), through the Weimar-influenced *The Magic Mountain* (1924), to *Doctor Faustus* (1947), an epic account of modernist genius emerging amidst the barbarism of Nazi Germany. Mann's own ideological and philosophical journey is also a model of modernist contradiction and struggle: from early German cultural and political nationalism, though the disillusionment of the First World War, Weimar idealism, fierce critique of the rise and consequences of German fascism, and alliance with Marxist Frankfurt School thinkers such as Theodor Adorno. *Minima Moralia* (1951), Adorno's crucial, aphoristic reflections on the conditions of a 'damaged life', came out of the same mid-1940s period as did *Doctor Faustus*, when Mann and Adorno had set up friendship and dialogue while exiled in America.

Mann's focus across the fiction remains remarkably steady: it is fixed, metaphorically, on a culture's recognition of, and attempts to scrutinize and come to terms with, the ill-health of civilized, liberal–humanist values. The archetype in these fictions is the bourgeois male, within whom is enacted a conflict between the norms of polite, respectable civic society and the demands of vital, life-giving creative and aesthetic energy. In *Death in Venice*, the writer Gustave Aschenbach finds himself imprisoned in plague-ridden Venice by his infatuation with Tadzio, the young boy who becomes for Aschenbach a symbol of idealized beauty, yet whose bluish and imperfect teeth reveal a corruption at the heart of this perfection. Sickness and cure are thus bound together in a contradiction which seems unreadable to conventional wisdom. *The Magic Mountain* is an extended reprise of this metaphor of sickness and imprisonment. Hans Castorp, set for a career in engineering, visits his cousin in a sanatorium in the Swiss Alps. The visitor, however, becomes the patient: Castorp is persuaded of his own sickness by Behrens, the head of the clinic, and in an overarching irony the three-week visit becomes a seven-year stay. This 'choice' of incarceration is also the occasion of Castorp's metamorphosis into an intellectual, along the lines of the distinction between *Kultur* and *civilization*; the inmates symbolize a cross-section of Europe's intelligentsia, and the sanatorium becomes a crucible of debate about the current status of knowledge and its relation to humanism, from science to aesthetics. In *Doctor Faustus*, the debate is enjoined again, but with more specific reference to modernist experimentation itself. Here irony is embedded in the perspective of the conventional narrator Zeitbolm, who tells the tragic story of his musician friend, Adrian Leverkuhn. In Leverkuhn, radical modernist experimentation (atonality and serialism; the character is based on Mann's friend the composer Arnold Schoenberg, who is discussed in the next chapter) is associated with anti-humanism in the form of a Faustian pact with the devil, through which he forfeits his soul in return for genius in musical composition. In an account mixing irony with chilling horror, Zeitbolm transcribes Leverkuhn's meeting with the devil, who appears as an aspect of the musician's own psyche.

A distinguishing modernist characteristic of Mann's fictions is their intellectual scope, as if the debates staged in the pages of *The Magic Mountain* and *Doctor Faustus* are attempting to encapsulate the contradictory forces of modernity and the logic of creative destruction. For Georg Lukács, this formed the basis of an endorse-ment of Mann as a supreme exponent of 'critical realism'. *The*

Magic Mountain, for example, refuses to conflate certain characters' experience of time as subjective with any claim that this subjectivity constitutes the absolute nature of time *per se* –a claim that Lukács associates with naive 'ideologies' of modernism. In the intriguing comparison staged in his essay 'Franz Kafka or Thomas Mann?', Lukács argues that the aspiring writer must always choose Mann over the 'aesthetically appealing, but decadent' modernism of a Kafka who, despite his marvellous sincerity and simplicity, exemplified the modern writer 'at the mercy of a blind and panic-stricken *angst*' (*The Meaning of Contemporary Realism*, p. 92, 77).

As an interesting example of the shift in literary criticism away from this highly judgemental, mid-twentieth century mode (F.R. Leavis, from a very different ideological position to that of Lukács, similarly insisted that readers must choose between James Joyce and D.H. Lawrence!), a more recent reading of Mann, by Sara Danius in *The Senses of Modernism: Technology, Perception and Aesthetics* (Ithaca, NY and London, Cornell University Press, 2002), reveals *The Magic Mountain* to be alive to changes, brought about by modern technologies, in the philosophy of vision. Noticing the novel's obsession with eyes, vision and visuality, Danius argues that it charts a dethroning of vision's God-like, transcendent attributes, as new technologies open out multiple new optic possibilities which are at the same time relativized and demystified. A supreme moment of irony in this context would be Clavdia Chauchat's presentation to Hans Castorp of an X-ray of her chest, as a keepsake to mark Hans' infatuation and the process of visual flirtation in which they have both been indulging.

Lukács' essay is worth revisiting, however, if only to assess his less favoured novelist, Franz Kafka (1883–1924), who is equally central to this tradition of irony, albeit in a different way. If we take irony to be a discourse of repression, insinuating or withholding what might otherwise be said outright, then Kafka presents an extreme face of irony in terms of an artistic mask of blankness or unfathomability, a mode of narration stranger and more elusive than Mann's generally realist manner. Kafka is the great obsessive fabulist of the modern world of alienated life and labour, as these are enshrined in the vast, anonymous bureaucracies of modern statehood or in the pitiless mechanisms of market capitalism. Born to German-Jewish parents in Prague, he pursued his writing and intellectual life while using his legal training to work up to a position of authority in the Workers' Accident Insurance Institute during a fourteen-year career. Kafka's intense writerliness is decidedly anti-Romantic in orientation – 'I have no literary interest', he wrote to his fiancé in 1913, 'but am made of literature, I am nothing else and cannot be anything else' – and this complex sense of imprisonment made for a troubled psychological life, composed of broken relationships and a distance from his father explored in the extraordinary document 'Letter to His Father'. Much of his greatest work was published posthumously – *The Trial* (1925), *The Castle* (1926) and *Amerika* (or *The Boy Who Sank Out of Sight*, 1927) – but the most fascinating introduction to Kafka's work is through the famous early novella *The Metamorphosis* (1915).

'There is no *answerable* question to be found anywhere in the works of Kafka', writes Erich Heller, an effect of an imaginative world shaped by overbearing paternal authority, 'in which the principle of sufficient cause is as good as abolished, above all the rule upon which all justice is founded: that there must be a correspondence between the seriousness of the offence and the degree of the penalty' (*Kafka*, London, Fontana, 1974, p. 27). The unanswerable question and the irrational, unjust world are crystallized in the opening line of *The Metamorphosis*, in which travelling salesman Gregor Samsa wakes in his family home 'from uneasy dreams' to find himself transformed into a gigantic insect. As Gregor deteriorates, his parents and sister, whose bankruptcy he has been rescuing through his labour, transform themselves into a functioning economic unit again. The immediately available allegorical reading – that Gregor has been dehumanized and discarded by capitalist society – is shadowed however by a more elusive one, in which it is Gregor that escapes into a transgressive condition of abjection, playful aesthetic autonomy and eventual non-existence, while his family remain condemned to the tedious cycle of production and reproduction (see Mark Anderson's excellent essay, 'Sliding Down the Evolutionary Ladder? Aesthetic Autonomy in *The Metamorphosis*', reproduced in Franz Kafka, *The Metamorphosis*, ed. Stanley Corngold, New York, Norton, 1996). I use 'abjection' here in the psychoanalytical sense developed by Julia Kristeva (see her *Powers of Horror*, 1980) to designate a state of seepage or leakage beyond the borders of the 'clean and proper body' of bourgeois respectability: Gregor, despite remaining human in his mind, becomes an offence to his family's sense of order and sanitation. The concept can in this sense link Gregor with Mann's Aschenbach, whose body is similarly breached by the Venice plague, as he makes his own helpless retreat from the symbolic order. A related and highly suggestive reading of Kafka's unsettling, transgressive irony is through the concept of 'deterritorialization' applied to his work by Gilles Deleuze and Félix Guattari in *Kafka: Towards a Minor Literature* (1986), where this concept denotes the tendency of his writing to grow beyond stable and hierarchical cultural meanings, flaunting its 'minority' status.

Other key works and figures in this ironic tradition would include *The Confessions of Zeno* (1923) by the Italian Italo Svevo (1861–1928), *Berlin-Alexanderplatz* (1929) by the German Alfred Döblin (1878–1957), *The Sleepwalkers* (1931–2) by the Austrian Hermann Broch (1886–1951) and *The Man Without Qualities* (1930–43) by Robert Musil (1880–1942), also Austrian, and *Auto-da-Fé* (1935) by the Bulgarian Elias Canetti (1905–94). Clearly very masculine in orientation, the emphasis is nevertheless on the anti-heroic bourgeois figure, a man 'without qualities', bound up (as in Canetti and Musil) in a psychoanalytic self-scrutiny that fits him ill for action in the world. The novels present variations on psychological vulnerability and the power of the irrational, reproducing Mann's emphasis on the means by which the psychology of fascism was able to take hold in Europe; significantly, towards the end of their writing lives both Broch and Canetti were working on studies of mass psychology (Broch's *Massenpsychologie* (1959)) and Canetti's *Crowds and Power* (1960)).

As a footnote to the Central European tradition of the ironic novel, I conclude this chapter with two kinds of variation from a British context. The first links the English writer D.H. Lawrence (1885–1930) with the British-Canadian modernist Wyndham Lewis (1882–1957). In a famous review of Thomas Mann's fiction (1913), Lawrence condemned Mann as the 'last sick sufferer from the complaint of Flaubert', who had 'stood away from life as from a leprosy' (*Phoenix: The Posthumous Papers, 1936*, ed. E.D. McDonald,

Harmondsworth, Penguin, 1980, p. 312). In this gesture, which may be guilty of the cardinal error of conflating Mann with one of his fictional characters, Aschenbach of *Death in Venice*, Lawrence sought to assert his own particular distance from a decadent modernist aestheticism – something he condemned, in the visual arts, through a critique of Roger Fry's worship of 'significant Form'. In distinctly Bergsonian terms, Lawrence complained of qualities of calculation and predictability in Mann's style: it lacked a 'fulsomeness of life', with 'none of the rhythm of a living thing, the rose of a poppy, then the after uplift of the bud' (*Phoenix*, p. 313). This distinctly unironic, vitalist–organicist aesthetic, allied to a working-class Midlands perspective alien to the largely bourgeois–metropolitan cultural field, informed a profoundly original fictional voice at work in the early short stories and two early, realist-oriented masterpieces, *Sons and Lovers* (1913) and *The Rainbow* (1915). With his war novel *Women in Love* (1920), however, a change of tone is apparent, more distanced and self-conscious, as if in tune with the stylized intellectual debates of the four main characters drawn from various fractions of the middle class, and whose interrelationships the novel maps. While often seen as Lawrence's most mature novel, *Women in Love* heralds a later style which becomes increasingly, stagily self-conscious. Always unpredictable in their plotlessness and tendency to harangue the reader (hardly an Eliotic model of modernist impersonality – and it was Eliot who notoriously accused Lawrence of being 'incapable of what is ordinarily called thinking'), the ironic self-consciousness of Lawrence's later fictions connected them precisely with the distanced aestheticism of the European modernism he continued to repudiate.

Wyndham Lewis was, like Lawrence, an insider–outsider, his highly ironic modernism motivated by a critique of modernism itself. Lewis had a much closer association with the English avant-garde, having been a leading member of the London Vorticists and founder of the extremely influential if short-lived journal *Blast* (1914–15). In a novel such as *Tarr* (1918), however, drawing on his earlier years in bohemian Paris, a mercilessly comedic treatment of modernist artists such as the central character, Frederick Tarr, combines with a very distinctive, concentrated aphoristic style. Like Lawrence, Lewis' considerable importance lay in an individualistic and high-principled oppositionalism, always vigilant about the distinction between a virile authenticity and effete pretentiousness in modernist art. *Time and Western Man* (1927) is a fascinating document in this respect, containing trenchant critiques of the subjectivism and affectation of artists such as Pound, Joyce, Stein and Diaghilev, alongside a treatise on the philosophy of time.

The second variation is, in effect, more of a radical alternative to the theme of irony. In developing your thoughts on the modernist novel, you might consider the relevance of the modernist aesthetic to two texts whose origin was very far from the metropolitan contexts of the European avant-garde. Robert Tressell's *The Ragged Trousered Philanthropists* (1914) became known as the 'Socialist's Bible', an avowedly politicized tale of a group of working men, house painters and decorators, in a south-coast town, and their struggles with the methods of unscrupulous employers. While this voluminous and rambling novel draws on a range of non-modernist fictional modes, from Dickensian satire and caricature through Victorian sentimentalism to Naturalism, these same instabilities, added to Tressell's varied use of graphic materials, such as a page-size reproduction of an empty time sheet, suggest parallels with the post-Cubist 'alienation techniques' of other radical left-wing modernists such as Eisenstein, Heartfield and Brecht. *A Scot's Quair* (1946) is a trilogy of novels written in the early 1930s by the Scottish Marxist, Lewis Grassic Gibbon. As in McDiarmid's poetry, Gibbon's novels merge Scots vernacular with modernist forms, in a narrative sweep that takes the female protagonist Chris Guthrie from her origins in the disappearing world of peasant agriculture to, in *Grey Granite*, a modern city rendered in distinctly Eliotic and Joycean tones. Far from ever being 'canonized' as modernist texts, the novels of Tressell and Gibbon nevertheless seem to demand a reappraisal of the requirement that the experimental text display the credentials of a distanced irony.

Selected reading

Head, Dominic, *The Modernist Short Story* (Cambridge, Cambridge University Press, 1992)
An authoritative study of modernist short fiction.

Lodge, David, *The Modes of Modern Writing: Metaphor, Metonymy, and the Typology of Modern Literature* (London, Arnold, 1977)

Tinged by the structural–linguistic approach favoured by Lodge and other critics in the 1970s; interesting sections on Stein and Joyce.

Parsons, Deborah, *Theorists of the Modernist Novel: James Joyce, Dorothy Richardson and Virginia Woolf* (London, Routledge, 2006)

A good study of ideas of these key theorists, with an emphasis on questions of realism, temporality, gender and subjectivity.

Shiach, Morag (ed.), *The Cambridge Companion to the Modernist Novel* (Cambridge, Cambridge University Press, 2007)

Comprehensive collection of newly commissioned essays, divided between historical and critical questions and essays on specific writers, including Wyndham Lewis and the novelists of the 'black Atlantic'.

Stevenson, Randall, *Modernist Fiction* (rev. edn; London, Prentice Hall, 1998)

A popular and accessible introductory survey.

Trotter, David, *The English Novel in History 1895–1920* (London, Routledge, 1993)

An original approach that places modernist fiction within a broader context of popular writing and cultural history.

8
Performing modernism

Total art

In the previous two chapters we have seen evidence of what David Trotter has called a 'will-to-literature': 'modernism', Trotter writes, 'was one of the fiercest campaigns ever mounted in favour of literature' ('The Modernist Novel', in Levenson, *Cambridge Companion to Modernism*, p. 74). Should we, however, be wary of associating too readily the intensity of 'high' modernist literariness with the interiority and inwardness that the private reading experience of poetry or fiction seems to call for? From a certain alternative perspective, it can seem that modernism was made to be performed, so that even the most 'literary' of forms – the complex textures of Eliot's *The Waste Land*, or the fictional technique of stream of consciousness, for example – can be seen to represent the dramatization of voices, in gestures of externalization and dialogization.

This chapter will suggest that, from the post-Impressionist conception of modern life as *spectacle* onwards, there is a characteristically public and performative face to modernism, which is able to exploit expanding means and technologies for the projection of artistic forms. I examine the importance of a performative principle under the headings of drama, film, music and dance. Yet if there is one defining characteristic of performative modernism, it may be the tendency towards individual works of collaborative and interdisciplinary originality which combine or baffle such familiar categories. A concept of 'totality' informing these developments may be traced back to the German poet and operatic composer Richard Wagner's (1813–83) late-Romantic concept of *Gesamstkunstwerk*.

Wagner's key works, *Tristan and Isolde* (1865) and the epic cycle *The Ring of Nibelung* (completed 1876) were immensely influential, and from as early as 1849 Wagner in his copious writings had firmly linked great art to the idea of social revolution. Such revolution was couched in universalist terms, proposing to free humankind both from 'every shackle of hampering nationality' and from the 'despotic abstract powers' of a culture of commerce and industry which 'employs the human mind as naught but steampower for its machinery' (Wagner, 'Art and Revolution', 1849, quoted in Kolocotroni *et al.*, *Modernism*, p. 9). This art would, Wagner claimed, represent the living strength of Nature finally overpowering an enfeebled culture. Such an idealized revolutionary force might be seen to typify the utopian, progressive side of modernism, and to bring with it ideological ambivalence: Wagner's music and ideas, like a certain simplified version of Nietzsche's philosophy of will, were to prove amenable to anti-Semitic Nazi thinking in the 1930s (see, for example, the use of his music in Leni Riefenstahl's film of the 1934 Nuremberg rally, *Triumph of the Will*). Equally, however, the Russian Constructivist director Vsevolod Meyerhold could write in 1929 that:

> There was a time when Wagner's idea of a new theatre which would be a dramatic synthesis of words, music, lighting, rhythmical movement and all the magic of the plastic arts was regarded as purely utopian. Now we can see that this is exactly what a production should be: we should employ all the elements which the other arts have to offer and fuse them to produce a concerted effect on the audience. ('The Reconstruction of the Theatre', in Kolocotroni *et al.*, *Modernism*, p. 241)

Meyerhold (1874–1940) had by this time become an influential force in Bolshevik culture, his own experimental theatre and film-making drawing on a preoccupation with the revolutionary potential of technology ('biomechanics') which was, perhaps equally paradoxically, informed by Taylorism in America (see chapter 3).

Another version of performative 'totality' is found in the concept of 'total theatre' in the work of the English theorist and stage designer Edward Gordon Craig (1872–1966), incorporating a series of revolutionary stage designs across Europe in the early 1900s, the foundation of a school of experimental theatre in Florence, and influential texts including *On the Art of the Theatre* (1911) and the periodical *The Mask* (1908–29). In Weimar Germany, Erwin Piscator's (1883–1966) conception of 'epic theatre' shared many aspects of this formal innovation, in combination with a revolutionary politics of the left. To move to a kind of obverse modernist extreme, however, consider Dada: it might be noted that the total rejection of political progressivism and bourgeois artistic value in the early days of the Zurich Cabaret Voltaire from 1915 carried a paradoxically totalizing charge, and was rooted in the immediacy and non-reproducibility of performance. As Michael North has illustrated, the concept of 'The New Man' in Richard Huelsenbeck's 1917 Dada manifesto is couched in the terms of a kind of universal underclass of the polyglot, the Dada group itself seeking to embody this experience 'of all outcasts, the dehumanized beings of Europe, the Africans, the Polynesians, all kinds'. Reflecting an international interest in pan-Africanism in the early twentieth century, the cabarets drew heavily on 'pseudo-African' artefacts and languages, using the latter as the basis of a nonsense poetry in which textuality was an adjunct to pure performance:

aao a ei iii oii
ou ou o ou ou e ou ie a ai
ha dzk drrr br obu br bouss boum
ha haha hi hi hi li li li leiomen
(Huelsenbeck's 'Chorus Sanctus', quoted in North, *The Dialect of
    Modernism*, pp. 29–30)

Before discussing our four categories, therefore, I offer here the example of four individual works which demonstrate the rich collusion of forms, and the unclassifiability, of modernist performance. You might follow up these annotations with some further research of your own on at least one from this list, in order to develop your sense of their particular contexts and details.

- *Murderer, Hope of Women* (1907), by Oskar Kokoschka, who as a young painter exhibiting at the 1908 Kuntschau exhibition in Vienna brought into play an Expressionist concern with eroticism and childhood which troubled bourgeois audiences. No more than what the critic Carl E. Schorske calls a 'playlet' (the entire text is included in Albright's 2004 anthology, *Modernism and Music*), *Murderer* dramatizes the encounter between an archetypal Woman and a warlord to whom she is powerfully and fatally sexually attracted. Repeated patterns of violent mythic imagery and gesture stand in for linear narrative and naturalistic character; the set depicts a menacing tower by torchlight; the intense curving lines and colours of Kokoshka's painterly Expressionism are transferred to the de-individualized actors with their lurid mask-like faces and muscular limbs, and whose high-pitched jagged delivery gave rise to the 'scream-theatre' of Expressionism ('in Europe', Antonin Artaud was later to write, 'no-one knows how to scream any more'). The bloody carnage at the end of this depiction of the mythic liaison between sex (Eros) and death (Thanatos) caused unrest when first performed in the liberal surroundings of the Kunstchau garden theatre in 1909. In 1919 the composer Paul Hindemith made an opera of the play, opening it with a chord, Albright writes, 'made of a semitone, the musical equivalent of a fingernail scraping a blackboard' (*Modernism and Music*, p. 265).

- *Victory over the Sun* (1913), by the Russian Futurist Aleksei Kruchenikh, with sets designed by Kasimir Malevich and music by V.N. Matiushin. Loosely described as an opera, *Victory over the Sun* presented through the aural cacophony of *zaum* poetry a chaotic dramatization of human victory over time. In heavily stylized form, a group of heroic individuals from the future triumph over others who through objection and argument seek to detain progress. The sun is robbed of its traditional iconographic role as the natural source of life and creativity; instead, in Act 2 Scene 5, a black triangle appears as half of Malevich's Cubist backdrop, signalling the forthcoming 'supreme' victory of human forces over nature, and of what Malevich saw as the darker power of 'pure feeling in creative art' over the dictatorship of rationalist enlightenment. The Cubist/Futurist designs of *Victory* were therefore the first illustration of Malevich's Suprematism. In his essay 'Russian Futurism', G.M. Hyde however suggests that the ultimate effect of *Victory* on its audience was more comic than suprematist; like *Parade* (below), its boisterous incoherence meant that it could be enjoyed 'as a kind of circus entertainment, an event in which the boundaries between high art and vaudeville were trampled under-foot in the enthusiastic melee' (Hyde, in Bradbury and McFarlane, *Modernism*, p. 267).

- *Parade* (1917), by Jean Cocteau, with music by Erik Satie, sets designed by Pablo Picasso, choreographed by Leonid Massine, and first performed by Serge Diaghilev's *Ballets Russes* in Paris in 1919. In a preface, Guillaume Apollinaire referred to 'a kind of *sur*-realism' to characterize *Parade*'s apparently random structure and Cubist design, this first use of the term having less to do with the Surrealist art of the 1930s than with Cocteau's claim that *Parade* was a more 'realistic' ballet than any previous form. Realism is reconfigured here, however, not as mimesis or illusionism, but as a stripped-down attempt to 'draw the greatest possible amount of aesthetic emotion from objects' (Apollinaire). Within Satie's mischievously atonal score, the outraged audience was assailed with various aspects of metropolitan modernity – typewriters, ticker tape machines, 'a magnificent vaudeville Chinaman' and 'the American girl cranking up her imaginary car' (Apollinaire). For Apollinaire, *Parade* amounted to a joyful 'new alliance' between painting and dance (Kolocotroni *et al.*, *Modernism*, pp. 212–13).

- *Triadic Ballet* (1922), by the Bauhaus director of theatre Oskar Schlemmer. Droste describes this work, first performed in Stuttgart and then at other Weimar venues throughout the 1920s, as 'really an anti-ballet, a form of "dance Constructivism" that could only have been created by a painter and sculptor' (Droste, *Bauhaus 1919–1933*, p. 101), combining dance, costume, pantomime and music. Principles of composition were based around seemingly abstract variations on the triad (group of three) and on a sequence of colours, from yellow through to pink and black; narrative and concrete situation are absent. The dancers were dressed as 'figurines', their human forms almost comically over-elaborated to resemble marionettes combining circus grotesquerie with futuristic mechanism. Yet, as Gronberg points out, it was in the human body as the 'measure of all things', and in the utopian artistic potential of the body once released though modern abstract dance from the 'historical ballast' of theatre and opera, that Schlemmer was primarily interested (Gronberg, 'Performing Modernism', p. 126). That the *Triadic Ballet* emerged from the radical decision to situate a theatre workshop in a design school (Bauhaus) shows how far modernism sought to challenge the conventional contexts of performance art.

Drama

Discussions of modernist drama tend to be haunted by the paradox that the established social context of the theatre, and the performing of words on a stage, were widely perceived to be incompatible with modernism. It can sometimes seem that modernist drama is composed of plays that were never performed or unperformable (Wassily Kandinsky's Expressionist *The Yellow Sound* (1909), for example, or Wyndham Lewis' Cubist *The Enemy of the Stars* (1915)), and playwrights who repudiated the stage. This provides another context for the rise of 'total' theatrical art, if seen as an attempt to transcend the limitations of drama alone.

Raymond Williams notes that, by the mid-nineteenth century, English drama was 'at perhaps its lowest ebb in six centuries', a condition shared with 'most European countries other than France'. The theatres, Williams writes, were filled with 'farces, melodramas, and huge archaeological productions of the great drama of the past' (Williams, *Drama from Ibsen to Eliot*, Harmondsworth, Penguin, 1964, p. 13). The extent to which theatre had become a possession and expression of orthodox middle-class culture was evident in the prevalent stage setting of the domestic interior. This 'drama of the living room' (Williams) implied an unchanging optic, in which the audience looks into a stable three-dimensional space as if the fourth wall of the room had been removed for their benefit: the 'old box form' (Erwin Piscator). It echoes, perhaps, the relatively passive role of the spectator gazing at the painted realist tableau. Between audience and play had invariably been, as Walter Benjamin observed, the orchestra pit, 'the abyss which separates the actors from the audience like the dead from the living' (*Understanding Brecht*, trans. Anna Bostock, London, Verso, 1984, p. 1). In fact, Piscator could claim, the theatre had 'existed for three hundred years on the fiction that there were no spectators in the house' ('Basic Principles of Sociological Drama', 1929, Kolocotroni *et al.*, *Modernism*, p. 244).

Modernist innovation in drama was therefore to be wider than linguistic or textual; it became a question of stage, space and apparatus as much as of 'the play'. It needed to address the imaginative implications of modern conceptions of time and space, so that the stage itself (and the tradition of the Aristotelian proscenium arch framing the action) could make way for new possibilities of relationship between audience and performance. With the modern filling-in of the orchestra pit, Benjamin argued, the elevated stage lost its sense of having risen from a mysterious depth and became instead a 'public platform'. This newly interactive space could also be more fully dialectical, not only bringing the stage closer to the real everyday world, but also vice versa, revealing the performative and ritualistic aspects of the real and the everyday. In practice, and as in many other fields of modernism, extremes of scale resulted: Dada produced cabaret, and Strindberg and Yeats developed 'chamber' plays, establishing intimate contact with a small audience without the obstructive effect of props, while Gordon Craig took the first scene of Ibsen's *Rosmersholm*, a comfortable sitting room, and transformed it into the arresting artifice of the interior of an enormous Egyptian temple ('without him', wrote the dancer Isadora Duncan of Craig, her sometime lover, 'we would still be back in the old realistic scenery, every leaf shimmering on the trees, all the houses with their doors opening and shutting' (Kolocotroni *et al.*, *Modernism*, p. 157)).

Another feature of innovation in modernist performance was a re-evaluation of the actor as a *material* within the dramatic apparatus. Gordon Craig repudiated the idea of acting as an art, seeing in the conventional aim of impersonation or 'getting under the skin of the part' another form of illusionistic realism. A number of experimental dramatists openly shared this impatience with the trappings of the 'actor'. The human body, because of the presence of emotion, uncertainty and chance, was, Craig asserted in 1907, '*by nature* utterly useless as a material for an art'; 'the actor must go, and in his place comes the inanimate figure – the Uber-marionette we may call him'. Craig's puppet figure thus became the model for 'a new form of acting, consisting for the main part of symbolical gesture' ('The Actor and the *Uber-Marionette*', in Kolocotroni *et al.*, *Modernism*, pp. 150–4). Across a range of modernist drama, from the outlandish, violent cartoonism of Alfred Jarry's *Ubu Roi* (1898) and the futuristically costumed stylizations of Dada and Constructivism, to the anti-illusionist forms of Bertolt Brecht and Antonin Artaud, the stripping-down and flattening-out of 'character' closely parallels the development of painterly abstraction from Cubism onwards. Luigi Pirandello's *Six Characters in Search of an Author* (1921) seemed to confer greater integrity on the dramatic artifice of character, immortalized in the text, than on the living person, who was by nature multiple and constantly changing, though the plays shifting frames of reference make of the distinction between appearance and reality an enigma that is ultimately impossible to resolve. The movements of modernist drama away from naturalistic character point thus towards more complex models of the self in its relation to art, yet at the same time back to a recuperation, for modernity, of the symbolic gesture of ancient ritual and Greek drama, as this had been figured in the work of thinkers such as Nietzsche or Jane Harrison.

Key characteristics of innovation in modernist drama

- de-individualization and de-naturalization of character, to be replaced, for example, by the archetype, the masked figure, the marionette;
- the staging of taboo subjects – sexuality, the body, violence – in a way that challenged bourgeois sensibility;
- foregoing of realist illusionism;
- foregrounding of artifice in props, setting, language and character;
- stylization of language; and
- creation of a mixed mode involving, for example, image, sound, ballet, mime.

STOP and THINK

An early instance that illustrates many aspects of modernist experimentalism in drama is August Strindberg's *A Dream Play* (1901), on which this Stop and Think section is based. The scenario is mythological and simple: the daughter of Indra, one of the eight Vedic gods who watch over the world, comes down to earth to find out why there is such a discrepancy between the beauty of the planet and the misery of its human inhabitants, whose 'mother tongue/Is called Complaint'. The play proposes that this discontent stems from perpetual contradictoriness. However, ordinary life, built on bourgeois aspirations such as married and familial happiness and linear progress, cannot easily admit the existence of these contradictions. They can only be acknowledged by access to the unconscious, which presents suppressed material in indirect and sublimated ways, and which is therefore gained by staging the play according to the form and 'logic' of a dream. It is striking that *A Dream Play* virtually coincides with Sigmund Freud's *Interpretation of Dreams*, although Strindberg had not read Freud.

Like a dream, therefore, Strindberg's play has continually and unpredictably shifting coordinates. Extremely detailed stage directions are required to enact the transformations of a highly stylized backdrop: a forest of giant, brightly coloured hollyhocks, within which a castle is also growing, with a flower bud at the top and its roots in manure, soon changes into an alleyway by a stage door, with a lime tree which in due course doubles as a hatstand when the scene transmutes again into a lawyer's office. Perhaps more transgressively, in the terms of Strindberg's textual note, the characters 'split, double, multiply, evaporate, condense, disperse, and converge' (*Miss Julie and Other Plays*, trans. Michael Robinson, Oxford, Oxford University Press, 1998, p. 176). These fluidities override conventional time and space and show the interpenetration of memory with the present: the Officer waits seven years for his fiancé to emerge from the door of the Opera, and speaks to his mother, who died ten years ago. These objectively impossible events are nevertheless psychologically true: the fiancé does not appear because desire, in order to exist, cannot be gratified (that is, because 'she loves me', in the words of the Officer), while the dialogue with the dead parent continues through life. Subjective logic holds sway: 'the autumn is *my* spring', 'to us on earth a minute can be as long as a year!'. In order for the play to cohere, therefore, the reader needs to adjust to the fact that the theatrical space of *A Dream Play* represents the space of the dreamer's unconscious mind.

- 'One should beware of setting anyone free', says the poet. Why? As one of the play's many highlighted contradictions, how is freedom shown to be dangerous while imprisonment might be liberating?
- 'I'm pasting . . .' How might we interpret Kristin's endlessly repeated activity?
- 'Help one person, and you hurt another . . .' Collect further evidence of such contradictions and consider them in the light of the refrain, 'Human beings are to be pitied . . .'
- 'All right-thinking people have twisted minds . . .' (the poet). How does this resonate in the play and, beyond, in modernist cultures?

Despite the previous emphasis on universal notions of a 'total' modernist theatre and dramatic language, and bearing in mind a pervasive tension between modernism and drama in the narrower sense, it is also possible to identify some distinctive geographical or national–cultural patterns. These cannot claim to provide a comprehensive survey, and should be supplemented with reference to the work of key dramatists in other national contexts such as Luigi Pirandello (Italy, 1867–1936), Vladimir Mayakovsky (Russia, 1893–1930), Frederico Garcia Lorca (1898–1936) and Eugene O'Neill (America, 1888–1953).

Scandinavia

Strindberg's work belongs to a distinctively Scandinavian revolutionary Naturalism whose main exponent was the great Norwegian Henrik Ibsen (1828–1906). Ibsen's concern with the intensities of ordinary experience and of pressing social issues such as women's rights and individual alienation in plays such as *A Doll's House* (1879), *Ghosts* (1881), *Rosmersholm* (1886) and *Hedda Gabler* (1890) were highly influential on James Joyce in his early work. Tony Pinkney argues that Ibsen was 'not so much *a* Modernist . . . as the whole gamut in a single extraordinary oeuvre of *all* its subsequent possibilities', in other words moving through Naturalism and Symbolism to Expressionism (Pinkney, 'Editor's Introduction: Modernism and Cultural Theory', in Raymond Williams, *The*

Politics of Modernism, p. 8). Strindberg could be said to follow a similar pattern, the earlier drama culminating in the 'Naturalistic Tragedy' of *Miss Julie* (1888), yet in the famous preface to the latter (in itself a key document of modernism), and in subsequent works such as *To Damascus I* and *II* (1898), *A Dream Play* and *The Ghost Sonata* (1907), Strindberg demonstrates a radical Expressionist break, at the same time showing how the stylized and symbolic form of *A Dream Play* might itself be seen as the necessarily *naturalistic* approach to issues of psychology and the unconscious.

France

Peter Nicholls identifies a post-Symbolist 'French hostility to narrative' as responsible for the exploration of 'depthlessness' in French modernist drama. Inaugurating this tendency were the extraordinary *Ubu* plays of Alfred Jarry (1873–1907) in the late 1890s, beginning with the performance of *Ubu Roi* in Paris in 1896. *Ubu Roi* should be read if only to complicate any association of (French) modernism with ethereal sophistication. The bare narrative structure is of a coup in which Ubu, a captain of the army of the Polish king Wenceslas, kills the king (having been egged on by his wife) and claims the Polish throne, but is then eventually overcome by a combination of Prince Boggerlas and the Russian army, and forced to flee on a ship across the Baltic, heading for France. From the opening word of the play, Ubu's 'Shit!', Jarry reduces political history to a series of childish fantasy fights interspersed with toilet humour: characters are mortally wounded but then suddenly find themselves recovered, while others are torn to pieces in seconds. W.B. Yeats famously noted after seeing the performance: 'After us the Savage God'. De-throning occurs on a variety of levels: not only the regicide of Wenceslas, but his replacement with the hapless and farcical Ubu, several of whose supporters 'die laughing' as in the final scene as storm wracks the vessel which Ubu has no idea how to control; further, as Nicholls notes, an idea of cultural authority is also displaced by Jarry's depiction of the shapelessness of history and its determination by visceral, childlike or animalistic forces. The play is not so much an Oedipal drama (as in Freud's reading of Sophocles, which stressed the determining role of the Father figure in social and sexual life) as a repudiation of the transcendence

of paternalistic authority per se (Nicholls, *Modernisms*, p. 236).
Jarry's work sets the tone for Dadaist, surrealist and absurdist
experiments in France, decreasing in intelligibility and naturalistic
reference points, although there is a significant gap until the appearance of works such as Apollinaire's *The Breasts of Tiresias* (1917),
the Dadaist 'manifestation' in 1920 including short plays such as
Tristan Tzara's *The First Celestial Adventure of Mr. Antipyrine* and
André Breton and Phillipe Soupault's *If You Please*, and Tzara's
The Gas Heart (1921). The most substantial transformation of this
aesthetic into a radically new theory of stage and performance was
however in the work of Antonin Artaud (1896–1948). Influenced by
the Balinese conception of physical theatre, Artaud railed against
the centrality of words and dialogue in Western theatre. These,
he argued, did not pertain exclusively to theatre, while everything
that did had been 'left in the background'; 'I maintain', he wrote,
'the stage is a tangible, physical space that needs to be filled and it
ought to be allowed to speak its own concrete language' (Artaud,
'Production and Metaphysics', in *The Theatre and Its Double*,
London, John Calder, 1995, pp. 26–7). Artaud sought a seriously
graphic and primitivist theatre that would 'wake us up heart and
nerves', and termed this Theatre of Cruelty. Pursuing collaboration with the surrealists through the 1920s, Artaud authored little
creative drama except the brief *Jet of Blood* (1925), and *The Cenci*
(1935), but was to continue to exert an influence on French philosophy, especially in the later anti-Oedipal thought of Félix Guattari
and Gilles Deleuze.

Germany

In Germany, experimental drama is overridingly political, from
Frank Wedekind (1864–1918) and Ernst Toller (1893–1939)
through to the theatre of the 1920s Weimar period and above all the
work of Bertolt Brecht. Brecht's early plays *Baal* and *Drums in the
Night*, both published in the modernist *annus mirabilis* of 1922, are
informed by an Expressionist aesthetic. But through the emergence
of a 'political' theatre in Germany as the decade progressed, the interiority of Expressionism gave way to a more collective and didactic
aesthetic, in works such as Piscator's *Flags* (1924) and Toller's
Hoppla! (1927). In such works, both the conventional trappings of

stage and scenery in bourgeois theatre, and the relationship between audience and production, are dismantled and reconfigured. As in the realm of modernist visual art, so in Weimar drama, the aim was to unmask the illusionism of realism or mimesis, to declare more openly the techniques and apparatuses of art: Piscator's play, based on the prosecution and hanging of a group of anarchists in Chicago, used scaffolding and platforms, stark and minimalist lighting, and the interpolation of film and radio excerpts, allowing them to enact another Cubist principle, the simultaneous or synchronic rather than linear or diachronic depiction of different situations. Brecht's *Threepenny Opera* (1928), which became another leitmotif of Weimar, with its famous Kurt Weill score ('Mac the Knife', for example), was beginning to show some signs of the radicalizing effects of Weimar political culture. But it was not until the great plays of the 1930s and 1940s, *St Joan of the Stockyards*, *Mother Courage*, *The Caucasian Chalk Circle* and *The Life of Galileo*, that the Weimar influence, and Brecht's embrace of Marxism, emerged in the coherent aesthetic of 'epic theatre', which Brecht had adopted from Piscator. Here Brecht gave a distinctive twist to an overused word in modernist studies, in his theory of the *alienation* effect, or estrangement. The politics of this theory lie in its opposition to the historical pessimism of Western tragic drama: rather than being weighed down by the inevitability of tragedy, the spectator, 'alienated' by a sudden shift in perspective or framing device, suddenly sees how history might have been otherwise. In *The Politics of Modernism*, Raymond Williams suggests that Brecht might have derived this principle from the similarly liberatory effect of Shklovsky's Russian Formalist *ostranenie*: art administers the 'shock' which changes our perception of the world, and makes the world seem changeable by human intervention. In 1930, in the notes to his opera *Mahagonny*, Brecht laid out the key distinctions of this aesthetic:

DRAMATIC THEATRE	EPIC THEATRE
Plot	Narrative
Implicates spectator in stage drama	Turns spectator into observer, but arouses capacity for action
Wears down capacity for action	
Provides spectator with sensations	Forces spectator to take decisions

Experience	Picture of the world
Spectator involved in something	Spectator made to face something
Suggestion	Argument
Instinctive feelings preserved	Brought to point of recognition
Spectator involved, sharing	Spectator outside, studying
Human being taken as read	Human being the object of enquiry
Human is unalterable	Human is alterable, able to alter
Eyes on the finish	Eyes on the course
One scene makes another	Each scene for itself
Growth	Montage
Linear development	In curves
Evolutionary determinism	Jumps
Human as a fixed point	Human as a process
Thought determines being	Social being determines thought (Marx)
Feeling	Reason

(Adapted from Bertolt Brecht, *Brecht on Theatre*, trans. John Willett, London, Methuen, 1964)

Ireland and Britain

If the modernist theatre of France and Germany is a distinct expression of possibility within those cultures, it is interesting to reflect on the relative modesty of radical innovation in Irish and British drama. Christopher Innes for example points to the clear success of George Bernard Shaw's plays as a triumph of compromise between traditional theatrical form and 'modernist spirit' (although Innes sees compromise as a broader desideratum, given that 'the theatrical life of each attempt to transpose the modernist vision to the stage was extremely brief or limited') ('Modernism in Drama', in Levenson, *Cambridge Companion to Modernism*, p. 147). Perhaps the most distinctive feature to emerge from the British Isles was the stylized poetic drama of T.S. Eliot and W.B. Yeats, each primarily known as a poet rather than theatre practitioner. Yeats and Bertolt Brecht were both present at the London performance of Eliot's first verse play, *Sweeney Agonistes*, in 1934. The set was Expressionistic, masks were worn, and Sweeney, the working-class protagonist mired in criminality and sexual violence, may have been the closest the English stage could get to the transgressions of Ubu. Yeats had similarly experimented with gestural and poeticized drama based on Japanese Noh theatre, for example in *At the Hawk's Well* (1916), and in the *Plays for Dancers*, culminating in *The Death of Cuchulain*, first performed in 1949. His attitude to dialect also bears interesting comparison with Eliot: while the latter's use of cockney or Negro could often be read as satirical, the poetry of Yeats' plays drew on his belief in the resources of Irish peasant speech. Despite his famous involvement in setting up the Abbey Theatre as a crucible for modern Irish drama in Dublin, however, Yeats' own performance work seemed to signal a retreat from modernity. After *Sweeney Agonistes*, and with *Murder in the Cathedral* (1935), Eliot's drama also became more culturally conservative. It could be argued that Irish and British drama had to wait for the first stage work of Samuel Beckett and Harold Pinter in the 1950s in order to connect with an earlier European avant-garde tradition.

Film

The first moving picture show, the documentary 'Arrival of the Train', was presented by the Lumière brothers in 1895. The apocryphal story surrounding this inaugural moment was that images of the train coming through a station and towards the screen induced fear and panic in some of its unsuspecting viewers. Whatever the truth of the story, it is a serviceable myth for representing both the defamiliarizing tendency of the modern, and the mesmerizing power that film was able to exert over the human psyche. Laura Marcus argues that 'film consciousness was everywhere' in the early twentieth century; perhaps more radically than the total art of theatre, it promised an international visual language that could transcend cultural boundaries, and acted as the perfect embodiment of the spectacle, in the sense that vision, seeing, became the defining condition of modernity itself ('Literature and Cinema', in Marcus and Nicholls, *Cambridge History of Twentieth-Century English Literature*, pp. 335–6).

In the rapid development of the film industry over the decades that followed, this collective power is frequently reflected upon, so that modernist discourses on the new medium oscillate between enthusiastic acceptance, and violent denial – between, for example, readings of a potential for art, or for entertainment, for consciousness-raising, or for inducing mass unconsciousness. More recently, film has become central to the new modernist studies, and at least three key emphases may be identified:

- *Movement*. If movement is one of the keynotes of early twentieth-century modernity – constant revolutionizing of production, machines and motor power, and the migration of peoples, for example – the 'motion picture' is seen as the appropriate medium to express this dynamism. At the cinema, wrote Virginia Woolf in 'The Cinema' (1926), the viewer glimpses a 'something vital', corresponding to that moment in a city when 'movements and colours, shapes and sounds had come together and waited for someone to seize them and convert their energy into art'.

- *The city*. As the above indicates, the city is the locus of this new dynamism often glimpsed as abstract shapes or conjunctions of forces. Not only is the city often the subject of film, as in the development of 'city symphonies' in the 1920s; there is, as Raymond Williams puts it, a 'direct relation between the motion picture, especially in its development in cutting and montage, and the characteristic movement of an observer in the close and miscellaneous environment of the streets' (*The Country and the City*, St Albans, Paladin, 1975, pp. 290–1).

- *Psychoanalysis*. Laura Marcus argues that there is more than historic coincidence to the rise of film and psychoanalysis, 'twin sciences and technologies of fantasy, dream, virtual reality and screen memory'. Through the device of the close-up in particular, film is seen to give access to hitherto obscured areas of inner life, the 'new and unsuspected formations of matter' (Siegfried Kracauer, *Theory of Film*, New York, Oxford University Press, 1960) paralleling the kinds of dream-work revealed by Freud. Psychoanalysis was thus crucial to the direction of the international film journal *Close Up* (see below), as Marcus' succinct and helpful introduction to a series of relevant extracts indicates (Donald *et al. Close Up 1927–1933*: *Cinema and Modernsim*, pp. 240–6).

Another key question concerning film and modernism might be put thus: are there modernist films and non-modernist films, or is film itself an inherently modernist phenomenon? Film is certainly that new artistic technology which most closely coincides with the central period of modernism. Yet by 1925, a spectrum had already emerged reinforcing the sense of a divide between modernism as experimental practice and the forms of mass entertainment. In the latter category, the commercial Hollywood industry was already established, while in the former, clear bodies of work are identifiable in Soviet Futurist–Constructivism, German Expressionism and French Surrealism.

The year 1927 might also exemplify a watershed moment: Warner Brothers produced *The Jazz Singer*, starring Al Jolson – the first 'talkie', that is, the first film to use synchronized speech and dialogue. In the same year, the international journal *Close Up* (1927–33), 'devoted to the art of films', was founded by Kenneth McPherson, the novelist Bryher and the poet H.D. *Close Up*'s explicit objective was to argue for what French avant-garde film makers such as Marcel L'Herbier had termed *photogénie*, the specific visual effect and language of film-as-art, a specificity typified by the 'close-up' itself, which delivered a sense of psychological, unconscious depth and an expansion of space unavailable to other art forms. Sound and music might be used and indeed had been used in film before the talkies, but in complementary or contrapuntal ways, accompanying the images while leaving the visual language intact. The 'talkie' therefore means the use of synchronized speech. This threatened to debase the visuality of film, making it easier to view film simply as a means of recording, visually and aurally, a more conventional theatricality, and indeed, as Walter Benjamin saw it, to reduce the political impact of film: 'the launching of the sound film', he wrote to Adorno in 1938, 'must be regarded as an operation of the cinema industry designed to break the revolutionary primacy of the silent films, which generated reactions that were hard to control and hence politically dangerous' (Adorno *et al.*, *Aesthetics and Politics*, p. 140). Thus in *Close Up* a characteristically modernist campaign emerged to preserve the 'purity' of silent filmic language, a position famously exemplified in Virginia Woolf's 1926 essay 'The Cinema', where a discussion of Robert Wiene's *The Cabinet of Dr Caligari* (1919) modulates into observations on the appearance of a tadpole-shaped blemish on the print itself, as if to confirm Woolf's interest in the abstract qualities of film.

The case of Charlie Chaplin

The paradox is crucial and worth reformulating: film and cinema were unprecedented technologies for the communication of performance as a collective experience, to mass audiences; yet they elicited from avant-garde thinkers a campaign closely comparable to that 'will-to-literature' described by David Trotter, in which their qualities align with the modernist intensities of literary symbolism or painterly abstraction. As a case study that combines both elements of this paradox, we might take the work of Charlie Chaplin (1889–1977). What is the current popular image of Chaplin, and how might this be modified by an understanding of his modernistic significance?

Chaplin began as a vaudeville artist in London music hall before travelling to America in 1910, soon to be engaged by the Keystone Comedy Company in Hollywood, and after gaining rapid international fame, established his own film company in 1918. Key Chaplin movies are: *A Dog's Life* (1918), *The Idle Class* (1921), *The Gold Rush* (1925), *City Lights* (1931), *Modern Times* (1936). In studies of modernism, Chaplin's widely loved tramp figure – bowler hat, ill-fitting suit and walking stick – tends to bear two principal forms of significance: as a critique of late-capitalist modernity, with its emphasis on ostentatious wealth achieved through the unrelenting, dehumanizing productivity of the Taylorist assembly line; and, with its extraordinarily gymnastic and mechanized movements, as a revelation of a complex bodily condition that only film itself could reveal. In an interesting work on the filmic sense in the work of four poets (Gertrude Stein, William Carlos Williams, H.D. and Marianne Moore), Susan McCabe argues that film 'made visible a body never visible before – one that is at once whole and in pieces', underlining the pervasive paradox that modernism sought to convey bodily experience while recognizing 'the unavailability of such experience except as mediated through mechanical reproduction' (*Cinematic Modernism: Modernist Poetry and Film*, Cambridge, Cambridge University Press, 2005, p. 3, 7). McCabe shows how Gertrude Stein identified closely with Chaplin, whose repertoire of movements, from the mechanical, nervous and compulsive to elliptical and even auto-erotic, 'like a disabled Model T, unable to be cranked up and started' (p. 70), seemed to echo Stein's repetitive non-teleological language of the 'continuous present'. Chaplin as a figure of the modern male hysteric, subverting the feminized meaning of hysteria as a condition of the 'wandering womb', thus connected with Stein's desire to de-naturalize or cut the body loose from heterosexual iconography.

Chaplin's comic undermining of humanistic stereotypes thus developed a broad appeal across modernism, especially insofar as he was able to encapsulate film's ability to explore the dialectic between the mechanism of the living and the animism of the non-living. In 1922 the 3rd number of the Russian Constructivist journal *Kino-fot* (Cinema-photo) was devoted to Chaplin, featuring a series of woodcuts by Varvara Stepanova. The drawings rendered Chaplin down into a series of dynamic geometrical shapes representing, as Alexandr Rodchenko wrote, the utopian potential of Chaplin's machine-like precision and economy of movement for a proletariat seeking to forge new structures of feeling based on the technologies of film and photography (see Gronberg, 'Performing Modernsim', and for two of Stepanova's illustrations, p. 137). In 1924, Fernand Léger used a Cubist vignette of Chaplin in *Ballet mecânique*, as a living yet fragmented and articulated puppet, half-organism, half-machine. These representations highlighted the inseparability of the avant-garde and the popular in Chaplin's appeal. For Walter Benjamin, Chaplin was one of the first to benefit from a deeply significant social change brought about by the mechanical reproduction of art and, in the case of film, by the determining of individual reactions by a collective response. The tendency to a 'reactionary attitude' towards a Picasso painting is transformed, Benjamin argues, into the 'progressive reaction' to a Chaplin movie, this reaction characterized by a unique combination of receptivity and criticism, 'the direct, intimate fusion of visual and emotional enjoyment with the orientation of the expert' (*Illuminations*, p. 236). Theodor Adorno, however, remained unconvinced, describing as 'out-and-out romanticization' the idea that 'a reactionary is turned into a member of the avant-garde by expert knowledge of Chaplin's films' (Adorno *et al.*, *Aesthetics and Politics*, p. 123), and repeating his view that the laughter of a cinema audience, for example at a Chaplin film, was itself a reactionary phenomenon.

STOP and THINK

Let us examine how far the concept of modernism might relate to the comparison of two key films: *The Cabinet of Dr Caligari*, directed by Robert Wiene and released in Germany in 1919; and Sergei Eisenstein's *Battleship Potemkin*, produced in the Soviet Union in 1927. After viewing these films you will almost certainly emerge with a sense of their radical differences in terms of technique and subject matter. In Wiene's Expressionist narrative, which became a motif of early Weimar culture, Caligari's hypnotized, somnambulist 'exhibit' Cesare wreaks murderous havoc on the inhabitants of a small town. Eisenstein's epic, a paradigm of the technique of montage, narrates a key episode in the 1905 revolutionary insurrection in Russia, the mutiny of the fleet at Odessa on the Black Sea, taking the vessel *Potemkin* as a focal point.

- Consider the differences in scene and setting between the two films: interior/exterior, the nature of the sets used, the kinds of deployment of actors (these directorial features together with camerawork are often called *mise-en-scéne*).
- Consider the differences between the uses of the camera and the editing (cutting and splicing, for example) of film. Do key set piece scenes stand out, and if so which and how?
- Compare the use of the close-up in each: for example, the scene in which Cesare's face is revealed for the first time, and the faces of the wounded women on the Odessa steps (Figures 17 and 18).
- Consider each in terms of narrative structure: for example, is there a linear story line, or is the telling of the story more complex? Is there a plot? Is one more didactic than another, for example?
- Consider each as a work of historical imagination: Germany after the war, and on the cusp of the Weimar Republic in 1919; Soviet Russia in 1925, Eisenstein's film a celebration of the twentieth anniversary of the 1905 revolution. How might the films express a historical situation?
- How helpful would the distinction between 'realism' and 'abstraction' be (thinking back to chapter 2, on visual art)

Figure 17 Still from *The Cabinet of Dr Caligari* (1919)

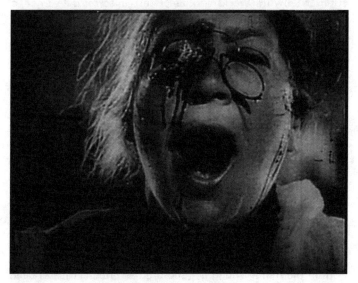

Figure 18 Still from *Battleship Potemkin* (1927)

in analysing these films? Does one film seem more 'modernist' than another, and if so why? (this may reveal as much about your thinking about modernism as about the films themselves!).

Here are some thoughts to back up your own reflections and conclusions. *Caligari* has tended to attract criticism from those upholding a more abstract filmic art, such as Ezra Pound and Eisenstein himself, who called the film a carnival of barbarism. This is because *Caligari* can be seen as more illusionistic: where montage in *Potemkin*, with abrupt juxtapositions or overt manipulation (for example, the sequence of images that animates the stone lion), draws attention to its own artifice (as in theatrical framing devices in Pirandello and Brecht, for example), *Caligari* uses the camera to mesmerize the viewer into the folds of the story, rather in the way that Caligari's mesmerism works on Cesare. The viewer of *Caligari* tends to be presented with conundrums – is Caligari walking along a street or a corridor? Are we inside or outside or, by analogy, in someone's mind, or out in the physical world? – while Eisenstein forces the viewer to see connections between otherwise disparate things: for example, the maggots in the sailors' food, and the arrogant statuary of a corrupt regime. At the same time, Wiene's Expressionist sets are highly stylized – the painted, distorted buildings, the use of shadow, the stools on which the clerks sit – suggesting a pervasive symbolic function, while the dramatic exterior scenes of *Potemkin* have the naturalistic feel of newsreel or documentary. In his extensive writing on film, Eisenstein insisted on clarity of political message despite the potential of the medium for artistic subtlety, and in *Potemkin* this can be seen to be communicated, not only in the revealing of state/military brutality in the Odessa steps scene, but in the emphasis on crowd scenes and patterns of movement, suggesting a socialist-collectivist rather than bourgeois-individualist vision. *Caligari* is clearly a more familiar and individuated narrative structure, with a traditional female love interest and the twist in the plot which focuses attention on the minds of Caligari and the narrator. Yet it has been argued (see Michael Minden, 'Politics and the Silent Cinema: *The*

Cabinet of Dr Caligari and *Battleship Potemkin*,' in Timms and Collier, *Visions and Blueprints*) that *Potemkin* relies more on an involved and emotional response in the viewer than Eisenstein's aesthetic might allow. Conversely, *Caligari* can be seen to dramatize what Minden calls the 'plight of the German bourgeois imagination', subject to the irrationality of state authority (the director of the asylum who may himself be insane and murderous), caught between internal paralysis and political action, or between illusion and truth, and struggling to escape from nightmare. A final consideration is that while Wiene's is a studio film made on a relatively low budget, Eisenstein as an official commemorator of the 1905 revolution had virtually unlimited resources for *Potemkin,* including access to the Winter Palace in St Petersburg and to an actual battleship of the Russian fleet.

A note on *montage*. This is an absolutely central term in the formation and analysis of modernist film. It clearly bears comparison with the layering and juxtapositional principle of *collage* in post-Cubist visual art. It is also slightly perilous for the non-specialist to use: while the Eisensteinian sense of montage as a principle of discontinuity has become dominant – 'an idea that arises from the collision of independent shots – shots even opposite to one another' (Eisenstein) – montage is also a more general term for the process of cutting and editing film in order to compose it into an artistic whole. For a useful discussion of the kinds of distinction that might need to be made between the uses of montage in media such as film, literature and photomontage, see Peter Bürger's section in ch. 4 of *Theory of the Avant-Garde*, pp. 73–82. You might further consider the uses of montage if you are able to delve into the following list of key films, chronologically ordered, which will extend your sense of the possibilities of cinematic modernism:

- *Manhatta*, Paul Strand and Charles Sheeler (1921): short film, first of the 'city symphonies', made by photographer Strand and painter Sheeler. Loosely based around the passage of a day in New York, using montage and high camera angles to give a vertiginous sense of skyscrapers, the docking of a ferry, the movement of traffic and pedestrians, and so on.

- *Ballet mécanique*, Fernand Léger (1924): Léger's realization of Cubist machine-age art in filmic form; stages a carefully choreographed 'dance' with human and inanimate subjects and references to Chaplin. An attempt to create a pure imaginative language of cinematography, breaking and reconstituting surfaces and forms.

- *The Gold Rush*, Charlie Chaplin (1925): Chaplin's rags-to-riches satire on the gold-prospecting age, with extensive use of montage for comic and allegorical effect; see Michael Wood, 'Modernism and Film', in Levenson, *Cambridge Companion to Modernism* (pp. 217–32).

- *Metropolis*, Fritz Lang (1926): German Expressionist narrative of a futuristic (year 2000) dystopian metropolis involving a Wellsian division between enslaved labour (underground) and leisured capital (overground). Controversies surround the film's images of a humanity determined and imprisoned by machines, and the gender politics of the 'vamp robot' figure: see e.g. Andreas Huyssen's essay 'The Vamp and the Machine: Fritz Lang's *Metropolis*', in *After the Great Divide* (1986).

- *Un Chien Andalou*, Luis Buñuel (1928): classic of surrealism, and Buñuel's collaboration with Salvador Dalí. Opens with the famous sequence of a razor being sharpened and then slicing a woman's eye, and throughout uses similar ingenious and highly symbolically suggestive dream effects. Very loosely based on a sexual relationship between the two protagonists, enclosed in a seemingly random and wildly shifting time-frame.

- *The Man with a Movie Camera*, Dziga Vertov (1929): classic of Russian Constructivism. Reflexive film using montage and framing devices to reveal the editor and cinematographer at work in its production, and emphasizing the increasing interaction with the machine in Soviet society. Malevich regarded the film as more radical/analytic in its form than Eisenstein's *Battleship Potemkin*.

- *Borderline*, Kenneth Macpherson (1930): 70-minute silent film made by POOL, the film-making group of *Close Up*, and featuring H.D. and Paul Robeson, only the latter's second film although he was already a singing star. Explores the 'borderline' of black–white sexual politics in a provincial town somewhere in Europe, with strong psychoanalytic overtones.

- *Triumph of the Will*, Leni Riefenstahl (1934): officially commissioned film of the 1934 Nazi party rally at Nuremberg. Conveys a sense of abstract modernism through its use of light and shade, numerous close-ups and angular approaches to Hitler himself, lingering gaze on fascist architecture and the peaceful massing of crowds. Is this modernist art, or in Benjamin's terms the 'asetheticization of politics'?

Music

'Music is written to be heard', wrote George Gershwin, and it is crucial that beginning modernism involves stopping to hear, listen to and think about its experimental music. While ostensibly the most immediate and accessible of performance forms (recall the Symbolists' interests, culminating in Pater's 'all art aspires to the condition of music', as discussed in chapter 6), music is also the most specialized in terms of the language that accompanies it. It is beyond the scope of this book to supply a knowledge of this language, and it cannot be assumed that the reader has a musical training. This section may therefore be the most interactive of the book, or the one that relies most on your own resources, in that it asks you first to seek out and listen to some examples of modernist composition.

STOP and THINK (and LISTEN)

Our discussion will be based on listening to three pieces:

- Arnold Schoenberg, *Three Piano Pieces, Opus 11* (1908)
- Igor Stravinsky, *The Rite of Spring* (1913)
- Claude Debussy, *La Mer* (1905)

If this music is unfamiliar to you, try to *suspend* that knowledge of other forms of music that you like or know, in order to keep an open mind about the effects of these pieces on you. Then, you might begin to consider how these sound-worlds compare with those forms with which you are more familiar.

- Arnold Schoenberg used the phrase 'the emancipation of dissonance' to refer to the fact that we have been led to expect from music a certain level of predictability, which can be supplied in various ways. Think about: the role of regular rhythms; the role of repetition, for example in the form of refrains or choruses; and the use of harmony, through which the music seems to resolve itself in pleasurable ways which we have somehow been led to expect. How do the Schoenberg piano pieces relate, or not, to these kinds of expectation?

- Above, I used the term 'sound-world'. What would be the effect of ceasing to think about the Schoenberg pieces in terms of the concept of 'music', and to think about them instead as shifting patterns of *sound* that evoke certain kinds of response or feeling in you?

- Experiment with using Stravinsky's *The Rite of Spring* as a kind of sound track to T.S. Eliot's *The Waste Land*. Like Eliot's poem, Stravinsky's work draws into proximity ideas of the primitive and the modern. Does this help us to hear the *Rite* in a certain way, for example as a combination of the sounds of tribal rituals and of modernity (cities, machinery) which may be difficult to disentangle? Does listening to the *Rite* help us to hear some of the ever-shifting poetic rhythms of *The Waste Land*?

- Consider the Stravinsky in the light of ideas of progress and development, which are usually assumed to inform a piece of classical music such as a symphony or concerto. Does the *Rite* go anywhere, or is it characterized more by circularity or stasis? Is there a sense of time, or a sense of timelessness?

- Consider the analogy between the placing of sounds (notes, chords) in Debussy's *La Mer* and the selection and application of colours from an artist's palette – say, the work of Paul Cézanne. Daniel Albright refers to Debussy writing with chords that resembled 'sonorous puddles' (*Modernism and Music*, p. 7), to continue this liquid analogy. How far do such analogies take us in thinking about the way harmony (or disharmony) works in Debussy's piece?

- Another question about time. 'Debussy's music does not propel the listener through the music' (Imogen Parker, 'The Time of Music: The Music of Time', *Critical Quarterly* 50:3, 2008, p. 59). Does this seem appropriate?

Tonality

Accounts of what happens in modernist music, either within a composition or over a historical period, are dominated by the word *tone*
and certain variants – tonality, atonal, twelve-tone system. Why is
this? Writing in 1932, the composer Anton Webern observed that
his tutor Arnold Schoenberg got a 'lot of fun' out of the description
of his work as 'atonal', because '"atonal" means "without notes";
but that's meaningless. What's meant is music in no definite key.
What has been given up? The key has disappeared!' (Albright,
Modernism and Music, pp. 203–4). Tonality, then, means music
written in a certain key, where 'key' is a pattern of notes that har-
monize around one key note, or more accurately around a 'triad' of
three notes: tonic, mediant and dominant. Traditionally in Western
music, keys have been identified as either major or minor, and are
situated on a 'diatonic' scale; movement within a key is always
through the eight notes of an octave. In the words of Webern again,
tonality provided *unity* to the music, and 'it was natural for the
composer to be anxious to demonstrate this key very explicitly. A
piece had a keynote: it was maintained, it was left and returned to. It
constantly reappeared, and this made it dominant'. In other words,
dissonance – departure from the triad – and modulation – change of
key – were permissible only if the keynote was returned to.

Carl E. Schorske sees tonality as a hierarchical system used, since
the Renaissance, to serve 'the purposes of established authority' and
as having a series of 'socio-cultural' parallels: the science of perspective in visual art; the geometric garden; the Baroque status system;
and legal absolutism in politics (*Fin-de-siècle*, p. 346). The diatonic
scale does not contain all the notes that exist, because the chromatic
scale, by comparison, consists of many more notes separated very
finely by semitones. These however are suppressed by tonality in
the interests – if we follow through Schorske's very political parallels – of established order and unity. From this perspective we may
see modernist music beginning to do two main kinds of thing: first,
finding more notes, thereby 'releasing' them in order to explore
their musical potential; and second, questioning the perpetual need
to seek consonance and harmony, by exploring *dissonant* or conflict-
ual sounds as expressions of alternative views of life (for example,
that life consistently does involve conflict; or, that breaking up

established structures is the only way to achieve revolutionary or creative change).

At this point it might be appropriate to invoke two rather thorny and closely related issues that have always confronted modernist music: pleasure and aesthetics. Is not harmony in music the essence of its sensual appeal? On what grounds should this be relinquished? Is there a necessary symbolic connection between political emancipation and the assault on tonality? And is it not in the nature of art to create new kinds of unity and order out of chaos? Clearly, these kinds of question have reverberated across our consideration of modernism as a whole, and modernist composers have responded in ways that may not seem surprising. 'Our age seeks many things', wrote Schoenberg in *Theory of Harmony* (1911): 'What it has found, however, above all, is *comfort* . . . The thinker, who keeps on searching, does the opposite. He shows that there are problems and that they are unsolved' (quoted in Ross, *The Rest is Noise*, p. 64). 'Is not beauty in music', wrote the American composer Charles Ives in 1922, 'too often confused with something which lets the ears lie back in an easy chair?' (Albright, *Modernism and Music*, p. 159).

That is to say, modernism challenges bourgeois complacency, and with it a whole conception of what constitutes aesthetic beauty; the notion of modernism as an art of difficulty, ceasing to make sense, is again in evidence. In addition, we might argue that conceptions of beauty can themselves be redefined: you may already feel that Debussy's *La Mer* has a tranquil beauty, perhaps largely because of the richness of its chords, but may not Stravinsky's *Rite* convey a pulse-quickening, powerful beauty, and Schoenberg's *Piano Pieces* an austere beauty? Nor is it necessarily the case that modernism aspires, through the force of its invention and will-to-truth, to displace other musical forms. You can listen to Tamla Motown one day, and Schoenberg the next. This may not be as superficial a point as it seems, because the question of how we might read modernism across the low–high cultural divide, and in a way that throws that divide into doubt, is raised by one particular musical form: jazz. A highly rhythmic improvisational form, jazz emerges from black American dance-band culture of the early years of the last century, associated with rag-time and the dance crazes surrounding it. Some within the music world, such as the American composer Daniel Gregory Mason, and Theodor Adorno, were quick to condemn jazz as a degenerate and commercialized form, thereby erecting the cultural divide.

However, an intriguing alternative response is found in the essay 'On a Negro Orchestra' (1919) by the French modernist Ernst Ansermet, who had conducted Satie–Cocteau's *Parade* and works by Stravinsky. Ansermet's is a lavish appreciation of having seen the Southern Syncopated Orchestra, led by Will Marion Cook, in Paris. While exoticizing and essentializing Negro music to some extent – there is 'a Negro way of playing the violin, a Negro way of singing', and all of this through being 'possessed' by the music to such an extent that they cannot help but 'dance inwardly' to it – Ansermet is also careful to couch his admiration in the strictest technical terms. In the Negro song, Ansermet notes the desire to emphasize or prolong certain syllables, leading to syncopation, the 'anticipation or delay of a fraction of rhythmic unity', so that the voice is in counterpoint to the body that keeps regular rhythm. In melody:

> [A]n old instinct pushes the Negro to pursue his pleasure outside the orthodox intervals: he performs thirds which are neither major nor minor and false seconds, and falls often by instinct on the natural harmonic sounds of a given note – it is here especially that no written music can give the idea of his playing . . . It is only in the field of harmony that the Negro hasn't yet created his own distinct means of expression. But even here, he uses a succession of seventh chords, and ambiguous major-minors with a deftness that many European musicians would envy. (Albright, *Modernism and Music*, pp. 368–73)

Ansermet finds these qualities crystallized in the young figure of Sidney Bechet (1897–1959), who was to become one of the great jazz clarinetist/saxophonists, and who could 'say nothing of his art' except that it was his 'own way'.

In returning therefore to the question of tone, and the way this narrative has been told, it is possible to see a greater complexity than the story of the hermetic pursuit of difficulty allows. Jazz is as much about the discovery of unorthodox notes and ambiguous chords as is the falsely named 'atonal' music, yet becomes the epitome of a *popular* musical modernism (and for a recent account of the multiform reach of 'jazz modernism', see James Donald, 'Jazz Modernism and Film Art: Dudley Murphy and *Ballet mécanique*', *Modernism/*

modernity 16:1, January 2009). Debussy wrote his own *Golliwog's Cake-Walk* in 1908; Stravinsky's ballet and orchestral music accumulates jazz passages and references (Debussy described the *Rite* as 'une musique nègre'), and by the time that George Gershwin (1898–1937) is writing of jazz as the 'result of the energy stored up' in machine-age America, he has integrated it seamlessly into works such as *An American in Paris* (1928). Perhaps the most adventurous of the avant-garde to use jazz was Darius Milhaud (1892–1974), one of a group of French composers hostile to Debussy and named 'Les Six', whose Brazilian-influenced music culminated in the multi-dimensional performance *The Creation of the World*, staged in Paris in 1923 by the Swedish Ballet, with Cubist sets by Fernand Léger and poetry by Blaise Cendrars. Tonal experimentation could be found as much in apparently simple forms, as evidenced in Béla Bartók's collection of Hungarian folk music between 1904 and 1919, whose undermining of the major–minor system informed his revolutionary work *The Magic Mandarin* (1919). As Christopher Butler argues, an academic model of music-as-language in the twentieth century led to a 'progressive story' about 'loosening the restrictive bonds of tonality', but this story is insufficiently pluralistic: citing 1912–13 as a moment of major technical innovation – Debussy's *Jeux*, Schoenberg's *Pierrot lunaire*, Stravinsky's *Rite* – Butler notes that these led off 'in all sorts of directions, not all of them atonal' ('Innovation and the Avant-Garde', pp. 74–7).

With such provisos in mind, let us finally return to the 'progressive story', and its terminus (at least as far as this account of modernist music can go) in the 'twelve-tone method'. This is a major breakthrough in Schoenberg's work, and is dated 1922–3, with the appearance of the *Five Piano Pieces* (Opus 23) and *Serenade* (Opus 24). The method takes the twelve notes of the chromatic scale within any octave (the seven white and five back keys on a keyboard octave), confers equal value on all of them, and devises a system for the permutation and recombination of notes without repeating one in any given 'row'. The number of permutations of twelve notes possible in the chromatic scale is, according to Ross, 479,001,600! In his essay 'Composition with Twelve Tones' (1941), Schoenberg writes that this method 'grew out of necessity', as a kind of inevitable development in musical history, and in his own terms as a continuing of the logic of unfolding dissonance over the past century. Examples of staging posts in this progressive narrative would be: Wagner's *Tristan und Isolde* (1865), which is already, Schorske argues, eroding the fixed key, and using chromatic half-tones in 'an egalitarian universe of sound' (*Fin-de-siècle*, p. 347); Franz Liszt's work of the late 1870s and early 1880s, including *Bagatelle sans tonalité*; the symphonic or 'tone' poems of Richard Strauss, leading to the opera *Salome*, first performed in 1906; and Debussy's works such as *Prelude to 'The Afternoon of a Faun'* (1894) and the opera *Pelléas and Mélisande* (1902). 'The ear', Schoenberg writes, 'had gradually become acquainted with a great number of dissonances, and so had lost the fear of their "sense-interrupting" effect. One no longer expected preparations of Wagner's dissonances or resolutions of Strauss' discords; one was not disturbed by Debussy's non-functional harmonies' (Albright, *Modernism and Music*, p. 196). The ground was prepared for his *Three Piano Pieces* of 1908, and the music of his pupils Webern and Berg around this time, which he describes as counterbalancing 'extreme emotionality with extreme shortness'.

The question of who 'one' might be in Schoenberg's account prompts some reflections on our guiding concept of performance. It would be easy to conclude that modernist music points in antithetical directions: in jazz, to a wider popular reception and dissemination; and in atonal and Schoenbergian music, towards limited reception by a private audience. Schoenberg's music has never become widely listened to, and in the 1920s he began to endorse the limited or private reception of music, on the grounds of a critique of professional performance culture based on competitiveness and commercialization. As Bryher noted of the demands to make film 'simple', this would obstruct the possibility of *thinking* through film; similarly, Schoenberg typified modernism as an intellectually engaged activity, in Albright's words a '*testing of the limits of aesthetic construction*' (p. 11). Theodor Adorno produced a particularly complex version of this in his *Philosophy of Modern Music* (1948), which is based entirely on a comparison of Schoenberg's music as 'progressive' with Stravinsky's as 'restorative': Schoenberg, Adorno claimed, worked on music to produce the endlessly new, while Stravinsky sought to make musical notes sound as they always had done. Conversely, in the late 1920s Schoenberg was engaged in bitter debate with the Weimar composer Kurt Weill, who claimed that a 'clear split' had developed between musicians who:

> full of disdain for their audience, continue as it were by shutting out the public sphere to work on the solution of aesthetic problems and, on the other, those who enter into contact with some sort of audience, integrating their work into some sort of larger concern, because they see that above the artistic there is also a common human attitude that springs from some sense of communal belonging and which has to be the determining factor behind the genesis of a work of art. ('Shifts in Musical Composition', 1927, in Albright, *Modernism and Music*, pp. 117–18).

Weill could not have drawn the battle lines around modernist 'elitism' more clearly, and his own work in creating a new kind of musical theatre in collaborations with writers such as Bertolt Brecht was aimed explicitly at 'satisfying the musical needs of broader levels of the population without giving up artistic substance' (Albright, p. 120). Yet the idea of Schoenberg as a musician in retreat from the public domain sits uneasily with the highly 'classical' and in a sense traditional aims of his work, to develop music along clear structural lines; while he persevered with this agenda, could it be said that the particular conditions of mass modernity placed 'the public sphere' in an attitude of retreat from classical music? Similarly, the 'technical' concerns of the twelve-tone system need not be interpreted as a deviation from the emotive or affective goals of music: as Albright puts it, Schoenberg was 'interested in intensifying the meaningfulness of music by making each moment of composition bear the weight of the whole', or in an intriguing statement of Schoenberg's own, 'The restrictions imposed on a composer by the obligation to use only one set in a composition are so severe that they can only be overcome by an imagination which has survived a tremendous number of adventures' (*Modernism and Music*, pp. 193, 200). Finally, as Alex Ross suggests, one technological conjuncture may have put all of us within the hearing of modernist musical performance more than we know: modern composition was soon widely used as film soundtracks, and 'horror movies need atonality as they need shadows on the walls of alleys' (*The Rest Is Noise*, p. 38)!

Dance

The early twentieth century saw a revolution in dance forms and in the social contexts of dance. Dance gained a wider prominence, and in current modernist studies a marked increase in the volume of biographies and critical works suggests a growing recognition of its importance. What a brief survey of dance and modernism also reveals is the extent to which dance shares with other modes of performance the ability to reveal the breadth and the paradoxes of modernism as a cultural category. To simplify, we could speak of a spectrum of dance, with 'popular' modernism at one end represented by the upsurge of new jazz and rag-time dances from America, and 'high' modernism at the other end represented by modifications to the ballet and classical music traditions. As is usual with modernism, what is then most interesting is to call into question the implicit hierarchy between 'low' and 'high', to show how these extremes might mirror or interact with each other, and to look at intermediate forms as of at least equal fascination. Dance also seems to crystallize a now-familiar set of critical issues and tensions within modernism. How does a renewed fascination with the ancient and the primitive relate to a sense of futuristic modernity? Is dance a collective form, enclosed by the discipline of choreography, or is it a means for the improvised expression of individual bodies? Is dance a highly specialized minority taste or activity, or is it a mass democratic form, to be enjoyed by one and all without the need of theory or education?

Black American culture and the new music of rag-time and jazz are the key reference points for the rapid emergence of popular modern dance. In the early twentieth century, a series of intensely rhythmic 'dance-crazes' spread through America and from there into Europe, closely associated with the music of the Negro ensembles discussed, for example, by Ernest Ansermet as we saw in the previous section, and beginning with the cakewalk, which was first performed in Paris as early as 1900. To glimpse the kind of external cultural barriers that prevailed, it is instructive to look at how a volume of the *Encyclopaedia Britannica* from the 1950s could narrate the rise of the 'dance-craze', proposing that from 1912 the United States:

[G]ave birth to a new form of dancing whose nervous and gyrating motions were well suited to express the emotions of a mechanical, urbanized civilisation. The first jazz dances of this century, the Turkey Trot, Bunny Hug, and Grizzly Bear, were often crude, vulgar and ugly. But the sense of exhilaration and release experienced by the dance of these steps caused them to sweep the country . . . From then on, dancing was taken over by the common people, and became an authentic expression of their moods and feelings. (1957, vol. 7, p. 22)

Considering the questionable features of this reading – the evaluation 'crude, ugly and vulgar'; the suggestion that the dancers are 'mechanical' as well as urbanized; the easy condescension of the phrase 'the common people'; and the uncertain nature of the transition from nervy mechanism to an 'authentic' expression of emotion – it is easy to construct our own, far more positive interpretations of these exciting origins of our later popular dance forms, from jive and disco to breakdance and hip-hop. (Revealingly, the *Encyclopaedia* goes on to see these early crudities as assuaged by the emergence of ballroom dancing!) For an analysis more typical of the exciting conjunctions at work in new modernist studies of Negro performance, see Rae Beth Gordon's account of the impact of black dancers on Parisian culture between 1875 and 1910, in 'Natural Rhythm: La Parisienne Dances with Darwin: 1875–1910', *Modernism/modernity* 10:4, November 2003.

Similar issues around mechanism were to arise in Siegfried Kracauer's Marxist critique of the Tiller Girls, a commercialized and rigidly choreographed American dance troupe. Kracaeur describes the troupe as 'mass ornament', or a systematized mode of capitalist distraction which, like capitalism, becomes an 'end in itself' (1927; see Harrison and Wood, *Art in Theory*, pp. 462–5); they were, he writes, 'no longer individual girls, but indissoluble female units whose movements are mathematical demonstrations'. Such standardized forms of capitalist entertainment, occurring in performances of simultaneous geometrical exactitude from America to Berlin, Australia and India, are objects of Kracauer's critique in the Weimar period. Yet, at the same time, Kracauer sought to avoid identification with reactionary theorists of mass society by insisting also that the performances provided '*legitimate . . . aesthetic* pleasure', preferable to 'artistic productions which cultivate obsolete noble sentiments in withered forms' (*Art in Theory*, pp. 464–5).

If the rise of jazz and commercial dance is primarily seen as a mass cultural phenomenon propagated through new technologies such as the phonograph and film as well as through live performance, the renovation of classical dance tends to be associated with individual dancers and choreographers such as Isadora Duncan, Loie Fuller and Ruth St. Denis in America, Mary Wigman in Germany, and Lydia Lopokova, Mikhail Fokine, Sergei Diaghilev, Vaslav Nijinsky and Leonide Massine in Russia. Duncan (1878–1927), for example, exerted an enormous galvanizing and international influence after an impoverished early life in California, London (from 1899) and Paris. Her innovations in dance were based on the interpretation of body poses drawn from images of ancient Greek and Roman cultures. Eschewing traditional ballet costume, Duncan danced in bare feet and simple flowing robes or tunics; she became renowned for her grace and athleticism of movement, whose air of spontaneity was deceptive (Figure 19). Duncan's pronouncements on avant-garde dance and music can seem to imply a surprising return to 'nature', spiritual and post-Romantic in orientation: as she wrote of students at the school she founded in Berlin in 1904 (others were to be established in Paris in 1914 and Moscow in 1921), 'they were to feel in their souls a secret attachment, unknowable to others, to initiate them into Nature's secrets; for all the parts of their supple bodies, trained as they would be, would respond to the melody of Nature and sing with her' (*My Life*, 1927, quoted in Kolocotroni *et al.*, *Modernism*, p. 156).

However, 'trained' here gives the clue to a counterbalancing emphasis. In the same memoir, Duncan observes that she could never perform without first being able to 'place a motor in my soul': 'When that begins to work my legs and arms and my whole body will move independently of my will'. As Carrie J. Preston has suggested, performers and artists of the modernist period tended not to observe any strict dichotomy between machines and the immaterial, and Duncan 'consistently positions her choreography at the juncture of motorized movement and soulful expression' ('The Motor in the Soul: Isadora Duncan and Modernist Performance', *Modernism/modernity* 12:2, April 2005, p. 273). Along with a more recent study of the American burlesque dancer Loie Fuller, *Electric*

Figure 19 Isadora Duncan

Salome: Loie Fuller's Performance of Modernism (Princeton, NJ, Princeton University Press, 2007), by Catherine Gunter Sodat, Preston interprets dance through an enlarged and varied sense of modernist performance in which the rational and the affective, the machine and the organic body, are fused.

Modernist dance is thus inevitably linked to the emergent 'healthy body' cultures of European modernism, and for example to the widely influential Swiss founder of kinesthetics or 'eurythmics', Emile Jacques-Dalcroze (1865–1950). This socially utopian method, perhaps more accurately described as dance-exercise or gymnastics, was a group-based approach to the understanding and improvization of rhythmic movement to music. In the terms of Dalcroze's essay of 1922, the human body was to become 'moving plastic', and work towards an autonomy (recall our discussion of this term in relation to the visual arts in chapter 2) which would eventually free it altogether from dependency on music ('The Technique of Moving Plastic', extract quoted in Albright, *Modernism and Music*, pp. 86–9). 'Do you mind if I do Dalcroze to that tune . . .?', asks D.H. Lawrence's Gudrun Brangwen as her sister Ursula sings, in *Women in Love* (1921). Nervously Gudrun proceeds to dance; as her feet 'pulse and flutter' rhythmically while her arms make slower, regular gestures, Lawrence captures precisely the simultaneous expression of different time signatures that Dalcroze required. The interpretation of the dance, however, combines incantation and rhapsody (Ursula catches an 'unconscious ritualistic suggestion') with a much more material, 'electric' hypnotic connection with a herd of Highland cattle which draws dangerously close.

Duncan's apparent classicism, stripping away the formality, decorativeness and cultural elitism of established ballet, might thus be compared with the impact of an Imagist poem by H.D. on the tradition of Edwardian poetry. Both artists used a reserved classicism to perform a revolutionary modernity, and both had formed their work within much more scientific/rationalistic milieus – healthy body culture and Imagism. In addition, both demonstrated a combination of the individual creative act with the group and collaborative identities crucial to much modernist activity, in Duncan's case revealing extraordinary entrepreneurial skills throughout a nomadic life. Most important in this respect was her

influence on Russian ballet. Following visits to St Petersburg in
1905 and 1907, Duncan's ideas were taken up by the dancer and
choreographer Michel Fokine, combining them with ideas from
folk dance to transform the ballet. In 1909, the travelling company
Ballets Russes, led by Serge Diaghilev (1872–1929), played its first
season in Paris (in the same year, Charles H. Caffin wrote an article
comparing the art of Duncan and Henri Matisse for the seminal
Alfred Stieglitz journal *Camera Work*). From that time on, and
especially after the arrival of Vaslav Nijinsky as principal dancer in
1913 and the iconoclastic performance of Igor Stravinsky's *The Rite
of Spring* in Paris in the same year, the *Ballets Russes* became a model
of avant-garde collaboration, with sets and costumes designed by
artists such as Picasso, Léger and Braque. Prior to the 1913 performance, Diaghilev and Nijinsky took the troupe for choreography to the *Deutscher Werkbund* workers' community in Hellerau,
where Dalcroze had become director of the Educational Institute
for Music and Rhythm. Personal as well as professional interrelationships are also a source of fascination in the transnational social
networks that motivated much metropolitan modernism: Duncan's
liaison with Edward Gordon Craig; Picasso's marriage in 1918 to
the *Ballets Russes* dancer Olga Koklova; Lydia Lopokova's marriage
to the economist and intellectual John Maynard Keynes, merging
the cultures of *Ballets Russes* and Bloomsbury.

Perhaps more than any other mode of modernist performance,
the *Ballets Russes*, in productions such as Cocteau–Satie's 1919
Parade for example, approached that Wagnerian vision of total art
with which we began this chapter. It seems appropriate therefore
that Isadora Duncan subscribed fully to the utopianism of 1917;
she was invited by Lenin to open her Moscow school in 1921 in the
palace of an ex-nobleman, and became a Soviet citizen, a continuing political attachment that proved problematic to her relationship
with her home country, despite the enthusiasm with which her
performances were received in modernist New York.

Selected reading

Albright, Daniel (ed.), *Modernism and Music: An Anthology of Sources*
  (Chicago, University of Chicago Press, 2004)

Albright's intelligent narrative links together this very useful anthology, mostly consisting of key composers writing about their work, and divided into chapters such as 'The New Music Theatre' and 'New Discipline: The Twelve-Tone Method'.

Ashby, Arved (ed.), *The Pleasure of Modernist Music: Listening, Memory, Intention, Ideology* (Rochester, NY, University of Rochester Press, 2004)

Stimulating collection of essays which endorse new approaches to listening to modernist music.

Butler, Christopher, 'Innovation and the Avant-Garde, 1900–1920', in eds N. Cooke and A. Pople, *The Cambridge History of Twentieth Century Music* (Cambridge, Cambridge University Press, 2004)

Useful and thought-provoking essay.

Donald, James, Anne Friedberg and Laura Marcus, eds, *Close Up 1927–1933: Cinema and Modernism* (London, Cassell, 1998)

An anthology of writings from this crucial journal, with thematized editorial introductions which provide a detailed commentary on the emerging discourse of film art and its critique of Hollywood/mainstream cinema.

Gronberg, Tag, 'Performing Modernism', in ed. Wilk, *Modernism 1914–1939: Designing a New World* (London, V&A, 2006)

A good survey of 1920s modernist performing arts, including the machine aesthetic, and with particular emphasis on the work of Kiesler, Léger and Schlemmer.

Humm, Maggie, *Modernist Women and Visual Cultures: Virginia Woolf, Vanessa Bell, Photography and Cinema* (Edinburgh, Edinburgh University Press, 2002)

Important discussion of women's ways of looking within modernist contexts, leading to the consideration of how film and photography relate to gendered subjectivities.

McCabe, Susan, *Cinematic Modernism: Modernist Poetry and Film* (Cambridge, Cambridge University Press, 2005)

Enlightening study of aesthetic cross-fertilization between film and poetry.

Marcus, Laura, *The Tenth Muse: Writing about Cinema in the modernist period* (Oxford, Oxford University Press, 2007)

Examines how a new discourse of and around film emerged through the conjunction of early film criticism and reviewing with the interests of writers such as H.G. Wells and Virginia Woolf.

Ross, Alex, *The Rest is Noise: Listening to the Twentieth Century* (London, Harper Perennial, 2009)

Exuberant account of innovatory music for those curious about 'this obscure pandemonium on the outskirts of culture'. Largely composer-based and anecdotal, but also includes good accessible music analysis and an online audio companion.

Watkins, Glenn, *Pyramids at the Louvre: Music, Culture and Collage from Stravinsky To the Postmodernists* (Belknap Press of Harvard University Press, Cambridge, MA, 1994)
Interesting cross-disciplinary study organized around the concept of collage.

9
Conclusion: continuing modernism

17 March 1986

I just wanted to put it on record that I perceive our only hope – or our one great hope – as residing in art. We must be resolute enough in promoting it . . .

25 April 1986

Art today – or so goes the party blather that has replaced the collective celebration of existence – is the new spontaneity and naïveté that we have. (I must break the habit, I must never read that sort of thing again, I must never look at a modern exhibition, above all I must throw away all those invitations unread.)

12 October 1986

What shall I paint? How shall I paint?
'What' is the hardest thing, because it is the essence. 'How' is easy by comparison . . . Even in my youth, when I somewhat naïvely had 'themes' (landscapes, self-portraits), I very soon became aware of this problem of having no subject. Of course, I took motifs and represented them, but this was mostly with the feeling that these were not the real ones, but imposed, dog-eared, artificial ones. The question 'What shall I paint?' showed me my own helplessness, and I often envied (still do envy) the most mediocre painters those 'concerns' of theirs, which they so tenaciously and mediocrely depict (I fundamentally despise them for it).

25 October 1986

These continuing difficulties. A constant work crisis that has lasted for decades, in fact ever since the start. Crisis personified. (Perhaps I am mistaken here; perhaps this is a perfectly normal way to work.)

(Gerhard Richter, *The Daily Practice of Painting: Writings and Interviews*, ed. Hans Ulrich-Obrist, trans. David Britt, London, Thames & Hudson, 2005, pp. 125, 129–30, 132.)

I want to conclude *Beginning Modernism* by speculating on the continuities of modernism. Having begun the book with reflections on the notorious difficulty of periodizing or defining modernism, that 'emptiest of all cultural categories' (Perry Anderson), I nevertheless offered various attempts at a working definition, starting with a reclamation of the 'high' modernist concern with *difficulty* ('the moment at which art stops making sense'), and borrowing ideas, such as those of Eugene Lunn, for identifying the formal characteristics of a modernist artefact. However, to define modernism simply in terms of its formal characteristics could become a rather 'academic' exercise, in the worst sense of that overused word, and I warned early on about taking a 'tick-box list' approach to the identification of a modernist text. What if, in attempting to summarize the many different strands we have explored in the course of this book, it would be more meaningful to regard modernism not as a set of such characteristics, but as *an orientation or approach towards the nature and potentialities of art within the modern world*? Below I present a different kind of list, speculating upon the main orientations or aspirations of modernism. These points are quite partial or subjective insofar as they are in some way a sketch of the reasons for my own continuing enthusiasm for modernist art and cultures, and in that sense you should strictly regard them as points to argue with – hence this last invitation to 'Stop and think'.

STOP and THINK

(On these as key features of the modernist outlook):

- A seriousness of conviction that art has an emancipatory and/or redemptive role to play in human life, and a self-conscious endorsement and theorizing of that role even where – as in Dada, for example – the ostensible aim is to call into question the concept of 'art' itself.
- A critical vigilance towards rapidly changing modes of cultural

production; an alertness as to how these changes might either positively or adversely affect thought and expression.

- As a result of the above, a distinctive combination of the rearguard action (for example the reclamation of myth, or the embrace of 'pre-modern' cultures) and the avant-garde.

- In experimentation, a determination not to patronize or talk down to the reader/viewer/listener; an assumption that intelligence needs exercising and stretching, and in this sense that 'difficulty' has the potential to be democratic as well as elitist.

- A sense of ambition which expresses itself in extremes and distortions of scale – the very small (minimalism, Imagism, the minute attention to the everyday), the very large (Proust, *Ulysses*, *Guernica*, Tatlin's tower).

- A utopian spirit, especially in design and architecture; the belief in the possibility of improved futures, to which art can materially contribute.

- In the wake of Romanticism and nineteenth-century industrialism, the emergence of a sophisticated and dialectical understanding of the *machine* as a product of human ingenuity; the deconstruction of the human–machine conceptual binary, and the embrace of the creative possibilities of the machine, notably in film, music and photography.

- An epistemological drive; an assumption that art is a mode of knowledge, and might consist in the continual process of problem-forming and problem-solving, even in contexts where the impossibility of resolution is glimpsed; in other words, an open encounter with paradox and contradiction (a version, perhaps, of the Italian Marxist Antonio Gramsci's formula, 'pessimism of the intellect, optimism of the will').

Together these imply a defence, of sorts, of Jürgen Habermas' theory that modernity, and with it cultural modernism, remains an 'incomplete project'; such orientations cannot easily be confined to a single chronological period. At the same time, however, we should be wary of advancing a relatively simplistic 'modernism-is-alive-and-well' argument. As Brecht would no doubt have it, modernism could not be *the same* today as it was a century ago: historical logic forbids it. Modernism might then only be identifiable in terms of its passage *through* certain much-changed contexts, the most obvious of these being what we now call postmodernism. Something of the complexity of this is hinted at in Michael Levenson's intriguing suggestion that, despite the need to disavow any nostalgic call for a 'return' to modernism, 'we are still learning how not to be modernist, which is reason all the more to see what such an ambition could mean' (*Cambridge Companion to Modernism*, p. 1). In a similar vein, Paul Wood observes of the contemporary German artist Gerhard Richter that Richter is in a fundamental sense 'not-modernist', but that 'this status is far from being merely chronological; and whatever it is that chronology has enabled, it would be mistaken to view it as a liberation from constraining modernism . . . The logic of Richter's being not-modernist is multiple' ('Truth and Beauty: The Ruined Abstraction of Gerhard Richter', in ed. John Roberts, *Art Has No History! The Making and Unmaking of Modern Art*, London, Verso, 1994, p. 182). Given the implication that some contemporary arts might carry the trace of modernism in their very negation of it, and in a sense that differentiates them from postmodernism, what might this 'not-modernism', a complex state of continuity, look like?

Rather than directly addressing contemporary literature here, I want instead to stimulate your thinking about literature through analogy with the work of the German painter Richter (born 1932), and that of the American composer John Adams (born 1947). Richter was based in Dresden in the German Democratic Republic (GDR) until he crossed the Cold War dividing line into West Germany in 1961. Since then he has become known for a particularly intense and varied output, within which two features in particular stand out: a sustained commitment to painting, albeit ranging across various modes of abstraction, and the deployment of photographs in the development of a distinctive form known as 'photo-painting'. Probably the most well known of these works is the sequence of fifteen paintings entitled *18 Oktober 1977* – beautiful, grainy and light grey, haunting and melancholy representations of members of the Baader–Meinhof terrorist group of the 1970s, based on police

Figure 20 Gerhard Richter, *Confrontation 1* (1988)

and press photographs taken shortly before their suicides in prison
(Figure 20).

Peter Osborne acknowledges that there is something 'historically exceptional' about Richter's art, and that a consideration of
this exceptionality can contribute to a 'rethinking of the history of
modernism' ('Painting Negation: Gerhard Richter's Negatives',
October 62, fall 1992, pp. 103–4). Richter, Osborne argues, embodies a complex response to a problem which is 'as old as modernism',
namely, the apparent threat posed by photography to painting in
the domain of representation. His works hover or hesitate, in a

delicate instability, between painting and photography, and certainly do not suggest the simple reproduction through paint of the photographic sheen of objectivity. Rather, Osborne describes the works' effect as 'an affirmation of photography by painting'; the act of painting establishes an (aesthetic) distance from the photograph across which a critical evaluation or even a celebration of photography might take place – though, at the same time, the exquisite painting of the photograph might act to reinstall painting, to 'rescue painting' (Osborne again) 'from its fallen position', so that painting is renewed and subtly enhanced even as it affirms the power of its modern challenger. In a utopian moment, we might then see this as the substitution of a symbiotic for an adversarial relationship.

In the course of this book we have noted that a complex response, such as Richter's, to the early twentieth-century moment of new, advanced-industrial and communication technologies is a defining feature of modernism. This might equally be discerned in the 1996 Piano Concerto, *Century Rolls*, which was composed by John Adams with 1920s pianola music in mind (the Pianola being a device fitted to a piano allowing a 'roll' to be mechanically played, and often thenceforth called a 'player piano'). Adams had become fascinated by how the mechanical reproduction of the piano roll 'radically altered the essence' of the music, giving it a 'bright, edgy quality and a rhythmic alertness' which 'could only have been the result of the black box through which it was channelled' (Adams, sleeve notes to *Century Rolls/Lollapalooza/Slominsky's Earbox*, New York, Nonesuch Records, 2000). Walter Benjamin's 'famous phrase' (art in the age of mechanical reproduction) came to Adams' mind, drawing him also to the 'energy and musical imagery' of the early twentieth century. As he sketches out the dynamics of the concerto, it is clear that the 'automatic' principle of the pianola – a form which similarly transforms all the 'content' it touches, whether Chopin, Gershwin or Fats Waller, just as Richter's photo-painting re-presents the difficult, recalcitrant material of the Baader-Meinhofs without discriminating between different levels of aesthetic subject – becomes identified with an impersonality in Adams' own relationship with the composition: the opening movement 'seemed urged on by some kind of electrical pulse', the music 'now seems to roll gently of its own free will', and so on. Listening to the music, one is aware of its automatism only as an expression of purpose and beauty, whether in the 'chirping, lightly pulsating twittering' of the first movement, the falling cadences of the slow second movement, which turns into a Satiean 'gymnopedie', or the urgent and erratic lurching of the final movement. Mechanism does not detract from something which is not mechanical – creativity? humanism? – but contributes its own aura of musicality. The modernist reference points – pianola, Debussy – are not fragments of style, enclosed in the quotation marks of postmodernism, but contribute to an un-rolling or developing whole.

In distinguishing between postmodernism and the condition of learning how-not-to-be-modernist, a crucial factor, Michael Levenson argues, is that we postmodern 'cultural sceptics' are able to see in modernism 'the force of cultural conviction' (*Cambridge Companion to Modernism*, p. 2). Does being not-modernist mean giving up on the transformative power of experimental art? On what grounds would we want to discard this conviction? Readings of Adams and Richter as *post*modernists are certainly available, notably in the case of Richter. Despite his commitment to painting as a 'historically significant' (Osborne) activity, the sheer diversity of Richter's work can suggest randomness and mannerism, which may seem to be at odds with modernist–expressivist conceptions of purposive style or signature. Of the abstract sketches that Richter began to paint in the mid-1970s, Paul Wood notes that Richter's previous practice seems to rule out 'any first-order sense of abstract expression' – indeed, the critic Benjamin Buchloh is cited as claiming that, in the period of post-Conceptual art, it was 'historically not possible for Richter abstractly to express mood or content, and mean it' ('Truth and Beauty', pp. 189, 194). So much, perhaps, for conviction: Wood writes of Richter's pragmatic approach to the abstracts, 'covering a surface with a series of marks which "worked" . . . almost as if he sought to replicate a convincing abstract painting but by starting from the opposite end' ('Truth and Beauty', p. 189).

Yet what we might say about Richter and Adams is that the sustained critical tension in their work – photograph–painting, piano roll–composition – is itself a sustaining of modernist conviction. Rather than some naïvely or unequivocally positive condition, this is often expressed as a productive state of *im*possibility. Osborne sees it in the 'double negation' of Richter's photo-paintings: the simultaneous negation of painting by photography, and of photography by painting. A similar case might be made for the relation between composition and mechanism in Adams' music. The prevailing of any one aspect in these dialectics would result in a loss of critical engagement, so that (in a deliciously modernist paradox), 'success (success in painting) is at risk of becoming the greatest failure of all', its outcome a 'merely affirmative' art. In the extracts from Richter's 1986 notebooks collected at the beginning of this chapter, we see something of this struggle recorded over a period of months: the belief that 'our one great hope' lies in art, involving a determined rejection of the 'party blather' of the postmodern culture industry; in pursuit of this goal, however, the seemingly inevitable encounter with the exhaustedness of the representational project, the banality of 'subject' – 'What shall I paint?' – and the temptation to see perpetual crisis or difficulty as the 'perfectly normal' substance of the pursuit of art.

No writer more fully embodies this sense of critical negation, and the dedicated struggle to avoid a 'merely affirmative' art, than Samuel Beckett. One beautifully illustrative text, appropriately very difficult to categorize, but which might nevertheless accompany our discussion of Richter and Adams, is 'Three Dialogues' (1949), by Beckett and Georges Duthuit, editor of the journal *Transitions*. The text takes the form of three short conversations between 'B' and 'D' about the painters Tal Coat, Masson, and Bram van Velde. We are immediately aware that the exchanges are not merely the transcription of actual dialogue, but are crafted and humorous responses to the dilemma of the modern artist. In the first dialogue 'B' insists, while admiring Tal Coat's work, that in seeking for 'a more adequate expression of natural experience' the painter only strains to 'enlarge the statement of a compromise' implicit in painting since the Renaissance. Such painters, 'B' notes, 'never stirred from the field of the possible', so that the 'revolutionary' modernism of Tal Coat and a comparable painter such as Matisse disturbs things 'only on the plane of the feasible'. When, perhaps understandably, 'D' enquires what other plane there might be for the artist, the dialogue ends thus:

B. – Logically none. Yet I speak of an art turning from it in disgust, weary of puny exploits, weary of pretending to be able, of being able, of doing a little better the same old thing, of going a little further along a dreary road.

D. – And preferring what?

B. – The expression that there is nothing to express, nothing with which to express, nothing from which to express, no power to express, no desire to express, together with the obligation to express.

D. – But that is a violently extreme and personal point of view, of no help to us in the matter of Tal Coat.

B. –

D. – Perhaps that is enough for today.

> (Samuel Beckett, *Proust and Three Dialogues*, p. 103)

Where 'B' concludes the first dialogue in silence, he 'exits' the second 'weeping'. They have been discussing Masson's aspiration to 'paint the void' or to find the 'inner emptiness, the prime condition, according to Chinese esthetics, of the act of painting' (p. 109). Masson is, in the words of 'B', 'in search of the difficulty rather than in its clutch'. Paradoxically, then, the obstacle to this search is precisely Masson's ease and competency as a painter, 'his own technical gifts, which have the richness, the precision, the density and the balance of the high classical manner' ('D', p. 111). This strange predicament leaves Masson 'literally skewered on the ferocious dilemma of expression' ('B'), unable to break free of an excellence which condemns him to the conventional field of painting and the 'capture of objects', beyond which he wishes to go. 'B' is finally forced to weep when 'D' tries to recuperate this familiar realm of art on the grounds of its life-affirming qualities: must we deplore the depiction of 'what is tolerable and radiant in the world'? 'B's tears, we feel, are not a denial of art's life-affirming potential, so much as an exasperation at the easy and undialectical approximation of it.

The third dialogue, the most performative and playful, ends with a long disquisition by 'B' on the art of Bram van Velde. Contrasting with Tal Coat and Masson, van Velde is, 'B' believes, the first to move beyond the prison of expressionism by 'accepting' a certain situation and 'consenting' to a certain act: 'The situation is that of him who is helpless, cannot act, in the event cannot paint, since he is obliged to paint. The act is of him who, helpless, unable to act,

acts, in the event paints, since he is obliged to paint' (p. 119). 'D'
demands clarification of this: does it, for example, mean that the
painting of van Velde is 'inexpressive'? 'B' replies in the affirmative
– but only 'a fortnight' later! Does 'B' realize the 'absurdity' of this
position? He replies that he hopes he does. Is not van Velde's position then 'expressive of the impossibility to express'? 'B' detects
in this the imperious hold that the concept of expression has over
our thinking about art. After much cajoling, and attempts at escap-
ing from the dialogue, 'B' is persuaded to speak further about his
theory of van Velde. The history of painting is the consistent effort
to bring the artist and the occasion of the painting into ever closer
relation; van Velde is the first to submit to the fundamental impossibility of this, 'the incoercible absence of relation', and hence to the
realization that 'to be an artist is to fail, as no other dare fail, that
failure is his work and the shrink from it desertion, art and craft,
good housekeeping, living' (p. 125). 'B' acknowledges, however,
that even this could be described as being 'expressed' by van Velde's
work. Is it ever possible to find an aesthetic which cannot be recuperated into 'expression'? Is there a form of words to describe such
an aesthetic? Apparently not: 'B' can only make the gesture of denying any precedents at all for van Velde's painting: 'For what is this
coloured plane, that was not there before. I don't know what it is,
having never seen anything like it before. It seems to have nothing
to do with art, in any case, if my memories are correct' (p. 126). The
dialogue ends inconclusively, in mid-stream, with 'B' remembering
that he has not even begun to say what he set out to say about van
Velde.

In artists such as Richter and Adams, it may be possible to trace
the continuity of that deeply paradoxical 'cultural conviction' found
in the late-modernist – or early postmodernist? – Beckett. Some
gratitude is due to Beckett, perhaps, for the rich, dark comedy with
which he helps to guide us through the strange contradictions and
seemingly unthinkable conclusions of modernism. Crisis, failure
and impossibility are not obstacles to but rather the enabling conditions of conviction in the transformative power of experimental art.
Without the stringent necessity of problems, perhaps insuperable,
to be formulated and addressed, art can collapse into the bland-
ness and banality of commodity production as easily as it can be

recuperated into 'expression' (Beckett) or 'concerns' (Richter). At the moment of modernism, the result is that peculiar combination of rearguard and avant-garde, a critique of modernity with an embrace of the modern, a surge of conviction in the ability to create art even as the new conditions, materials and techniques of the modern suggest its irrevocable transformation and, perhaps, demise. 'High' modernism may often be satirized for its aloof, elitist or heroic stances, yet the inherent acknowledgement of difficulty and impossibility can also, curiously enough, imply precisely those qualities of openness and undecidability that are claimed by its detractors. If, then, 'high' modernism is a self-created myth, how far is it also a myth conveniently generated by a postmodern culture? Peter Brooker's observations on the entire, epic project that is made up of Ezra Pound's *Pisan Cantos* may be apposite: 'Like other key modernist texts it is a "record of struggle", and in the end a self-acknowledged "failure" as both artistic and ideological unity. To see the *Cantos* as a disengaged, hermetically sealed art object, as some postmodernist critics choose to see the texts of modernism is, perversely, to endorse the selective reading which canonized "traditionalist modernism"' (*Modernism/Postmodernism*, p. 27). Heroism and anti-heroism, conviction and the pathetic, are often disinctively entwined in the modernist text. There is, then, no last modernist word, but if there were, it might be attributed to Beckett. 'There are many ways in which the thing I am trying in vain to say may be tried in vain to be said' (*Three Dialogues*, p. 123); 'you must go on, I can't go on, I'll go on' (*The Beckett Trilogy*, 1959, London, John Calder, 1976, p. 382).

Index